Successful

10 FCE
Practice Tests

10 complete Practice Tests for the
Cambridge English
First

including
FCE Exam Guide

analysing all the different exam tasks for the 4 Papers of
the **FCE** exam: **Reading & Use of English**, **Writing**,
Listening, **& Speaking** with example questions, exam
tips and strategies that help students understand what
the test is like and what is required from them.

GlobalELT
English Language Teaching Books

Andrew Betsis
Lawrence Mamas

CONTENTS

Published by
GLOBAL ELT LTD
Brighton, East Sussex
www.globalelt.co.uk
email: orders@globalelt.co.uk
Copyright © **GLOBAL ELT LTD, 2014**

Successful Cambridge English FIRST - 2015 Format - 10 Practice Tests - Student's Book ISBN: 9781781641569
Successful Cambridge English FIRST - 2015 Format - 10 Practice Tests - Teacher's Book ISBN: 9781781641576

Every effort has been made to trace the copyright holders and we apologise in advance for any unintentional omission.
We will be happy to insert the appropriate acknowledgements in any subsequent editions.

The authors and publishers wish to acknowledge the following use of material in the Speaking section(p. 3-32):
For the photos in Tests: 1-10 in the Speaking section: © Ingram Publishing Image Library and © www.123RF.com photo library

The authors and publishers also wish to acknowledge the following use of material in the Reading section of the practice tests.
Extensive adaptation has taken place on most occurrences.

Test 1 - Part 5: extract from 'Of Human Bondage' by W. Somerset Maugham
Test 1 - Part 6: 'The skydiving experience' by Ian Loft.
Test 2 - Part 5: extract from '1984' by George Orwell
Test 2 - Part 6: extract from 'Emergent Forest at Rangitoto Island'
http://www.nzgeographic.co.nz/resources-for-students/emergent-forest-at-rangitoto-island
Test 3 - Part 5: extract from 'Alice in Wonderland' by Lewis Carroll
Test 3 - Part 6: 'Lucid Dreaming' http://dreamsnightmares.com/luciddreaming.html
Test 4 - Part 5: extract from 'A Tale of Two Cities' by Charles Dickens

Test 5 - Part 5: extract from 'The Northern Lights from Arctic Sweden' by Peter Potterfield
Test 5 - Part 6: adapted from 'Whaling' (Wikipedia)
Test 6 - Part 5: 'Does Reality TV Make People More Accepting Of Surveillance?'
by Randall Parker
Test 6 - Part 6: 'Susan Boyle and John Wayne Gacy: The Similarities' by Phil
http://averypublicsociologist.blogspot.com/2009/06/susan-boyle-and-john-wayne-gacy.html
Test 10 - Part 5: extract from 'Howards End', by E. M. Forster
Test 10 - Part 6: adapted from 'Origin of music'
http://en.citizendium.org/wiki/Origin_of_music

Paper 4 Speaking

Test 1

Paper 4 Speaking	PART 1	2 minutes (3 minutes for groups of three)

Part 1 – Interview

In this first part of the Speaking test, the examiner will ask you questions about topics such as family life, daily routines, or how you spend your free time. You will be expected to provide information about yourself and give your opinions.

Interlocutor: Good morning/afternoon/evening. My name is .... and this is my colleague .... Can I have your mark sheets, please? Thank you. And your names are ....? Thank you.

First of all, we'd like to know something about you. *(to Candidate A)* Where are you from?
(to Candidate B) And you? .... And what do you like about living there?
(to Candidate A) And what about you?
Thank you.

(Ask each candidate one or more of the following questions, as appropriate.)

Home life
❖ How many people are there in your family? (Who are they?)
❖ Which family member do you spend the most time with?
❖ Could you tell me about your family home?
❖ Do you like your neighbourhood?
❖ Is there anything you would like to change about your neighbourhood?

Paper 4 Speaking	PART 2	4 minutes (6 minutes for groups of three)

Part 2 – Long turn

In this part of the test you have to speak for 1 minute without interruption. The examiner will give you two photographs and you have to compare and contrast them as well as talk about your reaction to them. Your partner will get a different set of photographs and has to do the same thing. When each of you has finished speaking, the other will be invited to comment on the topic of the photographs.

Interlocutor:　　In this part of the test, I'm going to give each of you two photographs. I'd like you to talk about your photographs on your own for about a minute and also to answer a question about your partner's photographs.

　　　　　　　Candidate A, it's your turn first. Here are your photographs. They show people who are in stressful situations.
　　　　　　　Candidate A has to look at the photographs on the next page.
　　　　　　　Candidate A, I'd like you to compare your photographs and say why each situation might be stressful. All right?

Candidate A:　(one minute) ....
　　　　　　　Thank you.

　　　　　　　Candidate B, which situation do you think would be more stressful?
Candidate B:　(approximately 30 seconds) ....
　　　　　　　Thank you.

　　　　　　　Now, **Candidate B**, here are your photographs. They show things that some people are afraid of.
　　　　　　　Candidate B has to look at the photographs on the next page.
　　　　　　　Candidate B, I'd like you to compare your photographs and say why people might be afraid of these things. All right?
Candidate B:　(one minute) ....
　　　　　　　Thank you.

　　　　　　　Candidate A, do you think either of these things is frightening?
Candidate A:　(approximately 30 seconds) ....
　　　　　　　Thank you.

Speaking Section

Candidate A   1 Why might each situation be stressful?

Candidate B   2 Why might people be afraid of these things?

Paper 4 Speaking   **PART 3**   4 minutes (5 minutes for groups of three)

Part 3 – Collaborative Task

Interlocutor: Now I'd like you to talk about something together for about two minutes. (3 minutes for groups of three). **I'd like you to think about TV programmes. Here are some types of TV programmes** and a question for you to discuss. First you have some time to look at the task.

Look at the task in the box below. You have 15 seconds.

Now, talk to each other about **why people would choose to watch these TV programmes**.

Candidates: .... *2 minutes (3 minutes for groups of three)*

Interlocutor: Thank you. Now you have about a minute *(for pairs and groups of three)* to decide **which type of TV show would be the most popular and would attract more advertisers to spend money on advertising their products**.

Candidates: .... I minute (for pairs and groups of three)

Thank you.

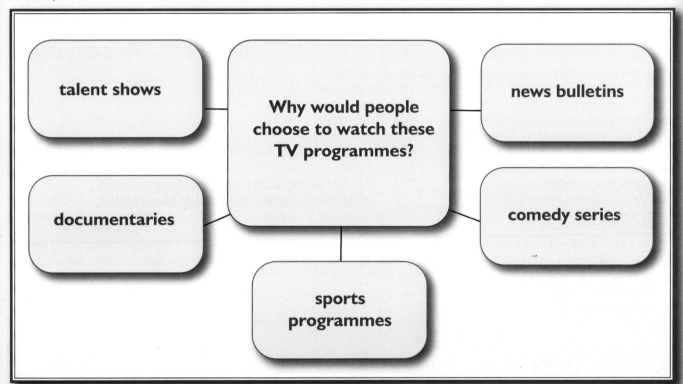

```
talent shows          Why would people         news bulletins
                      choose to watch these
documentaries         TV programmes?           comedy series

                      sports
                      programmes
```

Paper 4 Speaking   **PART 4**   4 minutes (6 minutes for groups of three)

Part 4 – Discussion

In this part of the test you have to take part in a discussion with the other candidate related to the topic of the task you did in Part 3. The examiner will ask you both some questions.

Interlocutor:
- Do you spend a lot of time watching television?
- What do you think about advertising on television?
- Do you think young people who watch a lot of violence on TV are more likely to be violent themselves?
- Why do you think watching television is such a popular pastime?

Thank you. That is the end of the test.

Select any of the following prompts, as appropriate:
- What do you think?
- Do you agree?
- And you?

Test 2

Speaking Section

| Paper 4 Speaking | PART 1 | 2 minutes (3 minutes for groups of three) |

Part 1 – Interview

In this first part of the Speaking test, the examiner will ask you questions about topics such as family life, daily routines, or how you spend your free time. You will be expected to provide information about yourself and give your opinions.

Interlocutor: Good morning/afternoon/evening. My name is ………… and this is my colleague ………… . Can I have your mark sheets, please? Thank you. And your names are ……….? Thank you.

First of all, we'd like to know something about you. *(to Candidate A)* Where are you from?
(to Candidate B) And you? ………… And what do you like about living there?
(to Candidate A) And what about you?
Thank you.

(Ask each candidate one or more of the following questions, as appropriate.)

Education

❖   What are your favourite and least favourite school subjects?
❖   What is the most important thing that you've learned at school?
❖   Where do you go when you have to study?   (Why do you like to study there?)
❖   Is there something new you'd really like to learn about?   (Why?)
❖   Do you plan to study in the future?   (What do you want to study?)

| Paper 4 Speaking | PART 2 | 4 minutes (6 minutes for groups of three) |

Part 2 – Long turn

In this part of the test you have to speak for 1 minute without interruption. The examiner will give you two photographs and you have to compare and contrast them as well as talk about your reaction to them. Your partner will get a different set of photographs and has to do the same thing. When each of you has finished speaking, the other will be invited to comment on the topic of the photographs.

Interlocutor: In this part of the test, I'm going to give each of you two photographs. I'd like you to talk about your photographs on your own for about a minute and also to answer a question about your partner's photographs.

                Candidate A, it's your turn first. Here are your photographs. They show places where people live in. *Candidate A has to look at the photographs on the next page.*
                Candidate A, I'd like you to compare your photographs and say what the advantages and disadvantages are of living in these two places. All right?

Candidate A: *(one minute)* ………………………………
                Thank you.

                Candidate B, which place would you dislike living in and why?

Candidate B: *(approximately 30 seconds)* ………………………………
                Thank you.

                Now, **Candidate B**, here are your photographs. They show different types of social problems. *Candidate B has to look at the photographs on the next page.*
                Candidate B, I'd like you to compare your photographs and say which you think is a more serious problem. All right?

Candidate B: *(one minute)* ………………………………
                Thank you.

                Candidate A, does your hometown have these kinds of problems?

Candidate A: *(approximately 30 seconds)* ………………………………
                Thank you.

Speaking Section

Candidate A

1 What are the advantages and disadvantages of living in these two places?

Candidate B

2 Which do you think is a more serious problem?

Speaking Section

Part 3 – Collaborative Task

Interlocutor: Now I'd like you to talk about something together for about two minutes. (3 minutes for groups of three). **Here are some ways that people spend their free time** and a question for you to discuss. First you have some time to look at the task.

Look at the task in the box below. You have 15 seconds.

Now, talk to each other about **how these ways of spending your free time can be entertaining or relaxing**.

Candidates: .... *2 minutes (3 minutes for groups of three)*

Interlocutor: Thank you. Now you have about a minute *(for pairs and groups of three)* to decide **which way of spending leisure time would be the most appealing to teenagers**.

Candidates: .... *1 minute (for pairs and groups of three)*

Thank you.

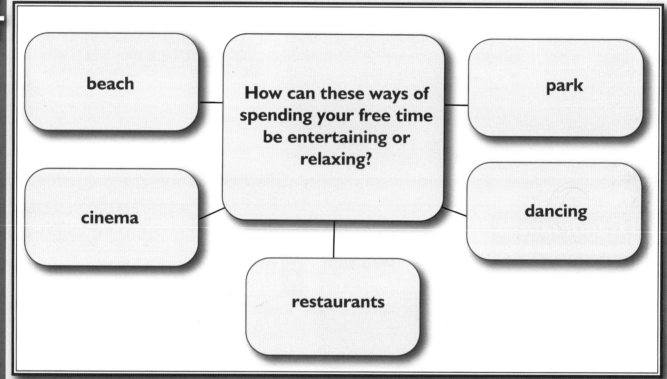

beach

park

How can these ways of spending your free time be entertaining or relaxing?

cinema

dancing

restaurants

Part 4 – Discussion

In this part of the test you have to take part in a discussion with the other candidate related to the topic of the task you did in Part 3. The examiner will ask you both some questions.

Interlocutor:

- Do people of different ages always have different interests?
- What kinds of activities do you enjoy doing with your parents?
- When you go out with your friends, how do you decide what to do?
- Do you enjoy going on excursions with a large group or do you prefer going by yourself or with a friend?

Select any of the following prompts, as appropriate:

- What do you think?
- Do you agree?
- And you?

Thank you. That is the end of the test.

Test 3

Paper 4 Speaking   PART 1   2 minutes (3 minutes for groups of three)

Part 1 – Interview

In this first part of the Speaking test, the examiner will ask you questions about topics such as family life, daily routines, or how you spend your free time. You will be expected to provide information about yourself and give your opinions.

Interlocutor: Good morning/afternoon/evening. My name is .... and this is my colleague .... Can I have your mark sheets, please? Thank you. And your names are ....? Thank you.

First of all, we'd like to know something about you. *(to Candidate A)* Where are you from?

(to Candidate B) And you? .... And what do you like about living there?

(to Candidate A) And what about you?

Thank you.

(Ask each candidate one or more of the following questions, as appropriate.)

<u>Work and employment</u>

❖   Would you prefer to work indoors or outdoors? (Why?)
❖   Do you prefer working on your own or with other people? (Why?)
❖   What kind of work would you like to do in the future?   (Why?)
❖   Is there a job you would never want to do?   (Why?)
❖   What do you think would be the most difficult job to do?   (Why?)

Paper 4 Speaking   PART 2   4 minutes (6 minutes for groups of three)

Part 2 – Long turn

In this part of the test you have to speak for 1 minute without interruption. The examiner will give you two photographs and you have to compare and contrast them as well as talk about your reaction to them. Your partner will get a different set of photographs and has to do the same thing. When each of you has finished speaking, the other will be invited to comment on the topic of the photographs.

Interlocutor: In this part of the test, I'm going to give each of you two photographs. I'd like you to talk about your photographs on your own for about a minute and also to answer a question about your partner's photographs.

Candidate A, it's your turn first. Here are your photographs. They show people spending time in different environments.
Candidate A has to look at the photographs on the next page.
Candidate A, I'd like you to compare your photographs and say how you think the environment is making people feel.
All right?

Candidate A: *(one minute)* ....
Thank you.

Candidate B, in which place would you prefer to be?
Candidate B: *(approximately 30 seconds)* ....
Thank you.

Now, **Candidate B**, here are your photographs. They show people who live in different countries.
Candidate B has to look at the photographs on the next page.
Candidate B, I'd like you to compare your photographs and say what reasons these people might have for moving abroad. All right?
Candidate B: *(one minute)* ....
Thank you.

Candidate A, would you like to live in a foreign country? Why/why not?
Candidate A: *(approximately 30 seconds)* ....
Thank you.

Speaking Section

Candidate A

1 How are the people's environments making them feel?

Candidate B

2 What reasons might these people have for moving abroad?

HIRE ME!

Paper 4 Speaking   PART 3   4 minutes (5 minutes for groups of three)

Part 3 – Collaborative Task

Interlocutor: Now I'd like you to talk about something together for about two minutes. (3 minutes for groups of three). **I'd like you to imagine that a family with children wants to move house. Here are some places they could move to** and a question for you to discuss. First you have some time to look at the task.

Look at the task in the box below. You have 15 seconds.

Now, talk to each other about **why a family with children would choose to live in these places**.

Candidates: .... *2 minutes (3 minutes for groups of three)*

Interlocutor: Thank you. Now you have about a minute *(for pairs and groups of three)* to decide **which place would be best for their children's education**.

Candidates: .... *1 minute (for pairs and groups of three)*

Thank you.

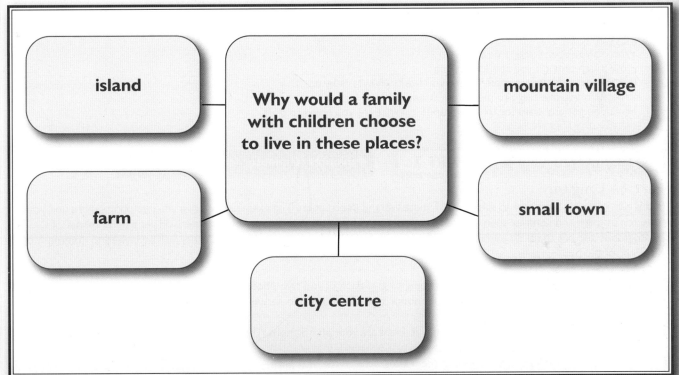

Paper 4 Speaking   PART 4   4 minutes (6 minutes for groups of three)

Part 4 – Discussion

In this part of the test you have to take part in a discussion with the other candidate related to the topic of the task you did in Part 3. The examiner will ask you both some questions.

Interlocutor:

- Do you think it is more difficult living in the countryside or in a big city? Why?
- Would it be easier for a foreign visitor to fit in a city or a village?
- Are there different social problems in cities and in the countryside? What are they?
- Where do you think most people will live in the future?

Thank you. That is the end of the test.

Select any of the following prompts, as appropriate:
- What do you think?
- Do you agree?
- And you?

Test 4

Speaking Section

| Paper 4 Speaking | **PART 1** | 2 minutes (3 minutes for groups of three) |

Part 1 – Interview

In this first part of the Speaking test, the examiner will ask you questions about topics such as family life, daily routines, or how you spend your free time. You will be expected to provide information about yourself and give your opinions.

Interlocutor: Good morning/afternoon/evening. My name is .... and this is my colleague .... Can I have your mark sheets, please? Thank you. And your names are ....? Thank you.

First of all, we'd like to know something about you. *(to Candidate A)* Where are you from?
(to Candidate B) And you? .... And what do you like about living there?
(to Candidate A) And what about you?
Thank you.

(Ask each candidate one or more of the following questions, as appropriate.)

Leisure time
❖   Who do you spend your free time with?
❖   How much time do you spend at home?
❖   Is it easy to meet new people where you live?   (Why? / Why not?)
❖   Where do you like to go to meet your friends?
❖   Have you got any plans for this weekend?   (What are you going to do?)

| Paper 4 Speaking | **PART 2** | 4 minutes (6 minutes for groups of three) |

Part 2 – Long turn

In this part of the test you have to speak for 1 minute without interruption. The examiner will give you two photographs and you have to compare and contrast them as well as talk about your reaction to them. Your partner will get a different set of photographs and has to do the same thing. When each of you has finished speaking, the other will be invited to comment on the topic of the photographs.

Interlocutor: In this part of the test, I'm going to give each of you two photographs. I'd like you to talk about your photographs on your own for about a minute and also to answer a question about your partner's photographs.

Candidate A, it's your turn first. Here are your photographs. They show different instances in which the environment is being damaged.
Candidate A has to look at the photographs on the next page.
Candidate A, I'd like you to compare your photographs and say which environmental problem you think is the most serious. All right?

Candidate A: *(one minute)* ....
Thank you.

Candidate B, are you worried about global warming?

Candidate B: *(approximately 30 seconds)* ....
Thank you.

Now, **Candidate B**, here are your photographs. They show things we can do to protect the environment.

Candidate B has to look at the photographs on the next page.
Candidate B, I'd like you to compare your photographs and say why these things are important for the protection of the environment.
All right?

Candidate B: *(one minute)* ....
Thank you.

Candidate A, do you do anything to try to protect the environment?

Candidate A: *(approximately 30 seconds)* ....
Thank you.

Candidate A

1 Which environmental problem do you think is the most serious?

Candidate B

2 Why are these things important for the protection of the environment?

Speaking Section

Part 3 – Collaborative Task

Interlocutor: Now I'd like you to talk about something together for about two minutes. (3 minutes for groups of three). **I'd like you to think about how humans treat the environment. Here are some environmental issues that affect the environment in a negative way** and a question for you to discuss. First you have some time to look at the task.

Look at the task in the box below. You have 15 seconds.

Now, discuss **how these environmental issues affect the environment**.

Candidates: .... *2 minutes (3 minutes for groups of three)*

Interlocutor: Thank you. Now you have about a minute *(for pairs and groups of three)* to decide **which environmental issue should receive more attention by governments**.

Candidates: .... 1 minute (for pairs and groups of three)

Thank you.

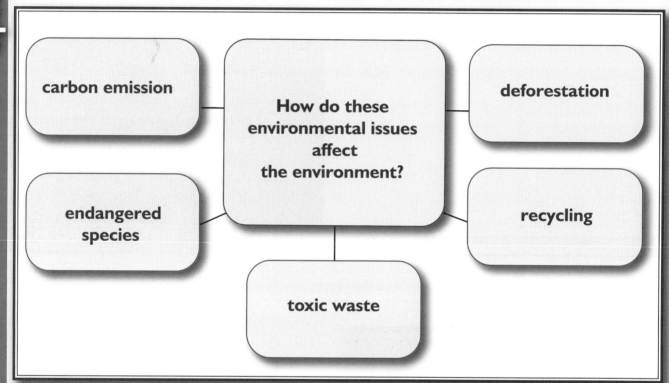

Part 4 – Discussion

In this part of the test you have to take part in a discussion with the other candidate related to the topic of the task you did in Part 3. The examiner will ask you both some questions.

Interlocutor:

- Air travel is very bad for the environment; so, is it wrong to fly abroad for a holiday?
- Many plants and animals are going extinct. Is this a problem? Why / why not?
- Do you think individual action can save the environment?
- How is the climate likely to change in the future due to global warming?

Thank you. That is the end of the test.

> *Select any of the following prompts, as appropriate:*
> - What do you think?
> - Do you agree?
> - And you?

Test 5

Paper 4 Speaking   PART 1   2 minutes (3 minutes for groups of three)

Part 1 – Interview

In this first part of the Speaking test, the examiner will ask you questions about topics such as family life, daily routines, or how you spend your free time. You will be expected to provide information about yourself and give your opinions.

Interlocutor: Good morning/afternoon/evening. My name is .... and this is my colleague .... Can I have your mark sheets, please? Thank you. And your names are ....? Thank you.

First of all, we'd like to know something about you. *(to Candidate A)* Where are you from?
(to Candidate B) And you? .... And what do you like about living there?
(to Candidate A) And what about you? Thank you.

(Ask each candidate one or more of the following questions, as appropriate.)

Travel
❖   What's your favourite way of travelling?   (Why do you like it?)
❖   What's the longest journey you've ever been on?   (Tell us about it.)
❖   How do you pass the time on a long journey?
❖   Do you prefer to travel abroad on holiday or to stay closer to home? (Why?)
❖   Where do you think you'll spend your holidays next year?

Paper 4 Speaking   PART 2   4 minutes (6 minutes for groups of three)

Part 2 – Long turn

In this part of the test you have to speak for 1 minute without interruption. The examiner will give you two photographs and you have to compare and contrast them as well as talk about your reaction to them. Your partner will get a different set of photographs and has to do the same thing. When each of you has finished speaking, the other will be invited to comment on the topic of the photographs.

Interlocutor: In this part of the test, I'm going to give each of you two photographs. I'd like you to talk about your photographs on your own for about a minute and also to answer a question about your partner's photographs.

Candidate A, it's your turn first. Here are your photographs. They show people taking part in different sports. *Candidate A has to look at the photographs on the next page.*
Candidate A, I'd like you to compare your photographs and say which sport is more interesting for people to watch.
All right?

Candidate A: *(one minute)* ....
Thank you.

Candidate B, do you prefer team sports or individual sports?

Candidate B: *(approximately 30 seconds)* ....
Thank you.

Now, **Candidate B**, here are your photographs. They show people competing in different kinds of sports. *Candidate B has to look at the photographs on the next page.*
Candidate B, I'd like you to compare your photographs and say which of these sports you think is the most challenging. All right?

Candidate B: *(one minute)* ....
Thank you.

Candidate A, do you prefer to play or to watch sports?

Candidate A: *(approximately 30 seconds)* ....
Thank you.

Speaking Section

Candidate A   **1** Which sport is more interesting for people to watch?

Candidate B   **2** Which of these sports do you think is the most challenging?

Paper 4 Speaking   **PART 3**   **4 minutes (5 minutes for groups of three)**

Part 3 – Collaborative Task

Interlocutor: Now I'd like you to talk about something together for about two minutes. (3 minutes for groups of three). **I'd like you to imagine that somebody wants to join a sports club. Here are some sports** and a question for you to discuss. First you have some time to look at the task.

Look at the task in the box below. You have 15 seconds.

Now, talk to each other about **what somebody needs to consider when choosing to do these sports**.

Candidates: .... *2 minutes (3 minutes for groups of three)*

Interlocutor: Thank you. Now you have about a minute *(for pairs and groups of three)* to decide **which sport is the least dangerous**.

Candidates: .... 1 minute (for pairs and groups of three)

Thank you.

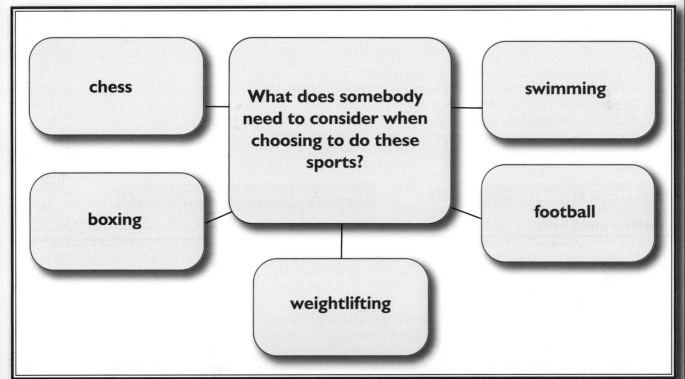

Paper 4 Speaking   **PART 4**   **4 minutes (6 minutes for groups of three)**

Part 4 – Discussion

In this part of the test you have to take part in a discussion with the other candidate related to the topic of the task you did in Part 3. The examiner will ask you both some questions.

Interlocutor:

- Do you think sport has an age limit, or should everyone be able to take part?
- In the sport world, is winning all that matters?
- Why do you think football fans often become violent?
- Why do you think athletes feel the need to take performance-enhancing drugs?

Select any of the following prompts, as appropriate:

- What do you think?
- Do you agree?
- And you?

Thank you. That is the end of the test.

Speaking Section

Test 6

Part I – Interview

In this first part of the Speaking test, the examiner will ask you questions about topics such as family life, daily routines, or how you spend your free time. You will be expected to provide information about yourself and give your opinions.

Interlocutor: Good morning/afternoon/evening. My name is ………… and this is my colleague ………… . Can I have your mark sheets, please? Thank you. And your names are ………..? Thank you.

First of all, we'd like to know something about you. *(to Candidate A)* Where are you from?
(to Candidate B) And you? …………………… And what do you like about living there?
(to Candidate A) And what about you?
Thank you.

(Ask each candidate one or more of the following questions, as appropriate.)

Media
❖   How do you find out what's happening in the world?
❖   Do you have a favourite newspaper or magazine?   (Why do you like it?)
❖   Do you use the Internet?   (What sort of things do you use it for?)
❖   What's the difference between reading the news in the newspaper or on the internet?
❖   Do you think computers will replace newspapers and TV in the future?

Part 2 – Long turn

In this part of the test you have to speak for 1 minute without interruption. The examiner will give you two photographs and you have to compare and contrast them as well as talk about your reaction to them. Your partner will get a different set of photographs and has to do the same thing. When each of you has finished speaking, the other will be invited to comment on the topic of the photographs.

Interlocutor: In this part of the test, I'm going to give each of you two photographs. I'd like you to talk about your photographs on your own for about a minute and also to answer a question about your partner's photographs.

Candidate A, it's your turn first. Here are your photographs. They show two different types of media.
Candidate A has to look at the photographs on the next page.
Candidate A, I'd like you to compare your photographs and say how influential these types of media are. All right?

Candidate A: *(one minute)* ……………………………….
Thank you.

Candidate B, do you watch the news on TV?

Candidate B: *(approximately 30 seconds)* ……………………………….
Thank you.

Now, **Candidate B**, here are your photographs. They show two special occasions.
Candidate B has to look at the photographs on the next page.
Candidate B, I'd like you to compare your photographs and say what makes an occasion special. All right?

Candidate B: *(one minute)* ……………………………….
Thank you.

Candidate A, what is the most important celebration in your country?

Candidate A: *(approximately 30 seconds)* ……………………………….
Thank you.

Candidate A   **1** How influential are these types of media?

Candidate B   **2** What makes an occasion special?

Speaking Section

Speaking Section

Paper 4 Speaking   **PART 3**   **4 minutes (5 minutes for groups of three)**

Part 3 – Collaborative Task

Interlocutor: Now I'd like you to talk about something together for about two minutes. (3 minutes for groups of three). **I'd like you to imagine that a company wants to advertise its products. Here are some forms of advertising they are thinking about** and a question for you to discuss. First you have some time to look at the task.

Look at the task in the box below. You have 15 seconds.

Now, talk to each other about **why a company would choose one of these methods to advertise its products**.

Candidates: .... *2 minutes (3 minutes for groups of three)*

Interlocutor: Thank you. Now you have about a minute *(for pairs and groups of three)* to decide **which form of advertising appeals more to young people**.

Candidates: .... 1 minute (for pairs and groups of three)

Thank you.

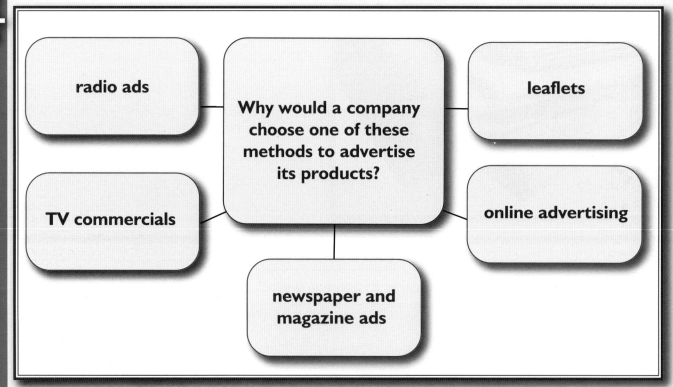

radio ads

TV commercials

Why would a company choose one of these methods to advertise its products?

newspaper and magazine ads

leaflets

online advertising

Paper 4 Speaking   **PART 4**   **4 minutes (6 minutes for groups of three)**

Part 4 – Discussion

In this part of the test you have to take part in a discussion with the other candidate related to the topic of the task you did in Part 3. The examiner will ask you both some questions.

Interlocutor:

- Why do you think there are regulations in place to control advertising?

- Do you think the media have a big impact on our everyday lives?

- Can you describe the most memorable advertisement you have seen?

- Have you ever bought something because of an advertisement that you saw on TV?

> *Select any of the following prompts, as appropriate:*
> - What do you think?
> - Do you agree?
> - And you?

Thank you. That is the end of the test.

Test 7

Paper 4 Speaking   **PART 1**   **2 minutes (3 minutes for groups of three)**

Part 1 – Interview

In this first part of the Speaking test, the examiner will ask you questions about topics such as family life, daily routines, or how you spend your free time. You will be expected to provide information about yourself and give your opinions.

Interlocutor: Good morning/afternoon/evening. My name is ………… and this is my colleague ………… . Can I have your mark sheets, please? Thank you. And your names are ………? Thank you.

First of all, we'd like to know something about you. *(to Candidate A)* Where are you from?
(to Candidate B) And you? ……………… And what do you like about living there?
(to Candidate A) And what about you?
Thank you.

(Ask each candidate one or more of the following questions, as appropriate.)

<u>Entertainment</u>
* How often do you go to the cinema?
* Tell us about a film you've seen recently.
* Would you rather go to the cinema or the theatre? Why?
* Have you ever been to a concert?

Paper 4 Speaking   **PART 2**   **4 minutes (6 minutes for groups of three)**

Part 2 – Long turn

In this part of the test you have to speak for 1 minute without interruption. The examiner will give you two photographs and you have to compare and contrast them as well as talk about your reaction to them. Your partner will get a different set of photographs and has to do the same thing. When each of you has finished speaking, the other will be invited to comment on the topic of the photographs.

Interlocutor: In this part of the test, I'm going to give each of you two photographs. I'd like you to talk about your photographs on your own for about a minute and also to answer a question about your partner's photographs.

     Candidate A, it's your turn first. Here are your photographs. They are both about crime.
     Candidate A has to look at the photographs on the next page.
     Candidate A, I'd like you to compare your photographs and say which one represents a more serious crime and why.
     All right?
Candidate A: *(one minute)* …………………………………
     Thank you.

     Candidate B, would you say that more serious and violent crimes are committed nowadays than in the past?
Candidate B: *(approximately 30 seconds)* …………………………………
     Thank you.

     Now, **Candidate B**, here are your photographs. They show people who are breaking a rule.
     Candidate B has to look at the photographs on the next page.
     Candidate B, I'd like you to compare your photographs and say why someone might break these rules.
     All right?
Candidate B: *(one minute)* …………………………………
     Thank you.

     Candidate A, do you think people who drink and drive should be arrested and sent to prison?
Candidate A: *(approximately 30 seconds)* …………………………………
     Thank you.

Speaking Section

Candidate A   **1**   Which photo represents a more serious crime and why?

Candidate B   **2**   Why might someone break these rules?

DON'T DRINK AND DRIVE

Paper 4 Speaking   PART 3   **4 minutes (5 minutes for groups of three)**

Part 3 – Collaborative Task

Interlocutor: Now I'd like you to talk about something together for about two minutes. (3 minutes for groups of three). **I'd like you to think about some recreational activities for young people. Here are some ideas** and a question for you to discuss. First you have some time to look at the task.

Look at the task in the box below. You have 15 seconds.

Now, discuss **whether these activities are beneficial for young people**.

Candidates: .... *2 minutes (3 minutes for groups of three)*

Interlocutor: Thank you. Now you have about a minute *(for pairs and groups of three)* to decide **which activity would be the most creative for young people**.

Candidates: .... 1 minute (for pairs and groups of three)

Thank you.

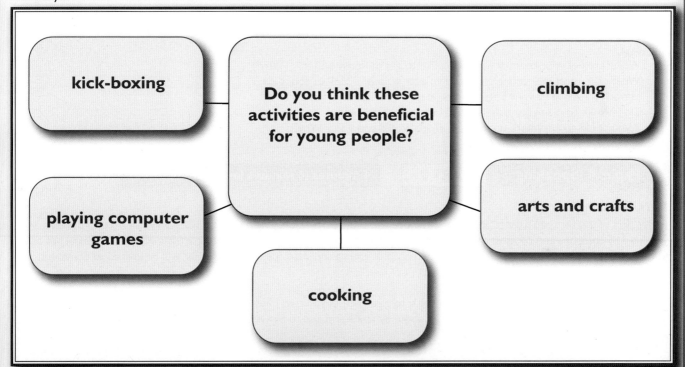

kick-boxing

Do you think these activities are beneficial for young people?

climbing

playing computer games

arts and crafts

cooking

Paper 4 Speaking   PART 4   **4 minutes (6 minutes for groups of three)**

Part 4 – Discussion

In this part of the test you have to take part in a discussion with the other candidate related to the topic of the task you did in Part 3. The examiner will ask you both some questions.

Interlocutor:

- Why do you think it is good for young people to do sports?

- Can artistic or musical skills be learned or are they something people either can or cannot do?

- Should people try to learn things that are hard for them, or should they focus on what they are good at?

- Are you ever too old to learn something new?

Select any of the following prompts, as appropriate:
- What do you think?
- Do you agree?
- And you?

Thank you. That is the end of the test.

Test 8

Paper 4 Speaking   **PART 1**   **2 minutes (3 minutes for groups of three)**

Part 1 – Interview

In this first part of the Speaking test, the examiner will ask you questions about topics such as family life, daily routines, or how you spend your free time. You will be expected to provide information about yourself and give your opinions.

Interlocutor: Good morning/afternoon/evening. My name is .... and this is my colleague .... Can I have your mark sheets, please? Thank you. And your names are ....? Thank you.

First of all, we'd like to know something about you. *(to Candidate A)* Where are you from?
(to Candidate B) And you? .... And what do you like about living there?
(to Candidate A) And what about you? Thank you.

(Ask each candidate one or more of the following questions, as appropriate.)

Holidays

❖   Which area of your country would you like to get to know better?   (Why?)
❖   What's the most interesting place you've ever visited?   (Tell us about it.)
❖   Have you ever used your English on holiday?   (What did you use it for?)
❖   Do you like to plan your holidays well in advance? (Why?)
❖   If you could go anywhere on holiday, where would you go?   (Why?)

Paper 4 Speaking   **PART 2**   **4 minutes (6 minutes for groups of three)**

Part 2 – Long turn

In this part of the test you have to speak for 1 minute without interruption. The examiner will give you two photographs and you have to compare and contrast them as well as talk about your reaction to them. Your partner will get a different set of photographs and has to do the same thing. When each of you has finished speaking, the other will be invited to comment on the topic of the photographs.

Interlocutor: In this part of the test, I'm going to give each of you two photographs. I'd like you to talk about your photographs on your own for about a minute and also to answer a question about your partner's photographs.

Candidate A, it's your turn first. Here are your photographs. They show people with different lifestyles.
Candidate A has to look at the photographs on the next page.
Candidate A, I'd like you to compare your photographs and say why you think it is important for people to do some form of exercise.
All right?

Candidate A: *(one minute)* ....
Thank you.

Candidate B, do you enjoy exercising?

Candidate B: *(approximately 30 seconds)* ....
Thank you.

Now, **Candidate B**, here are your photographs. They show people who are wearing different styles of clothes.
Candidate B has to look at the photographs on the next page.
Candidate B, I'd like you to compare your photographs and say why the people in the photos chose to dress this way.
All right?

Candidate B: *(one minute)* ....
Thank you.

Candidate A, do you follow fashion?

Candidate A: *(approximately 30 seconds)* ....
Thank you.

Candidate A   **1** Why is it important for people to do some form of exercise?

Candidate B   **2** Why did the people choose to dress this way?

Speaking Section

Speaking Section

| Paper 4 Speaking | **PART 3** | **4 minutes (5 minutes for groups of three)** |

Part 3 – Collaborative Task

Interlocutor: Now I'd like you to talk about something together for about two minutes. (3 minutes for groups of three). **I'd like you to think about clothes and how people dress. Here are different types of clothes** and a question for you to discuss. First you have some time to look at the task.

Look at the task in the box below. You have 15 seconds.

Now, talk to each other about **why people would choose to wear these clothes or accessories.**

Candidates: .... *2 minutes (3 minutes for groups of three)*

Interlocutor: Thank you. Now you have about a minute *(for pairs and groups of three)* to decide **which choice would be the most expensive.**

Candidates: .... *1 minute (for pairs and groups of three)*

Thank you.

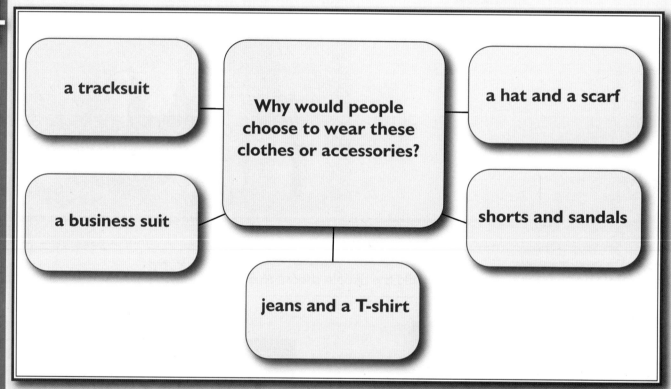

a tracksuit

Why would people choose to wear these clothes or accessories?

a hat and a scarf

a business suit

shorts and sandals

jeans and a T-shirt

| Paper 4 Speaking | **PART 4** | **4 minutes (6 minutes for groups of three)** |

Part 4 – Discussion

In this part of the test you have to take part in a discussion with the other candidate related to the topic of the task you did in Part 3. The examiner will ask you both some questions.

Interlocutor:

- Do you think looking good is important? Why/why not?
- Do you think there is too much pressure on young people to look a certain way?
- What do you think about fashion and the fashion industry?
- Have you ever judged someone only by their appearance and been incorrect?

Thank you. That is the end of the test.

> *Select any of the following prompts, as appropriate:*
> - What do you think?
> - Do you agree?
> - And you?

Test 9

Paper 4 Speaking	**PART 1**	2 minutes (3 minutes for groups of three)

Part 1 – Interview

In this first part of the Speaking test, the examiner will ask you questions about topics such as family life, daily routines, or how you spend your free time. You will be expected to provide information about yourself and give your opinions.

Interlocutor: Good morning/afternoon/evening. My name is ………… and this is my colleague …………. . Can I have your mark sheets, please? Thank you. And your names are ……….? Thank you.

First of all, we'd like to know something about you. *(to Candidate A)* Where are you from?
(to Candidate B) And you? …………………… And what do you like about living there?
(to Candidate A) And what about you?
Thank you.

(Ask each candidate one or more of the following questions, as appropriate.)

Likes and dislikes
❖   What sort of music do you listen to?   (Why do you enjoy it?)
❖   Do you like shopping?   (What sort of things do you buy?)
❖   What's your favourite food?   (Why do you like it?)
❖   What do you like to do at the weekend?
❖   Tell us about a day you've really enjoyed recently.

Paper 4 Speaking	**PART 2**	4 minutes (6 minutes for groups of three)

Part 2 – Long turn

In this part of the test you have to speak for 1 minute without interruption. The examiner will give you two photographs and you have to compare and contrast them as well as talk about your reaction to them. Your partner will get a different set of photographs and has to do the same thing. When each of you has finished speaking, the other will be invited to comment on the topic of the photographs.

Interlocutor: In this part of the test, I'm going to give each of you two photographs. I'd like you to talk about your photographs on your own for about a minute and also to answer a question about your partner's photographs.

Candidate A, it's your turn first. Here are your photographs. They show people using technology.
Candidate A has to look at the photographs on the next page.
Candidate A, I'd like you to compare your photographs and say why these forms of technology are important to people.
All right?

Candidate A: *(one minute)* ……………………………………
Thank you.

Candidate B, which of these things could people more easily do without?

Candidate B: *(approximately 30 seconds)* ……………………………
Thank you.

Now, **Candidate B**, here are your photographs. They show people working in different situations.
Candidate B has to look at the photographs on the next page.
Candidate B, I'd like you to compare your photographs and say which of these inventions has affected our lives the most and why?
All right?

Candidate B: *(one minute)* ……………………………
Thank you.

Candidate A, what kind of technology do you use at school/work?

Candidate A: *(approximately 30 seconds)* ……………………………
Thank you.

Speaking Section

Candidate A   **1**   Why are these forms of technology important to people?

Candidate B   **2**   Which of these inventions has affected our lives the most and why?

Paper 4 Speaking   **PART 3**   **4 minutes (5 minutes for groups of three)**

Part 3 – Collaborative Task

Interlocutor: Now I'd like you to talk about something together for about two minutes. (3 minutes for groups of three). **I'd like you to imagine that you are organising a competition at the community centre in your town, and you need to choose some presents that would attract more people to take part. Here are some gadgets you could offer** and a question for you to discuss. First you have some time to look at the task.

Look at the task in the box below. You have 15 seconds.

Now, discuss **whether you think that these presents would attract more people to take part in the competition**.

Candidates: .... *2 minutes (3 minutes for groups of three)*

Interlocutor: Thank you. Now you have about a minute *(for pairs and groups of three)* to decide **which gadget is the most complicated to use**.

Candidates: .... I minute (for pairs and groups of three)

Thank you.

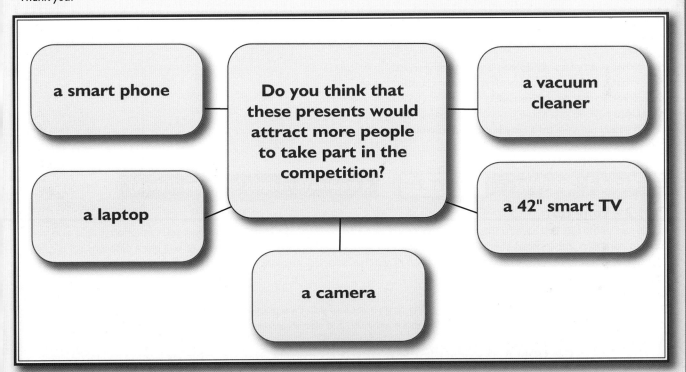

a smart phone

Do you think that these presents would attract more people to take part in the competition?

a vacuum cleaner

a laptop

a 42" smart TV

a camera

Paper 4 Speaking   **PART 4**   **4 minutes (6 minutes for groups of three)**

Part 4 – Discussion

In this part of the test you have to take part in a discussion with the other candidate related to the topic of the task you did in Part 3. The examiner will ask you both some questions.

Interlocutor:

- What do you think about internet access being restricted in some countries of the world?

- Are blogs, instant messaging and social networking sites threatening traditional face-to-face communication?

- Technology creates more problems than it solves. Do you agree or disagree?

- Can you think of an example of technology that should never have been created?

Select any of the following prompts, as appropriate:
- What do you think?
- Do you agree?
- And you?

Thank you. That is the end of the test.

Test 10

Speaking Section

| Paper 4 Speaking | **PART 1** | 2 minutes (3 minutes for groups of three) |

Part 1 – Interview

In this first part of the Speaking test, the examiner will ask you questions about topics such as family life, daily routines, or how you spend your free time. You will be expected to provide information about yourself and give your opinions.

Interlocutor: Good morning/afternoon/evening. My name is ………… and this is my colleague ………… . Can I have your mark sheets, please? Thank you. And your names are ………? Thank you.

First of all, we'd like to know something about you. *(to Candidate A)* Where are you from?
(to Candidate B) And you? ……………… And what do you like about living there?
(to Candidate A) And what about you?
Thank you.

(Ask each candidate one or more of the following questions, as appropriate.)

Hobbies
❖   What sorts of books do you enjoy reading most?
❖   What is the most popular sport in your country?
❖   What do you do to exercise?
❖   Does anyone you know have an interesting hobby?
❖   If you could take up a new hobby, what would you do?

| Paper 4 Speaking | **PART 2** | 4 minutes (6 minutes for groups of three) |

Part 2 – Long turn

In this part of the test you have to speak for 1 minute without interruption. The examiner will give you two photographs and you have to compare and contrast them as well as talk about your reaction to them. Your partner will get a different set of photographs and has to do the same thing. When each of you has finished speaking, the other will be invited to comment on the topic of the photographs.

Interlocutor: In this part of the test, I'm going to give each of you two photographs. I'd like you to talk about your photographs on your own for about a minute and also to answer a question about your partner's photographs.

Candidate A, it's your turn first. Here are your photographs. They show different kinds of natural disasters. *Candidate A has to look at the photographs on the next page.*
Candidate A, I'd like you to compare your photographs and say which of these natural disasters is the easiest to prepare for. All right?

Candidate A: *(one minute)* …………………………………
Thank you.

Candidate B, would you live near a volcano?

Candidate B: *(approximately 30 seconds)* …………………………………
Thank you.

Now, **Candidate B**, here are your photographs. They show areas in the world with extreme weather. *Candidate B has to look at the photographs on the next page.*
Candidate B, I'd like you to compare your photographs and say who would be able to live in these places. All right?

Candidate B: *(one minute)* …………………………………
Thank you.

Candidate A, would you like to explore either of these places?

Candidate A: *(approximately 30 seconds)* …………………………………
Thank you.

Speaking Section

Candidate A | **1** Which of these natural disasters is easiest to prepare for?

Candidate B | **2** Who would be able to live in these places?

Speaking Section

Part 3 – Collaborative Task

Interlocutor: Now I'd like you to talk about something together for about two minutes. (3 minutes for groups of three). **I'd like you to imagine that a city council is thinking of some ways to reduce air pollution in their city. Here are some ideas** and a question for you to discuss. First you have some time to look at the task.

Look at the task in the box below. You have 15 seconds.

Now, discuss how **these methods could reduce air pollution in a city**.

Candidates: .... *2 minutes (3 minutes for groups of three)*

Interlocutor: Thank you. Now you have about a minute *(for pairs and groups of three)* to decide **which method would be the most effective**.

Candidates: .... I minute (for pairs and groups of three)

Thank you.

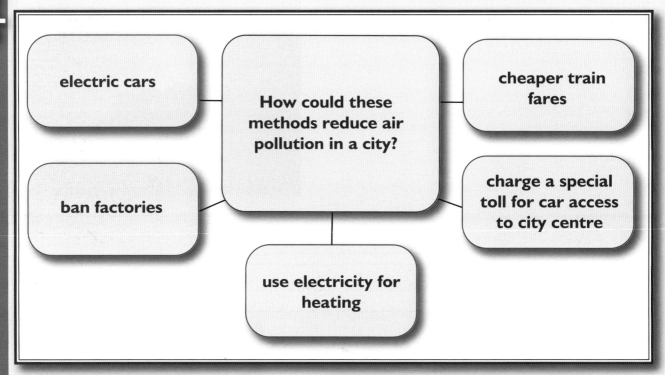

Part 4 – Discussion

In this part of the test you have to take part in a discussion with the other candidate related to the topic of the task you did in Part 3. The examiner will ask you both some questions.

Interlocutor:

Select any of the following prompts, as appropriate:
- What do you think?
- Do you agree?
- And you?

- How could the environment be improved in your city?

- Are open spaces and parks important for our cities? Why / why not?

- What can be done to make dangerous areas in a city safer?

- When lots of people move into the suburbs, how does this change a city centre?

- Do you think preserving a city's history is important?

Thank you. That is the end of the test.

Cambridge English:
First - FCE
EXAM GUIDE

This section contains a detailed analysis of the **Cambridge English: First** exam with exam tips and guidance for all 4 Papers:

Paper 1: Reading & Use of English
Paper 2: Writing
Paper 3: Listening
Paper 4: Speaking

Paper/timing	Part	Test content	Test focus
READING AND USE OF ENGLISH 1 hr 15 mins	1	A modified cloze test containing eight gaps followed by eight multiple-choice questions.	Candidates are expected to be able to: demonstrate the ability to apply their knowledge and control of the language system by completing a number of tasks at text and sentence level; demonstrate a variety of reading skills including understanding of specific information, text organisation features, implication, attitude and text structure.
	2	A modified cloze test containing eight gaps.	
	3	A text containing eight gaps. Each gap corresponds to a word. The stems of the missing words are given beside the text and must be changed to form the missing word.	
	4	Six separate questions, each with a lead-in sentence and a gapped second sentence to be completed in two to five words, one of which is a given 'key' word.	
	5	A text followed by six 4-option multiple-choice questions.	
	6	A text from which six sentences have been removed and placed in jumbled order, together with an additional sentence, after the text.	
	7	A text or several short texts, preceded by 10 multiple-matching questions.	

Paper 1 - Reading & Use of English

General Description

Parts: 7   **Timing: 1 hour 15 minutes**
Number of Questions: 52

Use of English
Parts 1 to 4: texts with accompanying grammar and vocabulary tasks,
and separate items with a grammar and vocabulary focus.
Reading
Parts 5 to 7: a range of texts and accompanying reading comprehension tasks.

TASK TYPES:
Multiple-choice cloze, open cloze, word formation, key word transformation,
multiple choice, gapped text, multiple matching.

WORD COUNT: 2,200–2,500

MARKS
Parts 1–3: each correct answer receives 1 mark.
Part 4: each correct answer receives up to 2 marks.
Parts 5–6: each correct answer receives 2 marks.
Part 7: each correct answer receives 1 mark.

Part 1

- Multiple-choice Cloze.

- Mainly a test of vocabulary (some grammatical knowledge required for certain questions).

- A text containing 8 gaps.

- Four options for each gap from which to choose the correct word to fill the gap.

- 8 Questions.

Part 1 (Test 1)

There will always be an example, which you can refer to if unsure of how to do the questions.

Always read the information BOTH before and after the gap.

Question 1 here is a test of vocabulary; that is, you must choose the word with the correct meaning. To do this, you must know or guess what the four words mean, and you must also know what the sentence is trying to say; therefore, meaning at word and sentence level is being tested.

For questions *1-8*, read the text below and decide which word A, B, C or D best fits each space. There is an example at the beginning (0).

Example:

0. A. or   B. and   C. in   D. nor   [0] [A] [B] [C] [D]

Each gap will have four corresponding options to choose from. Read all the options before choosing.

Royal Residences

Buckingham Palace, Windsor Castle (0) .... the Palace of Holyroodhouse are these (1) .... of the sovereign and, as such, serve as both home and office for the Queen, whose personal flag flies (2) .... her Majesty is in residence.

These buildings are used extensively for State ceremonies and official entertaining and are opened to the (3) .... as much as these commitments allow. They are furnished with fine pictures and works of art from the Royal Collection, assembled over four centuries by successive sovereigns. Many of the State Apartments and rooms at the official residences have been in continuous use since their conception and many of the paintings are (4) .... in the rooms for which they were originally (5) ....

The official residences are in regular use and the style and manner in which they are shown to visitors reflects their working status. Rooms are kept as close to their normal (6) .... as possible. Inevitably, opening times are subject to change at short notice depending on circumstances.

The Royal Collection, which is owned by the Queen as Sovereign in trust for her successors and the Nation, is administered by the Royal Collection Trust to which a proportion of the admission fee and other (7) .... from visitors is directed. The remainder of this money funds the majority of the cost of restoring Windsor Castle which was badly (8) .... by fire in November 1992.

#	A	B	C	D
1.	A. venues	B. residences	C. situations	D. occupation
2.	A. whatever	B. however	C. whoever	D. whenever
3.	A. humans	B. public	C. peoples	D. strangers
4.	A. created	B. explored	C. produced	D. displayed
5.	A. instructed	B. intended	C. performed	D. guarded
6.	A. feature	B. location	C. destination	D. appearance
7.	A. salary	B. budget	C. income	D. wages
8.	A. destroyed	B. ruined	C. damaged	D. collapsed

Task Focus:

(i) meaning at word and / or sentence level

(ii) your knowledge at phrasal level i.e. collocations like 'pay attention to', phrasal verbs like 'give up' and linking phrases like 'even if'.

(iii) grammar whether you can choose an option that fits correctly with the verb or preposition which follows the gap.

Some questions will test your knowledge at phrase level and you will be expected to recognise set phrases and collocations.

Your grammar knowledge may also be tested i.e. if you have to choose an option to fit correctly with a preposition or verb which follows directly after the gap.

Part 2

- Open cloze.

- A test of both vocabulary and grammar.

- A text containing 8 gaps.

- No options to choose from - you must think of the right word to fit in the gap yourself.

- May be more than one correct answer, but just write down one.

- 8 Questions.

Task Focus

This task tests your knowledge of the structure of the language, and also your understanding of the text. The focus of each gapped word will either be grammatical (article/preposition/pronoun/verb tense or form etc.) or phrasal (i.e. phrasal verbs, linking phrases, words within fixed phrases etc.).

Part 2 (Test 1)

Paper 1 Reading and Use of English | PART 2

*For questions **9-16**, read the text below and think of the word which best fits each space. Use only **one** word in each space. There is an example at the beginning (0).*

Example: | **0** | m o s t |

Inspiration

I have had what, I think, is the (0) ......*most*...... extraordinary day of my life. While the events are (9) .... clear in my mind, I wish to write them down. Let me introduce (10) ....

My name is Lawrence Terrel. I am thirty-five years old, and in perfect health. I have never been ill in my life, not even for a day. I am an artist. I am (11) .... very successful, but I earn enough money to (12) .... care of my needs. My only near relative, a sister, (13) .... three years ago. So I have no family.

I ate breakfast this morning at eight. After I had read the morning paper, I smoked my pipe and let my mind wander. I hoped I would think of (14) .... to draw. The room was very hot,

If the answer is not obvious, ask yourself what kind of word is needed i.e. a noun, pronoun, adjective, verb etc. In this case, a pronoun is needed.

The answer will always be a single word.

Always read before and after the gap. With gap 11, for example, we can only find out whether the missing word is positive or negative by reading on.

The answer for gap 12 is a phrasal verb. Familiarise yourself with as many common phrasal and idiomatic expressions, and collocations, as you can.

Part 3

- Word formation.

- A test of (mainly) vocabulary.

- A text containing 8 gaps.

- Each gap represents a missing word.

- The stems of the words are provided.

- You must put the stems into the correct form.

- 8 questions.

Task Focus

This task focuses mainly on vocabulary, though an understanding of structure is also required. You should know how prefixes, suffixes, internal changes and compounds are used to form new words from a stem.

Part 3 (Test 1)

Try to familiarise yourself with the pre-fixes and suffixes used before certain words. For example, is it 'unrefutable' or 'irrefutable' or 'derefutable' etc.

Paper 1 Reading and Use of English   **PART 3**

For questions **17-24**, read the text below. Use the word given in capitals at the end of some lines to form a word that fits in the space in the same line. There is an example at the beginning **(0)**.

Example: **0**   e n t e r t a i n m e n t

Your answer must be **one word** and that word must be a form of the corresponding word given in the right-hand column.

People in the world of **(0)** _entertainment_ have to be very **(17)** .... ENTERTAIN/OBSERVE

in the way that they dress. It's an **(18)** .... fact that image is REFUTE

more than just a case of **(19)** .... for a celebrity. How they DECORATE

present themselves is all part of their artistic personality.

It would be **(20)** .... though to think that somebody can be FOOL

a successful celebrity just because of the clothes they wear. They don't **(21)** .... NECESSARY

have to wear **(22)** .... clothing but they do need to be ALTER

talented and communicative and they also need to have an

(23) .... of their fans who make them successful. APPRECIATE

They also need to be **(24)** .... so that they can cope ADAPT

with all the public attention.

As with all gap-fill exercises, you should read the information BOTH before and after the gap; this will help you determine important details about the correct form of the word.

Look carefully for clues as to what the correct form of the word is. For example, Q23 is preceded by 'an'; therefore, a noun is required. Q24 is preceded by 'to be'; probably an adjective is also required and so on...

Part 4 (example from Test 1)

25. My parents last spoke to me a month ago.   heard

    I .... my parents for a month.

Your answer must have the same meaning as the original sentence.

You must write no less than 2 and no more than 5 words.

You must use the given word in your answer.

Part 4

- Key word transformations.

- A test of grammar and vocabulary.

- 6 separate tasks (6 questions).

- Each task has a lead-in sentence and a gapped sentence.

- The gapped sentence must be completed in 2-5 words using a given key word.

Task Focus

This task tests a range of different structures, and has both a grammatical and lexical (vocabulary-based) focus. You must demonstrate that you have the ability to express messages in different ways without compromising their meaning.

General Comments

- Always look at the title (Parts 1, 2 and 3) as this will indicate the main subject of the text.
- Read through each text (Parts 1, 2 and 3) before attempting the questions.
  (this will help you get a clear idea of what it is about)
- Parts 2 and 4 - there may be more than one correct answer.
  (however, only give one answer; if you give two and one is wrong, you will get no marks)
- Each part of the test has an example - study the example closely if you are unsure of what to do.
- If you want to change your answer:
  1) For Part 1; rub out the mark you have made and mark a different box.
  2) For Parts 2-4; rub out and replace the existing words (do not try to write over or change them or put the new words in brackets).
- You must allow time at the end of the test to:
  1) Check your answers.
  2) Transfer your answers to the answer sheet.
- Remember: Correct spelling is essential in all parts of Paper 1 where you must write an answer.
- Your handwriting should be clear and easy to read.

Preparation

The best way to build up your vocabulary and become familiar with the many different types of structures used in this paper is to read extensively (a lot). Don't limit yourself to reading school books; find subjects you are genuinely interested in to read about. Read novels, magazines etc. Not only will your performance in this section be helped, so will your performance across the test.

When you are reading, it is useful to have dictionaries or grammar books to refer to, but also try to get used to guessing the meaning of unknown words and phrases from the context they are found in. This is the strategy you will have to employ on exam day as no dictionaries are allowed, so it is wise to get some practice beforehand.

Paper 1 Reading Tasks

PART 5: Task type: **4-option multiple choice**   **Number of Questions: 6**

Focus: This part has a wide range of focus; it is possible for questions to be asked in relation to detail, opinion, gist, attitude, tone, purpose, main idea, meaning from context, text organisation, comparison, reference, exemplification etc.

PART 6: Task type: **gapped text**   **Number of Questions: 6**

Sentences have been removed from the text and placed in random order. You must decide where the sentences were removed from.
Focus: The focus is on text structure, cohesion and coherence - your understanding of the text, where information should fit and how the text should flow.

Part 5

- Always look at the Part 5 text before looking at the questions. Read the text for gist (overall or general understanding) first, and then turn to the questions. Why? Because three of the four options for each question are wrong and this is too much information to absorb at once.

- After you have read the text for gist, read the first question. Once you are satisfied you understand it, skim through the text until you find the section to which the question relates, then read this section carefully.

- Don't assume that if you spot a word or phrase in the text that is the same as one of the answer options, the answer option must be the right one; you need to check that the meaning of the option is reflected in the text, not that the words are the same in both. Words from the text will often be paraphrased in the multiple choice options.

Part 6

- Always read through the text with the gaps in it before starting to do the task. This will help you get an overall understanding of the structure of the text and how the writer's ideas develop.

- After you have read the text for gist, go to the first gap. Look carefully at the information both before and after the gap. The correct answer must not just fit logically with the information that has gone before, but with the following sentences also.

- Avoid word-spotting; just because a word in one of the options is mentioned nearby in the text, does not automatically mean it is the correct choice. Instead, ask yourself questions like:

  - Does the tense match?
  - Is the time period the same?
  - Does this option complete an incomplete argument or point?
  - Does it contain the missing introduction to an existing argument or point?
  - Is it an example or supporting point for what was just said?

Part 5 Method

Read the passage for gist.

Read the first question.

Scan the passage to locate the section with the answer (or skim if harder to locate).

Read this section carefully.

Select the option that most closely reflects the information in the text.

Move to question 2, 3 etc.

Part 6 Method

Read the passage for gist.

Go to the first gap and read the information BEFORE and AFTER it carefully.

Read through the options and select the most logical fit.

Move to gap 2, 3 etc.

You must match prompts (pieces of information) to the section of the text or (if there is more than one text) the actual text to which the prompts relate.

Focus: You will have to scan for specific information, or identify the location of a specific detail, opinion or attitude.

Part 7

■ This task is essentially a skimming and scanning exercise.

■ It may be helpful to read through the questions first and have them in mind for when you first read the text or texts.

■ Read the text or texts quickly, marking any section where you think you may have found an answer.

■ Look carefully at the sections you marked to confirm your answers.

■ For any questions that are still unanswered, scan the text(s) again for key words and/or phrases from each unanswered question, and keep in mind that you may have to scan for meaning as some of the question words may be paraphrased. Read carefully over the relevant section of the text when you think you have found an answer.

Reading for gist

Reading for gist involves reading the text quickly to get an overall understanding of what has been written. When gist-reading, do not be concerned about the meanings of individual words you don't immediately understand so long as you can grasp the general points that the writer is making.

Generally speaking, it is useful to have a broad understanding of what a text is about regardless of the exact nature of the questions which follow it as this understanding provides context and clarity for the exam-taker.

Gist-reading is particularly helpful when answering questions about the following:

(i) the writer's main point or argument
(ii) the writer's general views
(iii) the writer's tone and style

When gist-reading, you may identify areas of the text that are important and which you should return to to conduct a more careful reading. Highlight these sections as you go along.

Part 7 Method

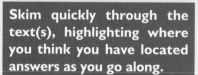

Skim over the questions to begin.

Skim quickly through the text(s), highlighting where you think you have located answers as you go along.

Read carefully over the highlighted areas to confirm the answers.

Scan the passage for key words and phrases from each remaining unanswered question.

Read carefully where you think you have found an answer.

Skimming

Skimming and reading for gist are often thought of as the same thing, but here we will use skimming to explain reading very quickly over a text you have seen before in order to confirm and/or identify where a piece of information is located within it. Skimming, then, is used to get a general understanding of specific points and where they are located in the text. It is often useful to skim when you want to find an area of text related to a question or when you want to find information from the question that is paraphrased in the text, as sometimes if a question is paraphrased very well, we cannot find what it relates to in the text using only key words taken from the question.

Scanning

Scanning involves looking for very small and specific pieces of information within a larger text; information such as key words or phrases found in a question. You don't read so much as glance over the text when you are scanning.

Scanning is useful in answering questions about:

(i) key facts or dates.
(ii) who said what.
(iii) the order of events etc.

You should try to scan for
(i) names.
(ii) dates.
(iii) technical terms.
(iv) places.
(v) people.
(vii) things.
(viii) words and phrases that are hard to paraphrase etc.

Reading for detail

Because you have limited time in the exam, it is not possible to read every part of every text very carefully. In fact, we only read for detail to do one of two things:

(i) confirm an answer we think we have identified.
(ii) understand an important but complicated section of the text.

Reading for detail, then, involves reading a small section of the text very carefully for a better understanding of what the writer is saying, and we only do it to help us answer a question.

Gist-reading

It is useful to start most tasks by reading for gist (PARTS 5 & 6 especially). This gives you a general understanding of the text, its layout and the writer's views.

Skimming

Use skimming to quickly read over short sections of text when you want to understand general points.

If there aren't many questions related to the text, skim through them before you start reading. This way the information you are looking for will be in the back of your mind as you read (PART 7 especially).

Reading for Detail

Once you have found where an answer is located in the text, read this section carefully to confirm the answer choice. Don't waste time reading the entire text in such detail though.

Scanning

When you are looking for specific pieces of information like names, dates, times etc, rather than read the entire text, scan through it quickly to locate the section you are looking for.

General Reading Tips

- Read a wide range of texts both in class and at home. You can find material in actual newspapers, magazines and other sources listed above.

- At home and in class, focus first on what is termed 'pre-reading'. Pre-reading involves looking quickly at the title, questions and any other simple information and trying to predict what the text might be about. This helps get your brain clued in to the subject matter quickly and activates your existing knowledge of the topic and topic vocabulary.

- Practise a wide range of reading skills such as scanning (quickly looking for specific words or details), skimming (quickly reading over sections of the text), gist-reading (reading for overall understanding), reading for detail (careful reading) etc. Reading for gist will be particularly important when you come to more complex texts where some of the words may be unknown to you. Do not dwell on unknown words but try to get an understanding of the general subject of the text.

THE QUESTIONS WILL ALWAYS BE ASKED IN THE ORDER THE ANSWERS APPEAR IN THE TEXT.

When trying to scan the text, be selective in the information you choose to look for.
The answer choices usually paraphrase the information which is mentioned in the text.

Though the questions are in order, the answer choices are not. A, B, C and D may appear in any order in the text, or, if they are distractors (put in the question to confuse you), they may not necessarily appear at all.

31. What does the writer mean by saying communities used to live in worlds inside a bigger world?
   A. In the past people knew little about faraway places.
   B. In the past people only cared about themselves.
   C. Most people didn't travel very much in the past.
   D. Most people cared about what was happening in the bigger world.

32. What changed after the experience of two world wars?
   A. Politicians felt determined to prevent another world war.
   B. Information technology brought the world closer together.
   C. Nobody was interested in conflict anymore.
   D. Nations wanted to become more independent.

33. What is suggested about the United Nations?
   A. It keeps the world peaceful and conflict-free.
   B. It will become a global government.
   C. It doesn't have a lot of meaningful influence.
   D. It is controlled by a few big powers.

Questions like this always require careful reading (reading for detail). Read the sentences before and after the word carefully. That way, if you are not familiar with the word, you should be able to work out its meaning in context.

34. What does the phrase 'took shape' mean in the context of paragraph 4, line 42?
   A. succeeded
   B. developed
   C. concluded
   D. changed

35. The arrival of new technology and the information age
   A. seemed unimportant compared to the political changes taking place.
   B. had a strong impact on the opposite side of the globe.
   C. brought people together in a way that politicians could not.
   D. saw people use the internet a lot in their living rooms.

36. What does the writer's tone in the final paragraph suggest?
   A. He is satisfied with what has been achieved.
   B. He is critical and pessimistic about the future.
   C. He is confused and upset.
   D. He is realistic about the situation.

A proper noun, i.e. United Nations, cannot be paraphrased. These are perfect key words to scan for in the text. Once you have found where the United Nations is discussed, you can read that section of the text for detail to make sure you get the right answer.

There are two types of multiple choice questions:

(i) finish the sentence.
(ii) answer the question.

Multiple choice questions like these can cover a broad range of functions. For example, questions 31 and 36 ask you to interpret the writer's views; question 34 tests your understanding of vocabulary and context; question 33 asks for factual information, and questions 32 and 35 have to do with cause and effect.

Reading Part 6 : Example (Test 7)

After reading the entire text quickly for gist and an understanding of how the writer's ideas are laid out.

Hope and Sadness

There's often a sense of the hopeless romantic associated with those who trek to the Highlands in search (more in hope than expectation) of the white stuff. More often than not, these ski and snowboard fanatics are met with disappointment. Either a thaw has set in and the rocks are visible or it's a total whiteout as gales blow and blizzards blast the poor expectant hopefuls. The Highlands, you see, is a tale of extremes; it's all or nothing up there.

37 [ ] But those patient folk – those old romantics whose sense of loyalty and optimism seems to know no bounds – are having the last laugh this winter. Picture this: fresh powder everywhere; 180cm of accumulated snow at the base of the resort; more falls forecast for later in the week; clear blue skies and a blazing sun. No, this isn't some upmarket French alpine retreat full of five-star chalets and bulging wallets. This is humble little Cairngorm, pride of Scotland. This is real, old-style skiing without the gloss. There's an infectious passion and enthusiasm here today. **38** [ ]

Despite all the talk of global warming spelling the end for Scotland's long-suffering winter sport industry, Cairngorm and its four sister resorts; the Lecht, Glenshee, Glencoe and the Nevis Range aren't about to go down without a fight. And, finally, nature has lent them a helping hand. As I am about to hop onto the chairlift, I can't resist the urge to pause and admire the scene around me; the Highlands at its best. **39** [ ] Back then, these slopes were crowded with thousands of skiers all season long; full to capacity – just as they are once again today. The cafes are overflowing with people enjoying their apres ski. You can see skiers of all sorts; beginners, wannabes and

Focus on the first gap. Read the information before and after it very carefully.

Even if the gap is at the start or end of a paragraph, read the 'before' and 'after' sentences. Paragraphs flow into one another and it is important to check that your chosen sentence fits well with what is said in the other paragraph.

A. The more we begin to feel the effects of global warming, the more it seems to be nothing instead of all.

B. Why have we wrecked this planet for future generations?

C. It's like going back in time to the glory days of the 1960s and 70s.

D. These people have waited a long time!

E. All of my happiest memories of winters growing up as a child were spent flying down the slopes.

F. Do you remember those hopeless romantics I described before?

G. But sadly there isn't the snow base to satisfy their passion or desire.

Sentences like these make the task slightly easier; they can only fit in the text where 'these people' have been mentioned immediately before. Look out for clues like this, then ask yourself who 'these people' might be.

When skimming through the sentences, look for repetition of words, phrases or ideas. But, BE CAREFUL, just because a word or phrase is repeated do not assume it is the right choice. Here, it is not just the words but the context and meaning that confirm the sentence as the right choice.

As you skim the sentences underline key words and phrases.

Therefore, as well as repetition of words/phrases/ideas, look out for sentences which introduce an idea when an introduction is missing; explain an idea when only the introduction is there; justify an argument or point made; exemplify (give an example of) an argument or point made; conclude an argument or point; link points together etc.

Some of the questions or statements will have more than one correct answer.

Highlight key words and ideas as you read each question or statement. Then read as much for the ideas (skimming) as for the words themselves (scanning) as often the words in the text(s) will not be exactly the same.

Which person:

is glad their nation is made up of people from lots of different backgrounds? | 43 |

is proud that their country has kept a particular political system? | 44 |

mentions something which attracts a lot of people to their country? | 45 |

Think about what kind of information you should scan for.

believes money has had an effect on something? | 46 |

thinks their country has an unfair reputation? | 47 |

believes their country has progressed very fast? | 48 |

believes geography has influenced their country's culture? | 49 |

feels their nation's identity is threatened by something? | 50 |

wishes their country was as successful as it once was? | 51 |

sees evidence of the work and achievements of their ancestors around them today? | 52 |

Scan for a time reference - a comparison between present and past.

As you practise you may find that some parts of the Reading section may take you longer than others. It is important to consider this before exam day and decide how you want to allocate your time. If you find **Part 6** particularly hard, you might aim to finish **Part 7** quickly so that you can spend time on the more difficult part, for example.

First - FCE - PAPER 2 Writing
EXAM GUIDE

Writing Section - Paper 2

Format: The paper contains two parts.   **Timing:** 1 hour 20 minutes   **Number of Parts: 2**

Task: You are required to complete two tasks: a **compulsory** task in **Part 1** and **one task from a choice of three** in **Part 2**.

Task Types: A range from the following: article; email/letter; essay; report; review.

Scoring: Each question on this paper carries equal marks.

Structure and tasks

Part 1: Write an essay giving opinion and providing reasons for the opinion.

You are asked to write an essay giving your opinion on the essay title using the ideas given and providing an idea of your own. The essay title will be on a subject of general interest not requiring any specialised knowledge.

Word Requirement: 140–190 words

Part 2: Writing one from a number of possible text types based on a contextualised writing task.

You have a choice of task. In questions 2–4, the tasks provide you with a clear context, topic, purpose and target reader for your writing. The output text types are:

• article   • report   • email/letter   • review

Word Requirement: 140–190 words

General Advice

- Where possible, choose tasks and topics that are suited to your interests and experience. In general, students who write about something they are familiar with do better.

- Always read the question carefully before starting to write. Underline the most important points. Then make a plan of your composition, ensuring that you are answering the question asked.

- Do not waste time rewriting all or part of your composition if you have to make corrections. Cross out your mistakes and write your corrections in as clearly as possible.

- Think carefully about who the target reader is each time you go to write; read the task carefully to identify the appropriate style and tone.

- At this level, you should be able to link your ideas together effectively. Use a variety of linking words and ensure that the flow of your ideas is logical. This creates a composition that is easy to follow and which leaves a positive impression on the reader.

- In the answer booklet, lined pages will follow each question-page. You should write your answers on these lined pages. If you want to make notes in the exam, there are blank pages at the back of the exam booklet. Your notes will not be marked. If you run out of space to write your answers, you can also use the blank pages at the back of the booklet for this purpose, but indicate clearly what you are doing.

- Only ever attempt two questions. You are marked on the compulsory task (Part 1) and ONE question from Part 2. If you do more questions, you will waste valuable time and gain nothing.

- Give equal amounts of your time to each question as both questions carry the same number of marks.

Expected word length

You should write approximately the right number of words. If you write considerably fewer words than the minimum, this is likely to mean that you have not successfully completed the task, resulting in a fail. An overlong composition, on the other hand, MAY include irrelevant information and repetition, and be poorly organised. If this is the case, it will have a negative effect on the reader and your grade.

Spelling and Punctuation

Spelling and punctuation are not actually marked. However, if poor spelling and punctuation impede communication (make it difficult for the reader to understand what you are saying), the Overall Impression mark will be negatively affected, so it is important not to be careless with either of these aspects of your writing.

*You **must** answer this question. Write your answer in **140-190** words in an appropriate style.*

1. In your English class you have been talking about the problem of obesity in young people. Now your English teacher has asked you to write an essay. Write an **essay** using **all** the notes and give reasons for your point of view.

Read the essay question and the notes very carefully in order to understand what you are expected to do.
It is important that in your essay all your ideas and opinions are relevant to the question.

In Europe and the USA a lot of young people have an obesity problem. What can be done to solve this problem?

Notes

Write about:
1. Drinking
2. Fast food
3. .... (your own idea)

Obesity is a serious issue affecting many young people in Europe and the U.S.A. I believe that the key to solving obesity is to educate the young. So what can be done to tackle this threat to the younger generations' health and reverse a worrying trend?

Medical issues apart, excessive intake of calories is to blame to a large extent for obesity in the young. The simple solution therefore is to educate young people to avoid fat-laden <u>fast food</u> and to opt for healthier salads and low-calorie foods instead.

However, it's not just bad eating habits that lead to obesity. <u>Alcohol is</u> packed with calories-3 glasses of wine are equivalent calorie-wise to one full meal! Those wishing to lose weight need to reduce alcohol intake too.

Furthermore, I believe that the key to solving obesity <u>is to educate the</u> young. If children are educated at school about healthy eating and drinking sensibly, then they are less likely to become obese when they are older.

I believe that if schools educate the young from an early age and individuals learn to take more responsibility for their own diet, obesity will become a thing of the past.

You will be provided with two ideas to write about. You have to write about the two ideas and also introduce a third one of your own. If any of the three essay ideas/prompts is not addressed, then you might be penalised.

You need to express your ideas in a clear and logical way. Essays should be well-organised and with linking words and phrases. Clear paragraphing is really important in an essay.

Make a plan

Analyse the task

Composition Type:	Essay
Writing to:	Your English teacher
Style:	Formal
Write about:	1. Drinking 2. Fast food 3. .... (your own idea) Educate young people about obesity.

Par 1	Introduction: Make a general statement about the problem of obesity.
Par 2	Write about: 2. Fast food Talk about bad eating habits / fast food.
Par 3	Write about: 1. Drinking How drinking leads to obesity.
Par 4	3. .... (your own idea) Educate young people about obesity.
Par 5	Reach a conclusion. Make your own suggestions or recommendations on what can be done to improve the situation.

Example Part 2 (taken from Test 1)

2. Your favourite music magazine has advertised a contest for readers to write a **review** of a concert they have seen recently.

Underline the key points in the question before you start to analyse the task.

"Soundcheck Magazine" is seeking reviews from readers!

Have you seen a <u>great concert</u> recently?
Have you seen a <u>terrible one</u>? We want to know!

Write the best review and win a trip to see your favourite band perform!

In **Part 2** questions, you have less input material and you are not told exactly what to write about.

Analyse the task

Composition Type:	Review
Writing to:	Magazine
Style:	Neutral or informal - look at the name 'Sound-check Magazine' - this doesn't sound like an academic publication, so a less formal style is appropriate. Also, it's a 'concert review'; this gives you another clue as to the register - think about what you know of concert reviews - are they normally very formal? No... Most reviews are neutral-to-informal.
Subject:	a concert review (good or bad)

Brainstorming

As you are not told exactly what to write about, it is important to come up with some ideas of your own. This is where brainstorming comes in. It should only take about a minute and what you should do is write as many ideas as you can think of down on a piece of paper. Once your brainstorm is over, decide what ideas to keep and which ones not to use. Then make a plan for your composition.

Notice in this task analysis, the 'Write about' row from the **Part 1** question is not there and has been replaced by 'Subject'. This is because Part 1 questions generally tell you exactly what you should write about, whereas Part 2 questions just give you a general subject and you must come up with what to say yourself.

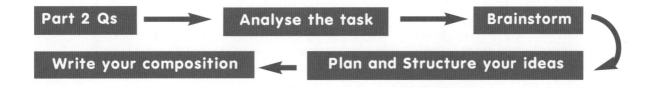

Part 2 Qs ⟶ Analyse the task ⟶ Brainstorm

Write your composition ⟵ Plan and Structure your ideas

Handwriting

The only thing you need to do is make sure that you write clearly so that the examiner can understand your answers.

Word-length preparation

Do not waste time counting words on the day of the exam. Know approximately what the word limits look like in your handwriting, and do not be overly concerned with exceeding the limit by a few words. Practise writing compositions that fit within the word limit in advance and you will become comfortable writing in this way.

Brainstorm

Who? - Metropolis / ~~Bandwidth~~ / Maxi ~~and the Monks~~

What? - rock concert

When? - last weekend - not planned - never heard of band - friend knew band member - nice surprise

What happened? - fantastic - unique style - lead singer - great voice - synthesizer, drums, ~~piano~~, ~~trumpet~~ - very creative

Cost? - bit ~~too expensive~~ - ~~£25 to get in~~ / great value - charged nothing

Would I recommend? - definitely - great show - though bad ~~language~~

- ~~not suitable~~ for young kids

Write down all your ideas.

Decide what to write about and cross out any ideas you don't want to use.

Make a plan

Par 1	The concert and why I went: - Metropolis - not planned - never heard of band - friend recommended - really surprised
Par 2	My experience: fantastic band - unique style of music - lead singer - great voice - man with synthesizer and drums - computer guy sampling - creative and improvised - great price too - free!
Par 3	My recommendation: see this band if you can - if you have to pay, absolutely worth it!

In your plan, you should decide exactly what to write about in each paragraph - the purpose of each paragraph.

The whole point of a review is to say whether something is good or bad in your opinion; in other words, whether you would recommend the thing you are writing about to other people. You must give your recommendation at the end of the review.

Whether you are reviewing a play / movie / concert / hotel / restaurant / book etc. it is always important to talk about the cost - is it good value for money?

The Review Plan

In general, unless you are told exactly what to discuss in the question, your review plan should look something like this:

- Par 1 - About the thing being reviewed - what/who? when? where? why?
- Main Body [usually 1-3 paragraphs] - Your experience - describe the good and bad aspects of your experience.
- Last Par - Your recommendation - would you recommend it? for whom? is it good value?

Writing Tips

- Avoid using abbreviated text-style language (e.g. 'luv' instead of 'love' - this is not acceptable).

- Always use clear paragraphing. This makes a positive impression on the reader and improves the cohesiveness and flow of your composition.

- Don't be afraid to attempt to use complex language. The examiner will give credit for complex language attempted, even if mistakes are made - so long as the mistakes do not impede communication (make it difficult for the examiner to understand what you are trying to say).

- You will not be asked to write about very specialised topics. Be familiar with general everyday topics like health and fitness, sport, music, technology and so on, and practise writing about them as much as you can.

Metropolis - A Great New Band

Last weekend I saw a live performance by the band "Metropolis". I had not planned to see a concert, and indeed, I had never heard of the band. Why I went is a long story; a friend of a friend knew someone who knew one of the band members and said we should check it out. It has been a long time since I have been so pleasantly surprised!

The band was fantastic. They were very unique, and played a style of music that cannot be categorised. There was a lead singer with a beautiful, mysterious voice, who sang mostly using abstract sounds instead of words and then there was a man with a synthesizer and drum machine, and another with a computer who was busy sampling the other two musicians, changing the sounds a bit, and then adding them to the music. It was all improvised and very creative! It was great value for money too, since the concert was free!

If you ever get the chance to see "Metropolis" perform, even if you have to pay, by all means do it! You will not regret it.

Every review should have a title - usually the name of the place or thing being reviewed.

Observe the language style; it is quite informal - 'a friend of a friend' and 'a long story'.

Use colourful descriptive language to keep the reader's attention.

Comment on what was good and bad about your experience - you may focus on the good or the bad, or discuss both.

Again, notice the use of linking words, as in the examples highlighted.

Formal Linking words

Giving Examples:
For example, ...
For instance, ...
Namely...

Giving a reason:
Due to (the fact that)...
Owing to (the fact that)...
... since/as/because ...
... because of ...

Adding information:
Moreover, ...
Furthermore, ...
In addition, ...
Additionally, ...

Summarising:
In short, ...
In conclusion, ...
To summarise, ...

Sequencing ideas:
First of all, ...
Secondly, ...
Last but not least, ...

Giving a result:
Therefore, ...
Consequently, ...
As a result, ...
As a consequence, ...

Contrasting:
However, ...
... whereas ...
... while ...
... but ...
... unlike ...
In theory ... but in practice...
Despite this ...
In spite of this ...
Nonetheless, ...

PART 1 — Essay

- Always written for a teacher, often as follow-up to a class activity.

- Formal or neutral style.

- Must be well-organised.

- Should contain a clear (i) introduction, (ii) development and (iii) conclusion.

- Main purpose is to develop an argument or discussion.

- It should answer the question given by addressing both content points and providing a new content point of your own.

Tip!
Planning and paragraphing are hugely important, and ideas must be linked together using appropriate linking words or phrases.

PART 2 — Article

- Usually written for an English-language magazine or newsletter.

- Tends to have a neutral-to-informal style.

- Main purpose is to engage the reader (make them interested).

- Usually requires you to comment on something or express an opinion.

- Successful articles:
  (1) engage the reader
  (2) use colourful language
  (3) have a catchy title
  (4) take a personal angle

Tip!
Use direct and indirect questions, descriptions, examples and anecdotes to add colour.

LETTERS

You don't need to write postal addresses in your letters and you don't need to write the sender's and the receiver's addresses and subject in your emails. Start with the opening salutation and end with a closing phrase.

Remember: in a formal letter, if you know the person's name you can start with 'Dear Mr/Mrs [last name],' and close 'Yours sincerely,'.
If you do not know the person's name, start with 'Dear Sir or Madam,' and close 'Yours faithfully,'. When writing an informal letter or email to a friend, just start with 'Hi [first name],' and end with a phrase like 'See you soon' or 'All my love' or 'Take care' etc.

PART 2 — Email

- Usually written in response to a situation outlined in the task.

- Might have to write to a college principal (formal), your own teacher (neutral), or a friend or colleague (informal); therefore, read the task carefully to decide whether to use neutral or informal language; style must be appropriate for target reader.

- Use an opening salutation.
  Informal: 'Hi [first name]',
  Neutral: 'Dear Mr/Mrs [surname]'
  ('Dear Sir or Madam' if name unknown)

- Close with a closing phrase.
  Informal: 'Bye for now' etc.
  Neutral: 'Kind Regards'

PART 2 — Letter

- Usually written in response to a situation outlined in the question.

- Must use the appropriate register and tone for the target reader.

  Informal Letter - usually written to an English-speaking friend or colleague.

- You must know appropriate informal language, such as informal linking words.

- A brief opening paragraph is appropriate, but most of the letter should focus on the task.
  Open: 'Hi' [first name],
  Close: 'See you soon!' etc.

  Formal Letter - may be written to an individual or organisation.

- Purpose might be to apply for work, a study or scholarship opportunity etc.

- Functions include describing skills and experience, expressing enthusiasm, persuading and complaining etc.

- You should know appropriate expressions to begin and end your letter.

Opening and Closing Formal Letters:
Open (name known): 'Dear Mr/Mrs [surname],'
Open (name unknown): 'Dear Sir or Madam,'
Close (name known): 'Yours sincerely,'
Close (name unknown): 'Yours faithfully,'

Recommending / Suggesting a course of action to a friend

'Why don't you... ?'	'Couldn't you...?'
'If I were you I would...'	'I think you should...'
'If you ask me, you should...'	'Maybe you could...'
'If it were me, I would...'	'It might be a good
'If I were in your shoes, I would...'	idea to...'
'Perhaps you should...'	'Why not try... ?'

PART 2 — Review

- Usually written for an English-language magazine, newspaper or website.
- Usually neutral-to-informal in style.
- Main purpose is to describe something you have experienced and express an opinion of it.
- Should contain a title.
- Reader must have a clear impression of what you are describing.
- Ends with a recommendation.
- Review topics include:
  (i) holidays (ii) books
  (iii) consumer goods (iv) TV programmes
  (v) films (vi) music
  (vii) restaurants (viii) hotels
  (ix) bands (x) concerts
  (xi) plays, etc.
- Language functions: describe, explain, give positive and negative opinions, make recommendations.

PART 2 — Report

- Usually written for a superior (e.g. a teacher) or a peer group (e.g. members of an English club).
- You must provide some factual information and make recommendations.
- It presents information and not an argument.
- A report should be well-organised (introduction, body and conclusion) and include headings.
- Avoid expressing personal opinions except in the conclusion.
- Instead of 'I think that…' use the impersonal 'It'.
- Use formal language only.

Informal Linking Words

Summarising:
In a nutshell, … Basically, …
At the end of the day, … After all's said and done, …
What it boils down to is…

Giving a reason:
… is down to … That's why…
That's the reason… because / as / since…

Contrasting
… but …
… though …
Even though…

Giving a result:
(And) so…
Because of this, …
Thanks to that…
When this happens…
The result is…
That causes…
Then…

Giving examples:
Let's say (for example)…
Take … for example; …
Say (for example)…
What if…
Here's an example; …

Sequencing ideas:
First up, …
The second thing is…
And another thing…
Last of all, …

Adding Information:
And another thing, …
What's more…
Not to mention (the fact that)…
Then there's also (the fact that)…
And what about…

First - FCE - PAPER 3
Listening
EXAM GUIDE

General Description

- The paper consists of four parts and lasts 40 minutes.

- There are 30 questions in total.

- These are made up of multiple choice, sentence completion and multiple matching tasks.

- You may hear monologues (i.e. answerphone messages, commentaries, radio features, instructions, lectures, news, announcements, advertisements, reports, speeches, stories etc.).

- Or you may hear recordings of interactive speakers (i.e. conversations, discussions, interviews, radio plays, transactions etc.).

- A variety of voices, styles of delivery and accents will be heard on the recording.

- There is one mark for every correct answer.

1 The instructions for each task are written on the question paper, and are also heard on the recording.

2 There will be pauses to enable you to read over the questions related to each task, and you will be told when these pauses are going to occur.

3 ALL parts are heard twice.

4 At the end of the listening paper, you will be given 5 minutes to transfer your answers onto a separate answer sheet.

Not only will the **context** and **focus** be written down clearly on the test paper, they will also be heard on the recording - the situation (context) and question (focus) will be clearly voiced.

When listening to a conversation, pay close **attention** to **which person** the question relates to. You may hear the other speaker talk about a wrong answer, but you are only concerned with what the woman says.

Part 1	Part 2	Part 3	Part 4
3-option Multiple Choice	Sentence completion	Multiple Matching	3-option Multiple Choice
A series of separate and unrelated extracts lasting about 30 seconds each.	A monologue lasting 3-4 minutes.	5 short related monologues lasting about 30 seconds each.	An extract lasting about 3-4 minutes.
One question per extract.	Listen to the recording and complete the sentences. Questions are asked in the order the answers appear on the recording.	For each question, select the correct option from a list of eight.	
8 questions in total	10 questions	5 questions	7 questions
[monologues and interactive exchanges]	[a monologue]	[5 monologues]	[an interview or interactive exchange]

Part 1
(Test 1 example)

The context of each question is explained very clearly, so you know exactly what situation is being presented to you in advance.

In each question, the focus is made very clear. For example, question 1 is 'The caller wants to buy' - You know exactly what to listen for (what she wants to buy).

Paper 3 LISTENING   PART 1

You will hear people talking in eight different situations. For questions 1-8, choose the best answer A, B or C.

1. You are in a shop when you overhear this man answering the telephone.
    What does the caller want to buy?
    A. a book about playing a guitar
    B. a book about guitar music
    C. a cassette of guitar music

2. You are listening to the radio when you hear this man speaking.
    What is he talking about?
    A. history
    B. shipbuilding
    C. politics

3. You are sitting in a cafe when you hear this woman speaking.
    She is telling her friend about
    A. the weather.
    B. buying a new coat.
    C. new windows.

5. You are sitting in a pub when you overhear this exchange.
    What does the woman want the man to do?
    A. go to the bar
    B. get her a drink
    C. replace her glass

6. You are staying in the home of a British family. You hear the mother answering the phone.
    The caller wants to take her daughter
    A. to the cinema.
    B. to a party.
    C. to a restaurant.

7. Listen to a policeman being interviewed on the evening television news.
    What is he describing?
    A. a car crash
    B. a bomb explosion
    C. a serious fire

Pay attention to who the speaker is:

Always listen to the whole extract before making your decision. You may hear a word(s) from more than one of the answer options mentioned, so it is important to listen closely for stressed words and key facts to ensure you choose wisely.

There is no penalty for choosing a wrong answer, so if you don't know, guess!

The focus (what the question asks you to listen for) can be anything from a specific detail (i.e. someone's age) to an opinion, place, attitude, relationship (i.e. work colleague or husband), genre (i.e. comedy or romance), topic, fact or detail, gist (overall understanding) etc.

Even if you don't have your own listening CD, you can still practise listening to Part-1-type tasks in your everyday life. Listen to weather and news reports, advertisements, announcements etc on the television, radio, internet etc.

The questions will always follow the order of the information in the text.

Answers should not exceed three words in length.

The word, number or phrase needed to fill the gap will be heard on the recording. Use the exact word(s) you hear; there should be no need to change the form of the word(s). If your answer doesn't make sense without changing the word form, then you have chosen the wrong word(s).

Minor spelling mistakes are not penalised so long as the word(s) you intended to write are clear to the examiner based on what you have written.

However, when a word is spelled out on the recording letter-by-letter (i.e. a person or place's name), your spelling must be correct.

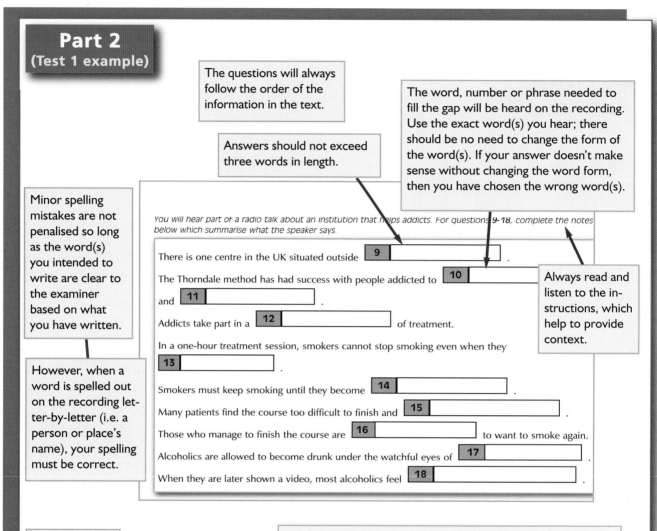

You will hear part of a radio talk about an institution that helps addicts. For questions 9-18, complete the notes below which summarise what the speaker says.

There is one centre in the UK situated outside | 9 | .

The Thorndale method has had success with people addicted to | 10 | and | 11 | .

Addicts take part in a | 12 | of treatment.

In a one-hour treatment session, smokers cannot stop smoking even when they | 13 | .

Smokers must keep smoking until they become | 14 | .

Many patients find the course too difficult to finish and | 15 | .

Those who manage to finish the course are | 16 | to want to smoke again.

Alcoholics are allowed to become drunk under the watchful eyes of | 17 | .

When they are later shown a video, most alcoholics feel | 18 | .

Always read and listen to the instructions, which help to provide context.

Always read the information before and after each gap when it is located in the middle of a sentence.

You should write your answers for Part 2 very clearly on the answer sheet and use CAPITAL LETTERS.

Use the time you are given (at the start of each part of the listening paper) wisely to read carefully over the questions. In this part, it may be useful to underline or highlight key words or phrases in the sentences as you read through them. This will give you something to focus on while you listen. It will also give you clues to help you follow the recording as it is played and identify which question is being talked about. Remember not to spend too much time on any one question because this is likely to cause you to miss other answers, too. If you don't find an answer the first time, move on; and then listen again the second time the recording is played.

Remember that you bring a lot to the listening yourself - before the recording even starts to play. Once you hear the instructions for each part of the paper, you should immediately start to think about what kinds of information you expect to hear. This will encourage your mind to start thinking of related vocabulary and provide you with focus for what information to listen out for. Similarly, reading the questions and anticipating the subject matter will help you to tune in to (focus on) the task and perform better.

Part 3
(Test 1 example)

All of the extracts will be in some way related; for example, the speakers may be talking about similar experiences (i.e. plane travel), similar subjects (i.e. various sports) etc. Or the similarity may be of function; for example, the speakers may be apologising or asking for information.

If the statements are long, you may want to underline or highlight key words to improve your focus. Here this is probably unnecessary though.

There will always be more options than you need: (**8 answer options; 5 questions**)

When you read over the task at the beginning, think about what kind of information you would expect to hear. The recording will often not use the exact same words as the answer options, but may contain words of similar meaning or context clues based on related vocabulary.

Paper 3 LISTENING   PART 3

You will hear five different men talking about visits they have made to a hospital. For questions 19-23, choose from the list A-H the reasons why each attended the hospital on the occasion described. Use the letters only once. There are three extra letters which you do not need to use.

A   have a medical check-up
B   collect somebody
C   deliver supplies
D   visit a relative
E   have an operation
F   do maintenance work
G   check a mental problem
H   collect some surgical knives

Speaker 1   [ ] 19
Speaker 2   [ ] 20
Speaker 3   [ ] 21
Speaker 4   [ ] 22
Speaker 5   [ ] 23

For example, option E; while we might not hear the word 'operation' we might hear an associated word such as 'surgery' or 'theatre' (operating theatre), or a phrase such as 'under the knife' (in surgery).

If you are unsure about an answer, don't be too quick to 'use up' an option that might be right for another question as this will usually cause you to get at least one additional question wrong. Instead, write the letter to the right side of the answer box and wait until the second hearing before making up your mind completely.

It is particularly important to **read through the questions** in this part of the paper because you need to have a clear idea of what to listen for (focus on).

For **Parts 1, 3** and **4**, it is important not to let yourself get distracted by one or two words or phrases from the recording that appear in incorrect options. Always listen out for the 'whole message' before making your decision. If you are unsure of an answer after the first time the recording is played, then try to identify the stressed words - the words which carry the message - the second time around.

Part 4
(Test 1 example)

The instructions in your test booklet provide you with essential information about the text/conversation you are going to hear. For example, in the instructions below you can find out a) what the speakers' names are: *Wendy, Mrs Turner and Adrian* and b) the topic of the conversation: *they are discussing a film they've just seen*

Try to understand the key points of the conversation; e.g. *What do they disagree about?*

Some questions require you to 'turn follow' or know which speaker is saying what. This can be more difficult than it sounds when two or three people speak in quick succession (e.g. here we have: Wendy, Mrs Turner and Adrian). If you are dealing with a two- or three-way conversation, always make a note of the accents or sounds of voice of the different speakers and their names at the beginning.

You will hear three people discussing a film they have just seen at the cinema (Wendy, Mrs Turner and Adrian). For questions 24-30, choose the best answer A, B or C.

24. What did Wendy's mum think of the film?
   A. It was not her favourite film.
   B. She loved the film.
   C. She absolutely hated it.

25. Adrian mentions doing a course in order to show that
   A. he wants to change the subject.
   B. Mrs Turner is wrong about the dinosaurs.
   C. he knows what he is talking about.

26. Adrian feels that watching a film at home
   A. is always better than going to the cinema.
   B. is not something he wants to do again.
   C. has advantages and disadvantages.

27. When Adrian suggests that Wendy was frightened, she
   A. admits that she felt scared.
   B. denies that she felt scared.
   C. complains about the length of the film.

28. What do Wendy and her mum disagree about?
   A. whether or not the film was frightening
   B. whether or not Wendy covered her eyes
   C. whether or not the film is P.G. rated

29. What is it suggested that they do now that the movie has ended?
   A. to go straight home
   B. to go for a drink
   C. to go for dinner

30. Adrian doesn't let Mrs Turner drive because
   A. he enjoys driving.
   B. she will drink alcohol.
   C. they could get in trouble.

Highlight the key words as you read through the questions in the time allowed at the start of the task.

Look for clues so you know when to listen carefully.

The questions follow the order of what is heard on the recording and are presented so that they either rephrase, report or summarise the speakers' ideas.

You may be asked to listen for general opinion, attitude, main idea and specific information.

Remember!

Always read the questions carefully in the time allowed at the beginning of each part.

Highlight any key words to help you focus on what to listen for.

Listen carefully to the recording each time it is played (all parts will be played twice).

Never leave an answer blank - even if you are guessing, you may be closer than you think.

The speaking test consists of four parts:

Part 1 Interlocutor and each Candidate

- a conversation between the interlocutor and each candidate
- candidates must answer the interlocutor's questions with basic personal information
- 2 minutes (about 1.5 per candidate)

Part 2 Candidate Alone

- 'long turn' for Candidate 1 (Candidate 1 speaks for 1 minute about a pair of photographs) - 4 minutes in total
- short response from Candidate 2 (30 seconds)
- 'long turn' for Candidate 2 (Candidate 2 speaks for 1 minute about a pair of photographs)
- short response from Candidate 1 (30 seconds)
- candidates must describe and compare their two photographs and give an opinion

Part 3 Candidate and Candidate

- a conversation between the two candidates
- candidates are given spoken instructions with written stimuli, which are used in discussion and decision-making tasks
- Candidates are expected to answer the question by exploring the different prompts (2 minutes) and reach a decision on the best one(s) (1 minute).
- 4 minutes

Part 4 Interlocutor and Candidates

- a discussion on topics related to Part 3
- candidates must express and explain their opinions, and agree or disagree with the opinions expressed by the other candidate and/or the interlocutor
- 4 minutes

The Speaking Test lasts around 14 minutes in total. In the event that there is an uneven number of candidates, the final group will be made up of three candidates and their test will last approximately 20 minutes.

General Advice

- There will be two examiners; an interlocutor and an assessor. You will only talk to one of the examiners during the test - the interlocutor. However, both of the examiners will grade your performance.

- Speak clearly and loud enough for both examiners to hear you.

- You will conduct the speaking test in a pair with one other candidate, unless there is an uneven number of students; then the last group will comprise three candidates.

- The interlocutor keeps to a scripted frame (has what to say written down for him/her). If you do not understand what he/she says, you may ask him/her to say it again. If you ask the examiner to repeat what he/she says, you will not lose any marks.

- Always listen carefully to the interlocutor's spoken instructions and read the questions above the pictures, so that you know exactly what you are being asked.

- When the other candidate is speaking, listen carefully, too, as you may have to speak in response to something they have said.

- If you get stuck and can't think of a word, paraphrase - don't stop and try to find the word you are looking for; say what you want to say using other words.

Part 1

The Interview

We call Part 1 the interview because the interlocutor will ask you questions - interview you - about yourself. You will not have to speak to the other candidate, though you may if you wish.

The questions will centre around your work/study, leisure time and future plans. You may be asked about the sports you enjoy, for example, or your travel and holiday experiences etc.

It is important that you give adequate answers; that means no 'yes' or 'no' responses. Use the 'Who?', 'What?', 'When?', 'Where?', 'Why?', 'How?' method to help you give more complete answers that show off your English. For example, if the examiner asks you where you live, rather than simply saying; 'I live in London, England's capital city.' You could say; 'I live in an area of London called Streatham, with my family - my mum, dad and baby sister. We live in a fourth-floor flat. It's nice and cosy, but sometimes I wish it was a little less noisy outside - there's so much traffic on the road.' In other words, say as much as you can.

Practise talking about yourself as often as possible, but avoid going into the exam with a list of answers that you have memorised. The examiner will spot this and will adjust your score downward. One of the best ways to practise is by brainstorming - thinking of as many things as possible to say in response to a question, making some notes if necessary. But after you have thought of the ideas and made some notes, try to speak without the aid of your notes and without having memorised them. With practice, you will find yourself improving your ability to think on your feet and paraphrase, as well as your overall fluency.

Part 1

Example Part 1 Examiner's Script (2 minutes)

Good morning / afternoon / evening. My name is .... and this is my colleague ....

And your names are?   Can I have your mark sheets, please?
Thank you.

First of all, I'd like to know something about you.

- Where are you from? (Candidate A)
- And you? (Candidate B)
- What do you like about living in .... (name of candidate's home town)?
- And what about you? (Candidate A/B)

Select one or more questions from any of the following categories as appropriate.

Likes and dislikes

- Do you prefer to spend time with your friends or family? (Why... ?)
- Do you like making things with your hands? (What... ?)
- What's your favourite food? (Why... ?)
- Do you like going to parties? (Why... ?)
- Tell me about a special day in your life that you really enjoyed?

Education and Work

- Do you find it easy to study where you live? (Why... ?)
- What do you like and dislike about your school/university? (Why... ?)
- What would you like to do when you finish school/university? (Why... ?)
- Do you prefer working on your own or with other people? (Why... ?)
- What would your perfect job be? (Why... ?)

Free Time

- Who do you spend your free time with?
- What sorts of things do you do together?
- Do you ever read books? (What kind... ? Why... ?)
- What is your favourite hobby? (Why... ? How often... ?)
- Have you got any plans for the weekend? (What... ?)
- Where do you hang out with your friends? (Why... ? What ... do... ?)

Holidays and Travel

- Which area of your country would you recommend to a tourist? (Why... ?)
- What is the most interesting place you've ever visited? (What ... do... ?)
- Have you ever had to speak English while on holiday? (When... ? Where... ?)
- Do you prefer beach holidays or holidays in the city? (Why... ?)
- Where would you most like to go on holiday in the future? (Why... ?)

Media and Entertainment

- How much T.V. do you watch each week?
- Tell me about a T.V. programme you've seen recently that you liked. (Why... like... ?)
- Do you often read the newspaper? (Why... ?)
- Have you got a computer at home?
- Do you use computers a lot?
- What do you do when you are surfing the internet?
- What sorts of websites do you look at? (Why... ?)

Everyday Life

- What do you usually do in the evenings?
- Do you get a lot of homework every week?
- How much time do you spend studying each night?
- Describe your daily routine.
- Do you often eat fast food?
- Who does the cooking in your home?
- What time do you normally go to bed at?
- How do you get to school / university / work every day?
- How often do you exercise?

Part 2

Long Turn

This section is called the 'long turn' because you will have to speak about two photographs for one minute without interruption. You will have to compare the photographs and then make a further comment on them.

The interlocutor will tell you what you need to do, but there will also be a written prompt, in the form of a direct question, above the photographs. Pay attention to this; it is very important to remember not just to compare the photographs, but to also answer the question.

Once your turn has finished, you should continue to listen carefully to your partner's turn because the examiner will ask you to comment briefly on something related to their photographs and what they have discussed.

Example Part 2

1 Animals in different environments
2 People celebrating   (4 minutes)

How are the animals feeling?

What are they celebrating?

Part 2 – Long turn

Interlocutor: In this part of the test, I'm going to give each of you two photographs. I'd like you to talk about your photographs on your own for about a minute and also to answer a question about your partner's photographs.

Candidate A, it's your turn first. Here are your photographs. They show animals in different environments.

Candidate A has to look at the photographs for Task 2.

Candidate A, I'd like you to compare your photographs, and say how you think the animals in each one might be feeling and why. All right?

Candidate A: *(one minute)* ....
Thank you.

Candidate B, which of the two places would you prefer to be - horse riding in the countryside or at the zoo - and why?

Candidate B: *(approximately 30 seconds)* ....
Thank you.

Now, **Candidate B**, here are your photographs. They show people celebrating different things.

Candidate B has to look at the photographs for Task 2.

Candidate B, I'd like you to compare the photographs, and say what you think the people are celebrating. All right?

Candidate B: *(one minute)* ....
Thank you.

Candidate A, what would you do to celebrate graduating from university?

Candidate A: *(approximately 30 seconds)* ....
Thank you.

Part 3

Collaborative Task

This part is called the 'collaborative task' because the two candidates have to work together and have a discussion about a number of options that the interlocutor presents to them.

You will be given a discussion question and five written prompts. You have to answer the question using the five prompts provided. You can choose which prompts to discuss but you are not required to discuss all five prompts in the time available; you should continue the discussion with the other candidate until asked to stop by the interlocutor. You have to express and justify your opinions and speculate in order to have a conversation which answers the discussion question. You will then be asked a second question which aims to help you summarise your discussion and reach a decision. Have in mind that you will not be penalised if you fail to reach a decision.

Timing: A 2-minute discussion followed by a 1-minute decision-making task. The total time for Part 3 is 4 minutes.

Part 3
(Test 1 example)

Part 3 – Collaborative Task

Interlocutor: Now I'd like you to talk about something together for about two minutes. (3 minutes for groups of three).
I'd like you to think about TV programmes. Here are some types of TV programmes and a question for you to discuss. First you have some time to look at the task.

Look at the task in the box below. You have 15 seconds.

Now, talk to each other about **why people would choose to watch these TV programmes**.

Candidates: .... *2 minutes (3 minutes for groups of three)*

Interlocutor: Thank you. Now you have about a minute *(for pairs and groups of three)* to decide **which type of TV show would be the most popular and would attract more advertisers to spend money on advertising their products**.

Candidates: .... 1 minute (for pairs and groups of three)
Thank you.

> You will then be asked a second question which aims to help you summarise your discussion and reach a decision.

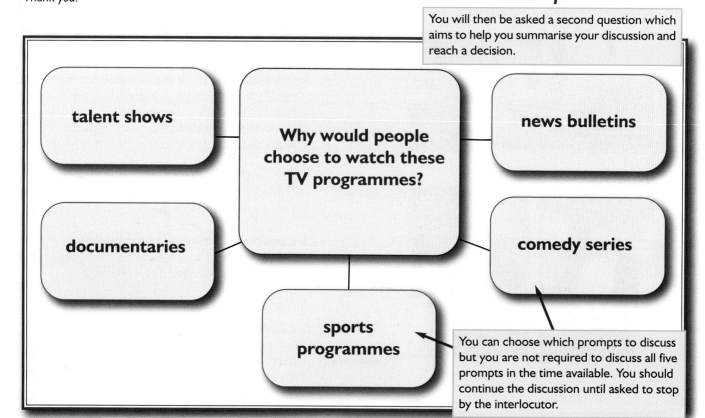

> You can choose which prompts to discuss but you are not required to discuss all five prompts in the time available. You should continue the discussion until asked to stop by the interlocutor.

Part 4

Discussion

The interlocutor asks questions which broaden the discussion of the topics introduced in Part 3. Whereas Part 1 questions mainly just ask for information, Part 4 questions require you to evaluate something.

Give as full an answer as possible to each question. Keep words like 'Why?', 'How?', 'When?' and 'Where?' in your head to help you think of your response. For example, if the interlocutor asked: 'Have you ever done any work for charity?', you could respond by saying:

'Yes. I did some work for a cancer charity last summer (when). My friends and I (who) organised a bag-packing event (what) at our local supermarket (where). I wanted to help raise money for the charity because my grand-mother had cancer a few years ago (why). Luckily, she made a full recovery, but ever since I've wanted to help other cancer sufferers.'

Example Part 4 (4 minutes)

Part 4 – Discussion

In this part of the test you have to take part in a discussion with the other candidate related to the topic of the task you did in Part 3. The examiner will ask you both some questions.

Interlocutor:

- Which of these fundraising activities would you most enjoy taking part in and why?
- Can you think of any other ways to raise money for charity?
- Which of these events would be most suitable for young people in their 20s? Why?
- Some people say we shouldn't go out asking for money for charity in public - it's rude. What do you think?
- Tell me some charities you would support and why.
- Do you think rich people should be more generous in supporting charity than poor people? Why?

Thank you. That is the end of the test.

> *Select any of the following prompts, as appropriate:*
> - What do you think?
> - Do you agree?
> - And you?

Part 2

Practise talking for as long as you can about selected topics.

Time your practice to get an idea of how long a minute of speaking uninterrupted is.

You don't have to give hugely detailed descriptions of the pictures; focus on comparing the pictures and giving your reaction to them.

Become as familiar as possible with the language of comparison and contrast.

Part 3

Familiarise yourself with ways to move a discussion forward i.e. 'Shall we move on to this one?'...

Show the examiner that you are capable of responding directly to what your partner says; agree / disagree with him, give your own opinion and justify yourself.

Understand how to manage a discussion - be alert to the importance of turn-taking.

Remain polite at all times and make a positive contribution to the discussion.

Part 4

Always give as full an answer as possible.

Remember there are no right answers to any questions, so you only get judged on your use of language, not your opinions themselves.

If you honestly do not know much about a particular question, you will not lose marks by being honest with the examiner and telling him/her so; however, always show off your English as much as possible when you have got something to say.

Useful Phrases

Turn-Taking (to begin)

Shall I begin?
May I start?
Would you like to start?

Turn-taking (to change turn)

What do you think?
Would you like to add something?
Wouldn't you agree?

Expressing your opinion

As far as I'm concerned...
The way I see it...
As far as I can see...
To my way of thinking...
To my mind...
If you ask me...
I strongly believe...

Agreeing

I see where you are coming from.
I see what you're saying.
I see what you mean.
I couldn't agree more.
I totally agree.
Absolutely.

Moving the discussion forward

Shall we move on to... ?
And what about... ?
Let's move on to... ?
Let's consider...
Why don't we look at... ?
How about... ?
Let's take a look at...

Inviting a general opinion

What's your take?
What do you think?
How do you see it?

Inviting agreement

Don't you think?
Wouldn't you agree?
Wouldn't you say?

Politely Disagreeing

I take your point, but...
I hear what you are saying, but...
I see where you are coming from, but...
I don't really agree with what you're saying because...

Reaching a decision

Shall we agree on... ?
Then we're agreed;...
Can we agree on... ?
Are we both agreed on... ?
So shall we say... ?
Let's decide on...
Why don't we go with... (an option)?

Contrasting pictures / images

In Picture 1 we see ... whereas in Picture 2... .
Picture 1 shows ... while in Picture 2 there is/are...
In Picture 1 there is/are... However, Picture 2 shows...
There is/are ... in Picture 1, while/whereas/but in Picture 2 there is/are...
In Picture 1 I can see... . In contrast, Picture 2 shows...
In the first picture ... can be seen, while the second picture shows...

Explaining (justifying) yourself

The reason I say that is because...
Let me explain;...
I think that because...
I am of this opinion because...
The reason I think that is...
I came to that conclusion because...

Finding similarities between pictures / images

In both pictures we can see...
Both pictures show...
There is/are ... in both pictures.
Picture 1 shows ... and in Picture 2 we can also see...
...can be seen in both pictures.
Both pictures have something in common; they show...
The pictures are similar in that they both show...
In Picture 1 there is/are... Similarly, Picture 2 shows...

Parts of a picture/image

'in the background'

'in the foreground'

In the top-left corner of the picture I can see...	Centre-top of the picture I can see...	In the top-right corner of the picture I can see...
Centre-left of the picture I can see...	In the centre of the picture I can see...	Centre-right of the picture I can see...
In the bottom-left corner of the picture I can see...	Centre-bottom of the picture I can see...	In the bottom-right corner of the picture I can see...

Successful
FCE
Practice Tests

Reading & Use of English
Writing - Listening

Test 1

Paper 1 Reading and Use of English   PART 1

For questions 1-8, read the text below and decide which word A, B, C or D best fits each space. There is an example at the beginning (0).

Example:

0.   A. or   B. and   C. in   D. nor

Royal Residences

Buckingham Palace, Windsor Castle (0) .... the Palace of Holyroodhouse are these (1) .... of the Sovereign and, as such, serve as both home and office for the Queen, whose personal flag flies (2) .... her Majesty is in residence.

These buildings are used extensively for State ceremonies and official entertaining and are opened to the (3) .... as much as these commitments allow. They are furnished with fine pictures and works of art from the Royal Collection, assembled over four centuries by successive sovereigns. Many of the State Apartments and rooms at the official residences have been in continuous use since their conception and many of the paintings are (4) .... in the rooms for which they were originally (5) ....

The official residences are in regular use and the style and manner in which they are shown to visitors reflects their working status. Rooms are kept as close to their normal (6) .... as possible. Inevitably, opening times are subject to change at short notice depending on circumstances.

The Royal Collection, which is owned by the Queen as Sovereign in trust for her successors and the Nation, is administered by the Royal Collection Trust to which a proportion of the admission fee and other (7) .... from visitors is directed. The remainder of this money funds the majority of the cost of restoring Windsor Castle which was badly (8) .... by fire in November 1992.

1.	A. venues	**B. residences**	C. situations	D. occupation
2.	A. whatever	B. however	C. whoever	**D. whenever**
3.	A. humans	**B. public**	C. peoples	D. strangers
4.	A. created	B. explored	C. produced	**D. displayed**
5.	A. instructed	**B. intended**	C. performed	D. guarded
6.	A. feature	B. location	C. destination	**D. appearance**
7.	A. salary	B. budget	**C. income**	D. wages
8.	A. destroyed	B. ruined	**C. damaged**	D. collapsed

Paper 1 Reading and Use of English   PART 2

*For questions 9-16, read the text below and think of the word which best fits each space. Use only **one** word in each space. There is an example at the beginning (0).*

Example: **0**   most

Inspiration

I have had what, I think, is the (0) ...*most*..... extraordinary day of my life. While the events are (9) ....**still**........ clear in my mind, I wish to write them down. Let me introduce (10) ......**myself**...... .

My name is Lawrence Terrel. I am thirty-five years old, and in perfect health. I have never been ill in my life, not even for a day. I am an artist. I am (11) ....**not**.............. very successful, but I earn enough money to (12) ....**take**............. care of my needs. My only near relative, a sister, (13) ....**died**.............. three years ago. So I have no family.

I ate breakfast this morning at eight. After I had read the morning paper, I smoked my pipe and let my mind wander. I hoped I would think of (14) ......**something**........ to draw. The room was very hot, even (15) ......**though/when**........ the door and window were open. I had decided to go to the public swimming pool when an idea for a drawing came to me.

I began to (16) ..**draw/work/sketch**... . I was so interested in my work that I forgot to eat lunch. I did not stop until the clock struck five. I looked at what I had done. For a hurried picture, I felt it was the best thing I had ever drawn.

Paper 1 Reading and Use of English   PART 3

For questions 17-24, read the text below. Use the word given in capitals at the end of some lines to form a word that fits in the space in the same line. There is an example at the beginning (0).

Example: **0**   e n t e r t a i n m e n t

People in the world of (0) *entertainment* have to be very (17) ....observant........	ENTERTAIN/OBSERVE
in the way that they dress. It's an (18) ....irrefutable........... fact that image is	REFUTE
more than just a case of (19) ....decoration........... for a celebrity. How they	DECORATE
present themselves is all part of their artistic personality.	
It would be (20) ....foolish........... though to think that somebody can be	FOOL
a successful celebrity just because of the clothes they wear. They don't (21) ....necessarily..........	NECESSARY
have to wear (22) ....alternative........... clothing but they do need to be	ALTER
talented and communicative and they also need to have an	
(23) ....appreciation........... of their fans who make them successful.	APPRECIATE
They also need to be (24) ....adaptable........... so that they can cope	ADAPT
with all the public attention.	

Paper 1 Reading and Use of English   PART 4

*For questions 25-30, complete the second sentence so that it has a similar meaning to the first sentence, using the word given. **Do not change the word given**. You must use between **two** and **five** words, including the word given. There is an example at the beginning (0).*

Example:

0 They think the owner of the house is in France.   thought

   The owner of the house .... in France.

*The gap can be filled by the words "**is thought to be**" so you write:*   **0**   i s   t h o u g h t   t o   b e

25. My parents last spoke to me a month ago.   **heard**

    I ....**haven't heard from**............................... my parents for a month.

26. All the students had a lot of respect for their teacher.   **looked**

    All the students ....**looked up to**............... their teacher.

27. Linda didn't feel like eating.   **mood**

    Linda wasn't ....**in the mood to**............... eat.

28. My brother was treated unfairly by his teachers.   **deserve**

    My brother ....**didn't deserve to be**............... treated that way by his teachers.

29. He couldn't buy the car he wanted because he didn't have enough money.   **too**

    The car he wanted was ....**too expensive for him to**........... buy.

30. We all agreed with my father's proposal apart from Joy.   **exception**

    With ....**the exception of Joy**..........., we all agreed with my father's proposal.

Paper 1 Reading and Use of English   PART 5

You are going to read an extract from a novel. For questions 31-36, choose the answer A, B, C or D which you think fits best according to the text.

"Come along, young fellow," shouted Mr. Watson. "I'll show you the school room."

3 He swept out of the drawing-room with giant strides, and Philip hurriedly limped behind him. He was taken into a long, bare room with two tables that ran along its whole length; on each side of them were wooden forms.

8 "Nobody much here yet," said Mr. Watson. "I'll just show you the playground, and then I'll leave you to shift for yourself."

Mr. Watson led the way. Philip found himself in a large playground with high brick walls on three sides of it. On the fourth was an iron railing through which you saw a vast lawn and beyond this some of the buildings of King's School. One small boy was wandering discon-solately, kicking up the gravel as he walked.

"Hulloa, Venning," shouted Mr. Watson. "When did you turn up?"

The small boy came forward and shook hands.

"Here's a new boy. He's older and bigger than you, so don't you bully him."

22 The headmaster glared amicably at the two children, filling them with fear by the roar of his voice, and then with a guffaw left them.

"What's your name?"

"Carey."

"What's your father?"

"He's dead."

"Oh! Does your mother wash?"

"My mother's dead, too."

Philip thought this answer would cause the boy a cer-tain awkwardness, but Venning was not to be turned from his facetiousness for so little.

"Well, did she wash?" he went on.

"Yes," said Philip indignantly.

"She was a washerwoman then?"

"No, she wasn't."

"Then she didn't wash."

The little boy crowed with delight at the success of his dialectic. Then he caught sight of Philip's feet.

"What's the matter with your foot?"

Philip instinctively tried to withdraw it from sight. He hid it behind the one which was whole.

"I've got a club foot," he answered.

"How did you get it?"

"I've always had it."

"Let's have a look."

"No."

"Don't then."

The little boy accompanied the words with a sharp kick on Philip's shin, which Philip did not expect and thus could not guard against. The pain was so great that it made him gasp, but greater than the pain was the sur-prise. He did not know why Venning kicked him. He had not the presence of mind to give him a black eye. Besides, the boy was smaller than he, and he had read in *The Boy's Own* paper that it was a mean thing to hit anyone smaller than yourself. While Philip was nursing his shin, a third boy appeared and his tormentor left him. In a little while he noticed that the pair were talk-ing about him, and he felt they were looking at his feet. He grew hot and uncomfortable.

But others arrived, a dozen together, and then more, and they began to talk about their doings during the holidays, where they had been, and what wonderful cricket they had played. A few new boys appeared, and with these presently Philip found himself talking. He was shy and nervous. He was anxious to make him-self pleasant, but he could not think of anything to say. He was asked a great many questions and answered them all quite willingly. One boy asked him whether he could play cricket.

"No," answered Philip. "I've got a club foot."

The boy looked down quickly and reddened. Philip saw that he felt he had asked an unseemly question. He was too shy to apologise and looked at Philip awk-wardly.

31. What does 'strides' mean in line 3, column 1?

A. brooms

B. leaps

C. steps

D. yells

32. When Philip is shown around the school, it is

A. mostly empty.

B. bright and cheerful.

C. small and cramped.

D. full of noise and activity.

33. Why were the children afraid of Mr. Watson?

A. He was very loud.

B. He was angry with them.

C. He was unkind to them.

D. He was very big and powerful.

34. What does 'his tormentor' in line 22 column 2 refer to?

A. Phillip's club foot

B. the boy called Venning

C. the third boy to arrive

D. the pain in Philip's shin

35. Why does Philip become hot and uncomfortable when the boys talked about his foot?

A. It was summertime.

B. He had been beaten.

C. He was embarrassed.

D. He felt left out.

36. How do the boys who interact with Philip directly react to his club foot?

A. They pay it little attention.

B. They are curious or embarrassed.

C. They are polite and sympathetic.

D. They are disgusted by it.

31. The correct answer is **C**. If you stride somewhere, you walk there with quick, long steps. It is not B because "leaps" means to jump high in the air over a long distance, which would be unusual in the context. It is not A as "brooms" are brushes used to sweep the floor. If you "yell", you shout loudly, either in anger, pain or excitement; he is not shouting but rather walking.

32. The correct answer is **A**. Line 8, column 1: "Nobody much here yet, said Mr. Watson". The room into which he is shown is described as long and bare, so for this reason wouldn't be B. The text describes areas of the school as "vast", "long" and "large"; the opposite of cramped or small. For this reason, it can't be C. As students are only just starting to return to the empty school, it can neither be noisy nor be full of activity as D suggests.

33. The correct answer is **A**. Lines 22-23, column 1: "The headmaster glared amicably at the two children, filling them with fear by the roar of his voice". It isn't B as the text says he looked "amicably", which means in a friendly way. For the same reason it can't be C either. The headmaster is said to have roared - to have made a very loud sound. It doesn't mention whether he is big and powerful (ruling out D), but we can assume he has a loud and strong voice.

34. The correct answer is **B**. His tormentor is Venning who teased Philip with jokes, pressured him to see his foot and then kicked him in the leg. The text says that he was nursing his foot when a third boy arrived and Venning, his tormentor, left. For this reason the answer can't be either A, C or D.

35. The correct answer is **C**. Lines 23-25, column 2: "...he noticed that the pair were talking about him, and he felt they were looking at his feet. He grew hot and uncomfortable". He grew hot and bothered because he felt awkward and self-conscious that people were talking about his foot. For this reason the answers can't be A, B or D.

36. The correct answer is **B**. Lines 37-40, column 2: "The boy looked down quickly and reddened. Philip saw that he felt he had asked an unseemly question. He was too shy to apologise and looked at Philip awkwardly". This boy was embarrassed while Venning had been curious. It isn't A as the subject of the foot keeps coming up in conversation. The boys show little sympathy, so C is incorrect, but neither do they react as if it is something terrible and disgusting, so choice D is also incorrect.

Paper 1 Reading and Use of English   **PART 6**

You are going to read a magazine article about one person's experiences of learning to skydive. Six sentences have been removed from the article. Choose from the sentences A-G the one which fits each gap 37-42. There is one extra sentence which you do not need to use.

The Skydiving Experience

The thrill of skydiving is beyond any possible description. Falling at 120 mph with the wind screaming past your body is an unbelievable experience of total freedom. The sport is not without an element of danger; indeed, it is this fear that makes it so addictive. Yet there are relatively few serious injuries in this activity because of the tight regulations and safety requirements mandated for skydiving and parachuting organisations.

I still recall my first jump from 2,500 feet using what is called a static line. **37** **B** The static line system is often used for those new to the sport. It is a means of helping them to deal with the sensation of falling, while ensuring that they will not actually hit anything.

38 **G** Still, there seems to be a little slice of missing time from the point where I let go of the aircraft to the parachute canopy actually opening. Pure terror sometimes does that! It was a moment where time ceased to exist, not quite a total blackout but still quite strange. Two days of training on the ground, the ceaseless drill of counting out "one thousand, two thousand, three thousand" and about all I seem to recall when I let go is something like "aaaaahhhhhh". After a second and many subsequent jumps, this sensation soon faded to a dim recollection as I became accustomed to falling.

The first real free fall commenced at about the fifth jump. This simply involved letting go of the aircraft and immediately deploying the canopy. **39** **D** Starting from three seconds (let go and pull the ripcord) to five seconds (let go, count to three then pull the ripcord) increasing to seven seconds and so on. Once I made it to ten seconds and beyond, it became important to use an altimeter.

Free fall became really interesting at the 15-second mark because that is when the real training started. Turning, tumbling and rocketing forward by using different body positions put a completely new challenge before me. I learned it was possible to put my body in a position where forward ground speed was around 80 mph with an increase of downward velocity close to 200 mph - the ears tend to get a little warm! It is also quite important to flare out, slow and adopt a more stable position before deploying the canopy. Doing so at really high velocity really hurts, and I suspect everyone does this at least once. It is quite a lot of stress on your body when pulling up from 120 mph to 10 mph in about two or three seconds. **40** **C**

One of my most fearful experiences occurred when I made a complete mess of trying to do a reverse tumble and became wildly unstable. Nothing I did seemed to correct the spinning and rolling, I was still at 5,000 feet and in desperation I deployed the canopy. **41** **F** The bag wrapped around one of my legs. Luckily, by this time I had enough free fall experience to have the presence of mind to see what was happening and it was not too difficult to reach down and disentangle the risers. I also knew there was plenty of time to correct the problem because I was far higher than the standard 2,500 deployment altitude. It turned out fine in the end.

I would say one of my most memorable free falling experiences was above the Mornington Peninsula in Victoria, Australia. **42** **E** From this altitude, I did some nice slow turns and drank in the scenery of Port Phillip Bay, out to sea, across the length of the peninsula to the city of Melbourne, all in an orange-red glow of the most amazing sunset I can ever remember. It was incredible.

A. There are few other ways to experience the total and utter freedom of flight.

B. This is a strong nylon tape that is attached to the aircraft on one end, and to the release pin of the jumper's canopy on the other.

C. I think my ears are still ringing from that mistake.

D. Altitudes increased gradually, as did time in free-fall.

E. It was a 40-second fall from 14,000 feet, right at sunset.

F. What happened next was not good at all.

G. My first experience is still very sharp in my memory.

37. The correct answer is **B**. The text speaks about a static line, used when the writer skydived. The gap must be filled by B as it describes what a static line is. Other options can be eliminated as they do not explain what a static line actually is.

38. The correct answer is **G**. The subject of this paragraph is the writer's experience of his or her first jump. This choice has something to do with the first jump - the others may be eliminated. The "still" which appears after the gap suggests that this sentence will contradict what comes before, so, choice G is most appropriate. The first experience is a sharp memory, still, a bit of it is missing because of pure terror!

39. The correct answer is **D**. This paragraph describes a sequence of jumps involving increasing time in free fall, which is exactly the meaning put across by choice D.

40. The correct answer is **C**. The paragraph is talking about more advanced training, such as learning to go faster, and then describes a painful error that everyone makes "at least once". Choice C describes the physical sensation of that mistake. It also fits because, several lines before, ear discomfort is mentioned, which is echoed again in choice C. Choice F may be eliminated because the gap occurs at the end of the description of the mistake, not in the middle as would be required for choice F. Choice G may be eliminated because at this point in the text the writer has quite a lot of experience.

41. The correct answer is **F**. Another mistake is being described; however, the gap here occurs in the middle of the explanation of what happened; the writer deployed the canopy, and a problem occurred; that is, the bag wrapped around his/her leg. Although it could have been very dangerous i.e. "not good at all", in the end it was ok. The key here is the flow of the narration of the fearful experience. Choice C would disrupt the chronology, while choice F helps it to flow.

42. The correct answer is **E**. The correct choice must provide an altitude since the gap is followed by "from this altitude". Also, sunset is mentioned in choice E and echoed later in the paragraph.

Paper 1 Reading and Use of English   **PART 7**

You are going to read some extracts about the fears or challenges that several people have faced. For questions 43–52, choose from the people A–D. The people may be chosen more than once.

Which person:

did not receive help willingly at first?	43	C
did not realise how difficult something would be?	44	B
did not feel a need to change?	45	A
helped others while being challenged?	46	B
can rely on a family member who does not share their phobia?	47	A
was afraid of being unsuccessful?	48	C
felt a sense of great happiness while taking part in an extreme activity?	49	D
initially tried to overcome his/her difficulty alone?	50	D
took advantage of an offer which had conditions attached to it?	51	C
had the support of a friend?	52	D

Confront your fears and face your challenges

KATIE   A

I'm afraid of spiders. You won't hear me scream, but I will certainly get out of the room until someone else has dealt with it. Once, when I was a teenager, and my parents were both working late, I sat on the front steps of the house for nearly five hours waiting for help. There was a spider on the ceiling in the hallway, you see! I couldn't get into the house! My father was quite angry with me when he got home; he thought I needed to learn to be more independent. "How will you ever survive if you have to live alone some day?" he asked. Well, I'm sure if I had to I would just deal with it, although it would be a challenge. But I've never had to live alone. I had flatmates at university, and now I'm married. <u>Luckily my husband has no problem with spiders, and is tolerant of my phobia!</u>

45, 47

Ellie   B

The most challenging thing I've ever done, by far, was trekking in the Himalayas. It was something I'd always dreamed of doing and I was incredibly fortunate <u>to have the opportunity to join a trek for charity.</u> **46** I always considered myself fit; I mean, I go to the gym two or three times a week. <u>But as soon as we set out I realised I was quite out of my depth;</u> I'd **44** never even carried a pack before. In retrospect, I can't imagine what I was thinking. On the first day, we had a six-hour walk and after four hours I was so exhausted I felt that I couldn't go on. I took off my pack, sat down, and cried. Apparently my reaction was fairly common so our group leader knew just how to deal with it. He calmly explained that we were only two more hours from our first camp, while I'd have to walk for four, alone, to go back! I had no choice. I had to continue. So I did, and when we eventually reached Everest base camp it was the proudest I've ever been.

DANIEL   C

After high school I was accepted into a very good music school, by merit of my audition. I almost declined; I didn't want to go to university. It was a terribly difficult time because nobody could understand why I would make that decision. <u>I was just so terrified that I would fail.</u> **48** I'm dyslexic, and I knew that even if I were studying music I would have to write essays for so many classes. I'd had some teachers in the past that were convinced that I was just careless, that I was lazy, when in fact I was spending much more time on the assignments than my classmates. In the end I went, but I had a terrible attitude. I missed a lot of classes; I wasn't even trying. Eventually I found my way to an office that offered support to students with special needs; I think someone told me that I <u>could get a free computer, or something.</u> **51** That turned my life around. To get the computer <u>I had to attend regular meetings with an advisor, which I hated at first,</u> **43** but eventually I learned to recognise my strengths and be realistic about my weaknesses; I realised I could get help when I needed it, and that was OK. That was the hardest thing; but once I'd understood it, there was no stopping me.

JACK   D

<u>My fear of heights was affecting my life</u> **50** because I had difficulty going up and down stairs or over bridges, particularly if I could see down, beneath me. I would just get paralysed. I would feel nauseous, and my feet would feel heavy, as if they were made of lead. I had read that it was possible to get over phobias by exposure, <u>so I put myself</u> **50** <u>into difficult situations on purpose.</u> It was exhausting, but I knew it was important. I noticed slight improvements, but only very slight. It was frustrating. Then I had the idea; I was going to try bungee jumping. <u>I got a</u> **52** <u>trusted friend to go with me;</u> to make sure I didn't change my mind. He told the people in charge they would have to push me, because I wouldn't jump. It was all very fast; there was no time to think. <u>The feeling was exhila-</u> **49** <u>rating,</u> to be honest. And I've had no trouble in my day-to-day life since then. Though, I admit, I have no desire to do it again.

Paper 2 WRITING PART 1

*You **must** answer this question. Write your answer in **140-190** words in an appropriate style.*

1. In your English class you have been talking about the problem of obesity in young people. Now your English teacher has asked you to write an essay.

   Write an **essay** using **all** the notes and give reasons for your point of view.

> In Europe and the USA a lot of young people have an obesity problem. What can be done to solve this problem?
>
> **Notes**
>
> Write about:
> 1. Drinking
> 2. Fast food
> 3. .... (your own idea)

Paper 2 WRITING PART 2

*Write an answer to **one** of the questions **2-4** in this part. Write your answer in **140-190** words in an appropriate style.*

2. Your favourite music magazine has advertised a contest for readers to write a **review** of a concert they have seen recently.

> *"Soundcheck Magazine"* is seeking reviews from readers!
>
> Have you seen a great concert recently?
> Have you seen a terrible one? We want to know!
>
> Write the best review and win a trip to see your favourite band perform!

Write your **review.**

3. The principal of your school is going to hire a new teacher to teach an elective class. He wants to be sure to offer a class that students will be interested in, so he has asked you to write a **report** explaining which subjects students would be most interested in learning and which would be most useful for them, and making a recommendation about what new class should be offered.

Write your **report.**

4. You saw this advertisement:

> **NEW ARTIST EXHIBITION at the DORCHESTER HOTEL**
>
> See works of art from the newest talent this weekend at this important conference! Buy paintings, sculpture and other media from artists throughout the world!

The exhibition was a great success and a lot of fun. Write to a friend telling him or her about it, and why it was such a great experience.

Write your **letter.** You do not need to include a postal address.

Listening

Paper 3 LISTENING PART 1

*You will hear people talking in eight different situations. For questions **1-8**, choose the best answer A, B or C.*

1. You are in a shop when you overhear this man answering the telephone.
   What does the caller want to buy?
   A. a book about playing a guitar
   B. a book about guitar music
   C. a cassette of guitar music

2. You are listening to the radio when you hear this man speaking.
   What is he talking about?
   A. history
   B. shipbuilding
   C. politics

3. You are sitting in a cafe when you hear this woman speaking.
   She is telling her friend about
   A. the weather.
   B. buying a new coat.
   C. new windows.

4. Listen to this woman introducing a college lecture.
   The visiting lecturer
   A. has recently changed career.
   B. has made a new discovery.
   C. was late for the lecture.

5. You will hear someone talking about soap operas.
   What does the speaker think about them?
   A. They are boring and meaningless to everyone.
   B. The plot is very exciting and unpredictable
   C. People become addicted to them without realising it.

6. You are staying in the home of a British family.
   You hear the mother answering the phone.
   The caller wants to take her daughter
   A. to the cinema.
   B. to a party.
   C. to a restaurant.

7. Listen to a policeman being interviewed on the evening television news.
   What is he describing?
   A. a car crash
   B. a bomb explosion
   C. a serious fire

8. You overhear this exchange in a major London railway station.
   The cause of the delay is
   A. snow.
   B. flooding.
   C. an accident.

PART 1 - JUSTIFICATION OF THE ANSWERS
1. The correct answer is **A**. We are told that the title is "Getting the Most out of Your Guitar". If you get the most out of something, you use it (in this case play it) in the most effective way possible. Therefore choice B is not a good answer; no mention is made of music. Choice C may be eliminated because the salesperson asks "Is it a recent publication?" A publication is a book or magazine which has been published. Also "available in paperback now" is another clue that it must be a book.
2. The correct answer is **C**. "...this makes what the minister said wrong..." and "...difficulties for the government..." both indicate that the topic of discussion is political. Choice A is not correct because it is "...currently happening..." or happening now. Choice B is not a good answer because while the dispute is related to shipbuilding, he is talking about the dispute itself.
3. The correct answer is **C**. "Not since Geoff got round to fitting the new windows..." Choice A is not a good answer because weather is discussed only in relation to the windows. Choice B is not a good answer because she wore a coat before she got new windows, but she does not mention buying one.
4. The correct answer is **B**. The speaker mentions "...Anne's staggering breakthrough..." A 'breakthrough' is an important development or achieve-

ment and something 'staggering' is surprising and amazing. Choice A is incorrect because Anne started her career there and hasn't left. Choice C is not correct because although the meeting is being held at "...short notice...", which means without much advance planning; no mention is made of lateness.
5. The correct answer is **C**: "... they become a habit". Choice A is not correct: " ... we actually enjoy them" therefore not boring to everyone. Choice B is wrong: "... the plot is often repetitive and predictable."
6. The correct answer is **A**. The mother says "He's one of her favourite actors." and "It's just come out, hasn't it?", so we can assume he asks to go to see a film at the cinema. No mention is made of the other answer choices.
7. The correct answer is **B**. "a blast" is a big explosion, especially caused by a bomb. Choice A is not correct because he found "remains of a...vehicle scattered over a wide area"; a crash would not do this. Choice C is not correct because there is no mention of any fire.
8. The correct answer is **B**. "The line's a foot under water" means that the track that the train runs on has flooded. Choice A is incorrect because there had been snow but it melted and choice C is incorrect because no trains are running, so accidents won't happen.

Paper 3 LISTENING   **PART 2**

You will hear part of a radio talk about an institution that helps addicts. For questions 9-18, complete the sentences with a word or short phrase.

There is one centre in the UK situated outside **9** **Bristol** .

The Thorndale method has had success with people addicted to **10** **alcohol**

and **11** **tobacco** .

Addicts take part in a **12** **ten-day course** of treatment.

In a one-hour treatment session, smokers cannot stop smoking even when they

13 **want no more** .

Smokers must keep smoking until they become **14** **physically sick** .

Many patients find the course too difficult to finish and **15** **give up early** .

Those who manage to finish the course are **16** **most unlikely** to want to smoke again.

Alcoholics are allowed to become drunk under the watchful eyes of **17** **trained personnel** .

When they are later shown a video, most alcoholics feel **18** **great embarrassment** .

PART 2 - JUSTIFICATION OF THE ANSWERS
9. "...the Thorndale clinic, situated on the outskirts of **Bristol**..."
10. "...the Thorndale clinic has the highest success rate in treating abusers of **alcohol** and tobacco."
11. "...the Thorndale clinic has the highest success rate in treating abusers of alcohol and **tobacco**."
12. "Addicts attending a **ten-day course** of treatment..."
13. "For example, a one-hour session for smokers involves smoking rapidly without stopping well beyond the point where they **want no more**."
14. "In fact, they are not allowed to stop smoking until they have been **physically sick**."
15. "...many people find the course too painful to complete, and those who do **give up early** are not considered cured..."
16. "On the other hand, smokers who keep going to the end of the course are **most unlikely** to want a cigarette again."
17. "...'patients' are encouraged to drink excessively in the setting of a bar. During this stage they are carefully monitored by **trained personnel**."
18. "Nearly all subjects feel **great embarrassment** when faced with forgotten scenes..."

Paper 3 LISTENING   **PART 3**

You will hear five different people talking about visits they have made to a hospital. For questions 19-23, choose from the list A-H the reasons why each attended the hospital on the occasion described. Use the letters only once. There are three extra letters which you do not need to use.

A collect some surgical knives
B collect somebody
C deliver supplies
D visit a relative
E have an operation
F do maintenance work
G check a mental problem
H have a medical check-up

Speaker 1   **H** **19**
Speaker 2   **E** **20**
Speaker 3   **D** **21**
Speaker 4   **F** **22**
Speaker 5   **C** **23**

PART 3 - JUSTIFICATION OF THE ANSWERS
19. The correct answer is H. "...because I needed a medical certificate." and "...an official piece of paper from any qualified doctor..."
20. The correct answer is E. "...they'd give me something to put me to sleep and when I came round everything would be over and all I would see would be a few stitches." The speaker was operated on.
21. The correct answer is D. "When, at last, I managed to find the right room I almost didn't recognise her." He expected to recognise her because he knew her well, so, of the options, it is most likely that she is a relative.
22. The correct answer is F. "...the call on my answerphone said there was this leaking roof in one of the wards." and "...I told them to get someone else to do it." The speaker was called to fix the roof.
23. The correct answer is C. "The address on the package says room 4J." and "...I take it up there and then there's nobody there to sign the documents to say they've received it."

Paper 3 LISTENING   PART 4

You will hear three people discussing a film they have just seen at the cinema (Wendy, Mrs Turner and Adrian).
For questions 24-30, choose the best answer A, B or C.

24. What did Wendy's mum think of the film?
   A. It was not her favourite film.
   B. She loved the film.
   C. She absolutely hated it.

25. Adrian mentions doing a course in order to show that
   A. he wants to change the subject.
   B. Mrs Turner is wrong about the dinosaurs.
   C. he knows what he is talking about.

26. Adrian feels that watching a film at home
   A. is always better than going to the cinema.
   B. is not something he wants to do again.
   C. has advantages and disadvantages.

27. When Adrian suggests that Wendy was frightened, she
   A. admits that she felt scared.
   B. denies that she felt scared.
   C. complains about the length of the film.

28. What do Wendy and her mum disagree about?
   A. whether or not the film was frightening
   B. whether or not Wendy covered her eyes
   C. whether or not the film is P.G. rated

29. What is it suggested that they do now that the movie has ended?
   A. go straight home
   B. go for a drink
   C. go for dinner

30. Adrian doesn't let Mrs Turner drive because
   A. he enjoys driving.
   B. she will drink alcohol.
   C. they could get in trouble.

PART 4 - JUSTIFICATION OF THE ANSWERS

24. The correct answer is **A**. She says "Well, I have seen better films. I mean, it wasn't as good as..." so choice B is not correct. However she concedes that "The dinosaurs were good." so choice C may be eliminated. Her feelings are neutral.

25. The correct answer is **C**. We may find the correct answer by the process of elimination. Choice A is not correct because the course he did was "computer graphics" which is how the dinosaurs - the subject of the current conversation - were created. Choice B is not correct because he is adding information to what Mrs Turner said, not contradicting her.

26. The correct answer is **C**. He says "...they looked much better on the big screen than they did on my mate's pirate video - but at least I could smoke at my mate's house." He mentions an advantage of going to the cinema and also an advantage of staying at home.

27. The correct answer is **B**. She says "No, I wasn't! What are you talking about?" and "I wasn't covering my eyes, I was laughing." Choice C is not correct because she says "Well, at least it wasn't too long..." which means she is happy that it was short.

28. The correct answer is **A**. We know from the previous question that Wendy claims that she was not frightened. Mrs Turner, on the other hand, says "Well, I couldn't look sometimes. I mean it was only a P.G. film but some of the scenes were...well...pretty..." In other words, she was frightened at times. Choice B is incorrect because this was a subject Wendy and Adrian were arguing about. Choice C is incorrect because Mrs Turner states that the film was P.G. as if this is a fact and no one contradicts her.

29. The correct answer is **B**. Mrs Turner says "Why don't we go for a quick one at the King's Head?" 'In context, we can infer that the King's Head is a pub and we can also guess that 'a quick one' refers to a drink of some sort.

30. The correct answer is **C**. Adrian says "...I'm afraid you're not insured to drive my car and if the police stopped us we'd both be in trouble." Choice B is not correct because she says "I'll have a fruit juice and I can drive us home." She offers not to drink. No mention is made of choice A.

Test 2

Paper 1 Reading and Use of English   PART 1

For questions 1-8, read the text below and decide which word A, B, C or D best fits each space. There is an example at the beginning (0).

Example:

0.   A. intended   B. wondered   C. decided   D. failed

New Cycling Schemes

The County Council has (0)........ to give a higher (1)........ to cycling and agreed a new strategy to guide the way ahead in East Sussex.

Cycling is a (2)........ , healthy and environmentally-friendly form of transport. It is intended to make it safer, more convenient and attractive, and to increase the (3)........ of journeys made by bicycle.

Cycling is being encouraged both for utility purposes (such as journeys to work, school and the shops) and for (4)........ trips for exercise and enjoyment, including longer trips by tourists.

Recent cycle schemes carried out in conjunction with District Councils and other bodies include the Brighton and Hove seafront route and the Cross Levels Way cycle route, in Eastbourne.

(5)........ people will be consulted as the strategy is implemented. The County Council will work with local cycling and other groups, and a countywide Cycling Forum will be formed to (6)........ that all bodies concerned with cycling are in regular (7)........ .

The objectives of the Cycling Strategy are given in a leaflet, and a (8)........ of the full strategy document can be seen in County Council Public Libraries.

1.	A. advantage	B. income	C. benefit	D. priority
2.	A. shortcut	B. high-speed	C. dangerous	D. low-cost
3.	A. size	B. proportion	C. provision	D. proposal
4.	A. recreational	B. useless	C. sufficient	D. promotional
5.	A. Abnormal	B. Proper	C. Country	D. Local
6.	A. improve	B. ensure	C. assert	D. maintain
7.	A. contact	B. basis	C. touch	D. account
8.	A. copy	B. book	C. letter	D. network

Paper 1 Reading and Use of English   PART 2

*For questions 9-16, read the text below and think of the word which best fits each space. Use only **one** word in each space. There is an example at the beginning (0).*

Example: | 0 | used |

Holidays with friends

I always (0) ...*used*.... to go to Porchester (9) .**for/during**. my summer holidays. It is a quiet little town, full of old and interesting buildings. Very (10) ....**few**........ visitors ever go there, so there are no crowds. I enjoyed its sleepy atmosphere. I work in a big city, so a holiday in Porchester was a complete change (11) ....**from**.......... my usual life. Besides, I found out about the history of the place. I wanted to learn how life used to be in Porchester - the stories of (12) ...**its/the**... people and buildings.

I made notes on all these things (13) ...**during/on**.. my holidays and I soon knew more about the history of Porchester than most of the people (14) ...**who/that**... lived there.

I am not a rich man and I cannot afford to stay in hotels. When Jack Thompson heard that I wanted to spend my holidays in Porchester again all these years later, he invited me to stay with (15) ..**him**.. . Jack and I were in the Army (16) ...**together**... during the war and we were good friends.

Paper 1 Reading and Use of English   PART 3

For questions **17-24**, read the text below. Use the word given in capitals at the end of some lines to form a word that fits in the space in the same line. There is an example at the beginning (0).

Example: | 0 | e x c i t a b l e |

Mr Greaves had always been an (0)..........*excitable*.......... man who should
never have had a (17)........**managerial / management**........ position.
His bad temper was only just (18).........**bearable**......... and there was often
a (19)........**temptation**........ to tell him to sit down and relax. His office
was chaotic with papers everywhere and had (20).........**absolutely**......... no
order to it.

Once he went to a (21)......**conference**...... in Paris and on his (22).....**arrival**.....
at the hotel he completely forgot who he worked for when the (23)**receptionist**.......
asked him.

When he tried to help he was a hindrance although his (24)........**intentions**........
were always good.

| EXCITE |
| MANAGE |
| BEAR |
| TEMPT |
| ABSOLUTE |
| CONFER / ARRIVE |
| RECEIVE |
| INTEND |

Paper 1 Reading and Use of English   PART 4

For questions **25-30**, complete the second sentence so that it has a similar meaning to the first sentence, using the word given. **Do not change the word given.** You must use between **two** and **five** words, including the word given. There is an example at the beginning (0).

Example:

0 They think the owner of the house is in France.   thought

The owner of the house .... in France.

The gap can be filled by the words "**is thought to be**" so you write: | 0 | i s   t h o u g h t   t o   b e |

25. Michael's wife finds getting up early every morning difficult.   used

Michael's wife ....**isn't used to getting**.......... up early every morning.

26. What a pity you didn't come to the party.   wish

I ....**wish you had come**.......... to the party.

27. The burglar failed to enter the house through the first floor window.   succeed

The burglar ......**didn't succeed in entering**...... the house through the first floor window.

28. My hair needs to be cut before the wedding reception.   must

I ......**must have/get my hair cut**...... before the wedding reception.

29. "Why didn't I ask her out last night?" John said to himself.   wondered

John ......**wondered why he hadn't**...... asked her out the night before.

30. They think that their school teacher is a very rich man.   believed

Their school teacher ......**is believed to be**...... a very rich man.

Paper 1 Reading and Use of English | PART 5

You are going to read an extract from a science fiction novel called "1984". For questions 31-36, choose the answer A, B, C or D which you think fits best according to the text.

'How is the Dictionary getting on?' said Winston, raising his voice to overcome the noise.

'Slowly,' said Syme. 'I'm on the adjectives. It's fascinating.'

He had brightened up immediately at the mention of Newspeak. He pushed his bowl aside, took up his hunk of bread in one delicate hand and his cheese in the other, and leaned across the table so as to be able to speak without shouting.

'The Eleventh Edition is the definitive edition,' he said. 'We're getting the language into its final shape - the shape it's going to have when nobody speaks anything else. When we've finished with it, people like you will have to learn it all over again. You think, I dare say, that our chief job is inventing new words. But not a bit of it! We're destroying words - scores of them, hundreds of them, every day. We're cutting the language down to the bone. The Eleventh Edition won't contain a single word that will become obsolete before the year 2050.'

He bit hungrily into his bread and swallowed a couple of mouthfuls, then continued speaking, with a sort of pedant's passion. His thin dark face had become animated, his eyes had lost their mocking expression and grown almost dreamy.

'It's a beautiful thing, the destruction of words. Of course the great wastage is in the verbs and adjectives, but there are hundreds of nouns that can be got rid of as well. It isn't only the synonyms; there are also the antonyms. After all, what justification is there for a word which is simply the opposite of some other word? A word contains its opposite in itself. Take "good", for instance. If you have a word like "good", what need is there for a word like "bad"? "Ungood" will do just as well - better, because it's an exact opposite, which the other is not. Or again, if you want a stronger version of "good", what sense is there in having a whole string of vague useless words like "excellent" and "splendid" and all the rest of them? "Plusgood" covers the meaning, or "doubleplusgood" if you want something stronger still. Of course we use those forms already. But in the final version of Newspeak there'll be nothing else. In the end the whole notion of goodness and badness will

be covered by only six words - in reality, only one word. Don't you see the beauty of that, Winston? It was B.B.'s idea originally, of course,' he added as an afterthought.

A sort of vapid eagerness flitted across Winston's face at the mention of Big Brother. Nevertheless Syme immediately detected a certain lack of enthusiasm.

'You haven't a real appreciation of Newspeak, Winston,' he said almost sadly. 'Even when you write it you're still thinking in Oldspeak. I've read some of those pieces that you write in "The Times" occasionally. They're good enough, but they're translations. In your heart you'd prefer to stick to Oldspeak, with all its vagueness and its useless shades of meaning. You don't grasp the beauty of the destruction of words. Do you know that Newspeak is the only language in the world whose vocabulary gets smaller every year?'

Winston did know that, of course. He smiled, sympathetically he hoped, not trusting himself to speak. Syme bit off another fragment of the dark-coloured bread, chewed it briefly, and went on:

'Don't you see that the whole aim of Newspeak is to narrow the range of thought? In the end we shall make thought crime literally impossible because there will be no words in which to express it. Every concept that can ever be needed, will be expressed by exactly one word, with its meaning rigidly defined and all its subsidiary meanings rubbed out and forgotten. Already, in the Eleventh Edition, we're not far from that point. But the process will still be continuing long after you and I are dead. Every year fewer and fewer words, and the range of consciousness always a little smaller. Even now, of course, there's no reason or excuse for committing thoughtcrime. It's merely a question of self-discipline, reality-control. But in the end there won't be any need even for that. The Revolution will be complete when the language is perfect. Newspeak is Ingsoc and Ingsoc is Newspeak,' he added with a sort of mystical satisfaction. 'Has it ever occurred to you, Winston, that by the year 2050, at the very latest, not a single human being will be alive who could understand such a conversation as we are having now?'

31. Winston and Syme are

   A. in a cafeteria.

   B. at a party.

   C. at school.

   D. in an office.

32. Syme likes

   A. the food.

   B. hearing Winston's opinions.

   C. talking about his work.

   D. to shout.

33. What kind of words are being the most greatly reduced?

   A. adjectives

   B. verbs and adjectives

   C. nouns

   D. everything except antonyms

34. What can be gathered about Winston's attitude towards Newspeak?

   A. He finds it exciting.

   B. He studies it eagerly.

   C. He is outspokenly against it.

   D. He accepts it unhappily.

35. Which of the following best describes Newspeak?

   A. It is a historical language being reconstructed.

   B. It is a highly simplified language designed to prevent thought.

   C. It was invented to help citizens escape an oppressive government.

   D. It is a new language that is incredibly difficult to learn.

36. What kind of future does Syme imagine?

   A. Everyone will be better educated.

   B. People will be safe because there will be no violent crime.

   C. People will not have enough language to think at all.

   D. People will communicate better and more effectively.

---

31. The correct answer is **A**. Paragraph 3: "He pushed his bowl aside, took up his hunk of bread in one delicate hand and his cheese in the other, and leaned across the table." This would suggest they are in a place where food is provided and they are chatting over lunch. However, the discussion is about work, which rules out options B and C and leaves us with the workplace cafeteria.

32. The correct answer is **C**. Paragraph 3: "He had brightened up immediately at the mention of Newspeak", in other words, he was very happy Winston had asked about his work. Also, Paragraph 5 "He continued speaking with a sort of pedant's passion." A pedant is someone who is too academic and concerned with rules and details. It isn't A as the text says he eats hungrily, but doesn't mention if he likes the food. B is incorrect as it is Syme who is doing the most talking. D is also incorrect since Syme leaned across the table in order to speak without shouting.

33. The correct answer is **B**. Paragraph 6: "Of course the great wastage is in the verbs and adjectives." In other words, there are a lot of verbs and adjectives to be got rid of, so these will be targeted the most - but not just the adjectives, which rules out A. And while Syme says "there are hundreds of nouns that can be got rid of as well', we can infer that this number is not as significant as the "great wastage" of verbs and adjectives he alluded to, ruling out C. Syme also mentions that antonyms should be done away with, which excludes D as a possible answer.

34. The correct answer is **D**. Paragraph 8: Syme comments on Winston's attitude: "I've read some of those pieces that you write...they're translations. In your heart you'd prefer to stick to Oldspeak, with all its vagueness and its useless shades of meaning." Winston is using Newspeak, but it is clear to Syme that he does not like it. Winston expresses neither excitement or disagreement in the conversation, eliminating answers A, B and C.

35. The correct answer is **B**. Paragraph 10: Syme says to Winston: "Don't you see that the whole aim of Newspeak is to narrow the range of thought?" The language is simple and has a limited number of words in order to stop people from thinking at all.

36. The correct answer is **C**. Last paragraph: "Every year fewer and fewer words, and the range of consciousness always a little smaller." He envisions that language will be so limited people won't be able to think at all. This is the opposite of choice A. Choice B is incorrect because the crimes in question are "thought crimes" which are not physical so cannot be violent. D is incorrect because people will not even "understand such a conversation as we are having now".

Paper 1 Reading and Use of English PART 6

You are going to read a magazine article about a volcano in New Zealand, now a nature reserve, and the experience of the native people in the past when it erupted. Six sentences have been removed from the article. Choose from the sentences A-G the one which fits each gap 37-42. There is one extra sentence which you do not need to use.

Rangitoto
By Alastair Jamieson

Off-track the ground is menacing. Lava, like angry waves frozen in mid-chop only moments ago, claws at the soles of my boots and threatens to shred my knees if I place a foot wrong. The surface is so uneven that progress is extraordinarily difficult. Occasional smooth stone channels course like petrified streams through the rougher ground, their solid surfaces a welcome pathway amid teetering plates of broken lava and treacherous bouldery rubble. Out of the shade of the dense thickets of bush, it's as hot as a furnace. All that black rock absorbs and radiates enough heat to melt Antarctica. It's as hostile a spot as you could find anywhere in New Zealand, yet when I turn around, there is downtown Auckland in plain view just a few kilometers away.

37 **F** Its symmetrical cone is a relaxed cousin of those higher and steeper volcanoes Taranaki and Ngauruhoe but Rangitoto is a truly astonishing wilderness right on the doorstep of the city. Landing on the island, the graceful sweeping curves seen from a distance quickly give way to a magnificent mosaic of the tortuous lava I've been scrambling through and scrubby, impenetrable pohutukawa forest.

Of course, it was not always like this. **38** **A** However, the emergence of the youngest and largest of the fifty-odd volcanoes in Auckland's volcanic field was witnessed by Maori living on adjacent Motutapu Island.

The persistent yelping of dogs might first have awoken them. Soon afterwards there would have been a thundering roar. The vibration of the sandy ground beneath them would surely have jolted them from their homes. **39** **E** A wind shift and the familiar smells of the camp—wood smoke, the sea, and even the penetrating stench of shark flesh drying on frames—were soon overpowered by the pungent, suffocating odour of sulphur dioxide.

Running across the beach and dragging boats into the sea, shoals of dead fish bumped against their legs as they waded into the cold shallows. **40** **D** Looking behind them, the cataclysm was becoming clearer in the first light of day. Black clouds were blasting out from the base of a roiling column of steam, flying boulders were arcing white streamers through the sky and splashing into the sea.

41 **G** The footprints of a small group of adults and children were found sandwiched between layers of Rangitoto ash. Markings show where the ground was prodded with sticks and that one of the dogs with the group paused to drink from a puddle. **42** **C** Whether these people were foolhardy or brave, lured by curiosity, or a desire to retrieve their treasured possessions, we'll never know.

A. The familiar form of Rangitoto did not exist for generations of Maori who first inhabited the surrounding lands.

B. The low black cliffs of Rangitoto are just 1500 m away, the centre of the eruption only 3 km further.

C. The impressions were so well preserved that the next blanket of ash must have spewed from Rangitoto soon after they were made.

D. Paddling hard towards safety, the first wet ash began to fall, sticky and abrasive.

E. Outside, the familiar stars above and the scatter of bright campfires along the shore to the west was hidden by a pall of steam, strobed by lightning and lit by a ferocious fiery glow from beneath.

F. No landform is more familiar to Aucklanders than Rangitoto Island and yet how many of them ever go there?

G. Proof exists that in the weeks or months following the onset of the eruption, people came back to their campsite on Motutapu Island.

37. The gap is best filled with choice **F**. The sentence that follows mentions the particular features of the mountain - "its symmetrical cone" this would then fit in with F that says it is a familiar landform to Aucklanders. The landform is visible in "plain view" from downtown Auckland, as it also says in the previous sentence.

38. The correct answer is **A**. The sentence before says that the volcano wasn't always the way it is seen today and A says that it did not exist when the first inhabitants, the Maori, came to the surrounding lands. A is then the most logical answer.

39. The correct answer is choice **E**. This sentence goes on to provide further information of what possible effects occurred from the volcano, which fits in here with the text describing how the smell of sulphur dioxide would have filled the air from the steam.

40. The gap is best filled with choice **D**. The text describes how people were trying to flee from the erupting volcano, D says that they were paddling for safety. For this reason D is the most logical answer.

41. The correct answer is **G**. G is the topic sentence; claiming that people returned after the eruption, and the text follows on from this to give evidence of their return in the form of footprints preserved in the volcano's dust. Choice C may be eliminated because "The impressions" have not yet been explained, so would make little sense here at the beginning of the paragraph - the reader would wonder "What impressions?".

42. The gap is best filled by choice **C**. The paragraph is speaking about the footprints that remained, and C refers to "The impressions" of the footprints preserved in the ash.

Paper 1 Reading and Use of English   PART 7

You are going to read five different people's opinions about time travel. For questions 43–52, choose from the people A–E. The people may be chosen more than once.

Which person:

thinks it is best to appreciate the present?	43	A
would make a different relationship decision?	44	E
would try to help a family member?	45	A
offers contemporary travel advice?	46	D
is probably at least 50 years old?	47	A
is interested in history?	48	B
is put off by old-fashioned clothes?	49	B
thinks of impressing others?	50	D
would make an investment?	51	E
would not expect time travellers in general to receive a friendly welcome?	52	C

Time Travel

Charlie   A

I'd travel back to the year I was born, and live my life again, but only if I could know then what I know now! I'd love to see my parents and grandparents again. **45** I'd persuade my dad to stop smoking, so that he wouldn't die so young. On the other hand, in the present, I have two wonderful grown-up children and two **47** precious grandchildren. Perhaps the answer is to make the best of the present and stop han- **43** kering after the past. If I could visit other times just for a day, I'd love to meet my parents as children, and go into the future to meet the great-great grandchildren I'll not live to see!

Chloe   B

48 I would not exchange today for any previous era. I have studied a lot of history and whilst I would be interested in certain eras there would be diffi-culties. For example, Tudor times - interesting, but as a Catholic I might have had my head chopped off; eighteenth and nineteenth **49** centuries - exciting, but too many petticoats to wear, never mind about corsets. Then there is the lack of education and opportunity for women to consider, and the lack of medical knowledge. No, today is the best time to live. Having said that, I would not mind the opportunity to take tea with Miss Austen - she would have been enormous fun.

Emily   C

Go back in time? Who'd want that? I mean, as soon as some people spotted you, you'd be the odd one out. And if you went back in time with all that futuristic equipment on and, for example, the alarm clock on your watch went off, you would be denounced as a devil; tortured, **52** quartered and drawn, and then burnt at the stake! Travel to the future and you'd be a museum artifact! You'd be seen as some sort of primitive beast! I'm fine where I am at the moment, thank you. Also, to those of you intending to prevent the election/birth of various politicians, it won't work; if you succeeded, then you would have no incentive to do so, and thus wouldn't have gone. That's the paradox.

Jack   D

I have always dreamed of being a sailor in the merchant navy between 1920 and 1940. At that time, travelling to foreign ports like Yokohama, Saigon, Rangoon, Surabaya and such would have been the same as space travel is today. Imagine coming home after a **50** long voyage, and telling the people in the pub all about your travels! You'd have such stories to tell! I have seen the majority of the world's cities now, and most look exactly the same as each other. If you want to travel somewhere that is still unique today, without the time machine, **46** see Asia but steer clear of package tours. And hurry; do it now before it all becomes McDonaldised.

Liam   E

I'd go back maybe about five years and try to do a better job this time. I would never have **44** ended the relationship with the love of my life. I wish I could've known better, and understood then what I understand now. I would also stay at college. I'd register 250 of the best **51** internet domains possible, so by now I'd be a billionaire without having done a thing. But I wouldn't be selfish; I would change the world for the better with the money. Money can save lives and do unbelievable things in the right hands. Plus, I would have the girl! Oh well, back to reality.

Paper 2 WRITING | PART 1

*You **must** answer this question. Write your answer in **140-190** words in an appropriate style.*

1. You have listened to a radio programme about the impact of smoking on people's health. Now, your English teacher has asked you to write an essay.

   Write an **essay** using **all** the notes and give reasons for your point of view.

   > Smoking is responsible for many health problems throughout the world. Do you think it should be made illegal?
   >
   > **Notes**
   >
   > Write about:
   > 1. lung cancer
   > 2. passive smoking
   > 3. .... (your own idea)

Paper 2 WRITING | PART 2

*Write an answer to **one** of the questions **2-4** in this part. Write your answer in **140-190** words in an appropriate style.*

2. You have been asked to write an article for a local paper about ways to improve the environment.
   Write the **article**, giving your opinion on this subject.

   > *The Daily News* is Seeking Articles!
   >
   > We need ideas from our readers about how to improve the environment.
   >
   > Write your article now and send it to us as soon as possible!
   > Prize for the best article is a bicycle!

Write your **article**.

3. You are interested in becoming a music critic and have been given an assignment by a new online magazine to review a new pop band in your city.

   > **The editor of the publication instructs you to consider the following when developing your review:**
   > - How well does the group sing and dance?
   > - What type of response does the group elicit from the audience?
   > - Would you change anything about the group's performance?
   > - Would you recommend the group to people you know?
   > - Why or why not?

Write your **review**.

4. Last night you left your bag at the cinema. Write a **letter** to the cinema, asking them if they have found it. Be sure to say where you left it, what it looks like and what was inside.

Write your **letter**.

Listening

Paper 3 LISTENING | **PART 1**

*You will hear people talking in eight different situations. For questions **1-8**, choose the best answer **A, B** or **C**.*

1. You need to see a doctor urgently. You telephone a surgery and hear this answer-phone message. What are you advised to do?
   A. go to 217 Jordan Street
   B. contact another doctor
   C. telephone 622919

2. You hear part of a news broadcast on TV about an accident at a chemical factory. The speaker is speaking
   A. in the chemical factory.
   B. outside the chemical factory.
   C. in the nearby town.

3. You are staying in Britain with a host family. You hear the father speaking to one of his children. The day of the week they are speaking on is
   A. Tuesday.
   B. Thursday.
   C. Wednesday.

4. You overhear a man at a call box telephoning an emergency break-down service to ask for a mechanic to fix his car. Where is the car?
   A. near the Green Lion pub
   B. opposite the Green Lion pub
   C. opposite the high street

5. Listen to a man outside a supermarket talking to a housewife. What does the man want to do?
   A. sell her some washing powder
   B. ask her about her family's washing habits
   C. visit her home

6. You are with a group of friends. One of them is telling you about something that happened to her at work. She works
   A. as a secretary.
   B. as a railway employee.
   C. for the police.

7. Listen to this man being interviewed on the radio. The man is
   A. a singer.
   B. a film star.
   C. an actor.

8. You are on a bus tour of a British historical city. You are currently looking at Saint Christopher's Memorial Hospital. The speaker's opinion of that building is that
   A. she is not clear on its appearance.
   B. the gardens are exceptionally beautiful.
   C. the architecture is a masterpiece.

PART 1 - JUSTIFICATION OF THE ANSWERS

1. The correct answer is **B**. "If you urgently need to see a doctor, dial...for doctors Smith and Parker". Choice A is not correct because you are advised to "go to 217 George Street." Choice C in incorrect because you should dial "622909".

2. The correct answer is **B**. "Looking though the chain-link fence..." indicates that they are outside the factory grounds looking in. Choice A is therefore incorrect. Choice C is incorrect because the nearby town is where the bodies have been taken for identification, not where the broadcast is happening from.

3. The correct answer is **C**. "...you'll have to go today or tomorrow because Friday's a public holiday..." So, we have today, tomorrow, then Friday, therefore today must be Wednesday. Also, we know that yesterday was Tuesday because the son says: "I couldn't go yesterday; it was closed." and "No, it's shut all day Tuesday."

4. The correct answer is **A**. His car is parked "...on the high street, you know, beside the Green Lion pub." Choice B is incorrect because the man says "No, not the one on Baker Street..." and choice C is incorrect because it is parked in the High Street.

5. The correct answer is **B**. "...we're currently carrying out a survey to determine...an average family's washing needs." Choice A is incorrect because he observes that she has already bought the washing powder and choice C is incorrect because he tells her "...it will not be necessary for one of our representatives to visit your home."

6. The correct answer is **C**. She says "I was working at the desk that day..." and "two officers brought a suspect into the station..." We know in this case that 'station' refers to the police station, not a railway station, because a suspect had been brought in by officers. A suspect is someone believed to have committed a crime.

7. The correct answer is **C**. We are told that the man gave "...a very impressive performance..." and he also says "...things that we do on stage..." Because he performs on a stage, he must be a theatre actor rather than a film star so choice B may be eliminated. Choice A may be eliminated because singers do not usually work with directors.

8. The correct answer is **A**. "The building has been hailed as a masterpiece, although I personally have reservations because it lacks the colour and flamboyance..." and therefore choice C is clearly incorrect. Choice B is incorrect because she says the gardens are "...particularly noted for the unusual layout..." which does not necessarily mean that they are beautiful.

Paper 3 LISTENING   PART 2

You are going to hear somebody giving their opinion about the media and its influence on society. For questions 9-18, complete the sentences with a word or short phrase.

The three forms of media are TV, radio and **9** newspapers .

Politicians use the media during political **10** campaigns .

Entertainers use it to stay in the **11** public eye .

The percentage of people who did not have a particular point of view about the privacy of

celebrities was **12** 4% .

The most influential form of media is **13** TV .

We can be deceived by TV when we are shown carefully selected **14** images/pictures .

Some TV stations turn true events into **15** fiction/lies .

A newspaper had to pay **16** £1,000,000 for printing lies about a pop singer.

Sometimes a paper can avoid being sued if it makes a public **17** apology .

There are two kinds of newspaper; the "quality" papers and the **18** tabloids .

PART 2 - JUSTIFICATION OF THE ANSWERS
9. "TV, radio and **newspapers** are the three main forms of media ..."
10." Politicians use it in their political **campaigns** in order to gain support"
11. "Entertainers and celebrities use it to promote themselves and keep themselves in the **public eye.**"
12. "**4%** had no opinion either way".

13. "... over two thirds asked said **TV**".
14. "... carefully chosen or edited **images** can deceive us".
15. "turns fact into **fiction**".
16. "awarded **one million pounds** when ...".
17. "get away with making a public **apology**".
18. "newspapers...tend to fall into two groups; the **tabloids** and the so called quality newspapers".

Paper 3 LISTENING   PART 3

You will hear five different women talking about the same wedding. For questions 19-23, choose from the list A-H who the speaker is speaking to. Use the letters only once. There are three extra letters which you do not need to use.

A	her husband	Speaker 1	**G**	19
B	her boyfriend	Speaker 2	**B**	20
C	a child	Speaker 3	**F**	21
D	her father	Speaker 4	**C**	22
E	her boss	Speaker 5	**E**	23
F	somebody she's just met			
G	her mother			
H	the vicar			

PART 3 - JUSTIFICATION OF THE ANSWERS
19. The correct answer is **G**. "Brian mentioned you in his speech...he still likes your cooking best." and "Of course, Dad was there..." indicate the speaker is addressing her mother.

20. The correct answer is **B**. The speaker says "when we get married a few little things are going to change..." so it must be her boyfriend she is speaking to.

21. The correct answer is **F**. The speaker asks the other person how he/she met Brian and provides the same info about herself - they didn't know each other.

22. The correct answer is **C**. "Did you take all these pictures yourself? You are clever." This would be inappropriate to say to an adult! Also, Julie is the other person's Auntie, he/she also has a granny and grandad, which suggests he/she is still a child.

23. The correct answer is **E**. "If you hadn't given me the Friday off...", so we can assume it is her boss.

You will hear three friends talking about their relationships. For questions 24-30, decide which of the choices A, B or C is the best answer.

24. What's Anne's problem?

A. She's got no one to go out with.

B. She's angry with her boyfriend.

C. She has hurt herself.

25. What does Mark do?

A. He gets angry with Anne.

B. He tries to change the subject.

C. He asks Sue about her boyfriend.

26. Who has been hard to get in touch with recently?

A. Mark

B. Dave

C. Anne

27. What does Dave say?

A. He will never get married to Sue.

B. He isn't sure if he is going to go on holiday or not.

C. He doesn't know where to go on holiday.

28. What is Mark's problem?

A. He smokes too much.

B. He goes out too often.

C. He has a medical problem.

29. How can Anne be described at the end?

A. sad

B. optimistic

C. nervous

30. What is Mark's attitude towards Anne?

A. He disapproves of her dating someone else so quickly.

B. He wants to try to help her.

C. He thinks it is unlikely that her cousin will be interested in her.

PART 4 - JUSTIFICATION OF THE ANSWERS

24. The correct answer is **A**. She says: "I'm fed up with staying in nearly every night. Since John and I broke up..." Choice B is not correct because she had split up with her boyfriend (see above). Choice C: there is no mention that she had hurt herself.

25. The correct answer is **B**. He is trying to change the subject: "Anyway, enough of my personal life. What about you..." There is no mention in the text about the other two choices.

26. The correct answer is **A**. "Well, well. That's why you *(referring to Mark)* are never home these days when I try to phone you"

27. The correct answer is **C**. Dave says: "We're trying to decide where to go on holiday." Choice A is not correct because Dave says: "I'm not saying we won't get married." Choice B is not correct: "We're trying to decide where (they have decided they will go) to go on holiday."

28. The correct answer is **C**: Mark: "...and I had to leave early because the smoke was making my asthma bad. I could hardly breathe and felt terrible the next day." The other two options are not mentioned.

29. The correct answer is **B**. She says: "The best cure for a broken heart is a new romance" so she is optimistic about the future and not sad or nervous.

30. The correct answer is **B**. "I'll see if I can arrange for him to be at the Christmas party..." The other options are clearly wrong.

Test 3

Paper 1 Reading and Use of English | PART 1

For questions **1-8**, read the text below and decide which word A, B, C or D best fits each space. There is an example at the beginning (**0**).

Example:

0.   A. major   B. frequent   C. similar   D. various

| 0 | **A** | B | C | D |

The Eighth Wonder of the World

The Thames Barrier is a (**0**).......... part of the flood defence scheme for protecting London (**1**).......... rising water levels. The defenses (**2**)................ include raised river embankments and additional flood gates at strategic points, including the Barking Barrier. The unique structure that is the Barrier spans the 520-metre wide Woolwich reach and (**3**).......... of 10 separate movable gates, each pivoting and supported between concrete structures which house the operating machinery.

When raised, the four main gates (**4**).......... stand as high as a five-storey building and as wide as the opening of Tower Bridge. Each (**5**).......... 3700 tonnes. During the first twelve years of (**6**).......... , the Barrier has been closed twenty nine times to protect London.

(**7**).......... the Barrier from the comfortable cafeteria. Picnic on the riverside embankment. Enjoy beautiful views from the riverside walk. Visit the shop which stocks a large selection of souvenirs, books and Barrier information.

There is a children's play area suitable for 4- to 12-year olds, located adjacent to the riverside walk. A visit to the spectacular Thames Barrier is a (**8**).......... experience.

1.	A. against	B. for	C. between	D. with
2.	A. and	B. also	C. still	D. too
3.	A. consists	B. includes	C. involves	D. contains
4.	A. which	B. every	C. each	D. none
5.	A. measures	B. costs	C. calculates	D. weighs
6.	A. operation	B. surgery	C. vocation	D. profession
7.	A. Sight	B. View	C. Hear	D. Explore
8.	A. forgettable	B. memorable	C. forgetful	D. memorised

Paper 1 Reading and Use of English | PART 2

For questions 9-16, read the text below and think of the word which best fits each space. Use **only** one word in each space. There is an example at the beginning (**0**).

Example: | 0 | *in* |

Datamac

Datamac was the greatest machine (**0**) .....*in*........ the world. Its business (**9**) ....**was**.......... facts: it accepted (**10**) ....**them**....... , stored them, tested them and delivered them.

It was located in Tokyo, where it received messages and questions from all (**11**) ....**over**.......... the world. It sent answers to every town and city in every (**12**) ..**country/region**... . An army of workers fed it with facts all the time. Other workers moved about inside Datamac and (**13**) .....**looked**....... after it.

Datamac had a very special duty. It was in (**14**) .....**charge/control/**.... of all the facts about every person **possession** in the world. Each day it brought these four thousand million facts together, and answered the question: "(**15**) ....**What**......... will happen tomorrow?" Every city in the world received the report for its own part of the country. And the complete World Report (**16**) ....**went**...... to the Chief of the Correction Force in Tokyo. John Williams had been Chief for only three weeks. By now he was not afraid of the World Report every morning. It was just a pile of papers, fifteen centimetres thick.

Paper 1 Reading and Use of English   PART 3

*For questions **17-24**, read the text below. Use the word given in capitals at the end of some lines to form a word that fits in the space in the same line. There is an example at the beginning (0).*

Example: | 0 | e n t h u s i a s t |

Being a DIY (0)....*enthusiast*.... I was happy to take on the challenge of	ENTHUSE
(17)......**modernising**...... an old but (18)..........**delightful**.......... cottage.	MODERN / DELIGHT
I had been given the (19)..........**invitation**.......... by a man who used to be	INVITE
an (20)..........**employee**.......... of mine before he stopped working for me.	EMPLOY
The cottage needed to be changed (21)..........**extensively**.......... , and my friend	EXTEND
had to remove all his (22)........**possessions**........ before I could start.	POSSESS
The requirements for such a task are many and before any (23)......**arrangements**......	ARRANGE
could be made some organisation was needed. The final (24)....**transformation**....	TRANSFORM
was worth the effort though.	

Paper 1 Reading and Use of English   PART 4

*For questions **25-30**, complete the second sentence so that it has a similar meaning to the first sentence, using the word given. Do not change the word given. You must use between **two** and **five** words, including the word given. There is an example at the beginning (0).*

Example:

0 They think the owner of the house is in France.   thought

   The owner of the house .... in France.

*The gap can be filled by the words "**is thought to be**" so you write:* | 0 | is thought to be |

25. The hairdresser did Mary's hair last Tuesday.   had

   Mary ....**had her hair done**............... last Tuesday.

26. Andrew's job is to supervise all the employees of the company.   responsible

   Andrew ....**is responsible for supervising**......... all the employees of the company.

27. Harry reads faster than his little sister.   reader

   Harry ....**is a faster reader than**............... his little sister.

28. "I didn't steal the lady's purse", said the boy.   denied

   The boy ....**denied stealing / having stolen**........ the lady's purse.

29. It was our first trip to Italy so we were very excited about it.   time

   It was the ....**first time we had travelled/been**........ to Italy so we were very excited about it.

30. "Whose car is this?" he asked.   belong

   "Who ....**does this car belong to**........... ?" he asked.

You are going to read an extract from the novel, "Alice in Wonderland". For questions 31-36, choose the answer A, B, C or D which you think fits best according to the text.

Before she had drunk half the bottle, she found her head pressing against the ceiling, and had to stoop to save her neck from being broken. She hastily put down the bottle, saying to herself 'That's quite enough - I hope I will not grow any more - as it is, I can't get out at the door - I do wish I hadn't drunk quite so much!'

Alas, it was too late to wish that! She went on growing, and growing, and very soon had to kneel down on the floor: in another minute there was not even room for this, and she tried the effect of lying down with one elbow against the door, and the other arm curled round her head. Still she went on growing, and, as a last resource, she put one arm out of the window, and one foot up the chimney, and said to herself 'Now I can do no more, whatever happens. What will become of me?'

Luckily for Alice, the little magic bottle had now had its full effect, and she grew no larger: Still it was very uncomfortable, and, as there seemed to be no sort of chance of her ever getting out of the room again, no wonder she felt unhappy.

'It was much pleasanter at home,' thought poor Alice, 'when one wasn't always growing larger and smaller, and being ordered about by mice and rabbits. I almost wish I hadn't gone down that rabbit-hole - and yet ... and yet - it's rather curious, you know, this sort of life! I do wonder what can have happened to me! When I used to read fairy-tales, I fancied that kind of thing never happened, and now here I am in the middle of one! There ought to be a book written about me, that there ought! And when I grow up, I'll write one ... but I'm grown up now,' she added in a sorrowful tone; 'at least there's no room to grow up any more in here.'

'But then,' thought Alice, 'will I never get any older than I am now? That'll be a comfort, one way ... never to be an old woman .... but then ... always to have lessons to learn! Oh, I shouldn't like that!'

'Oh, you foolish Alice!' she answered herself. 'How can you learn lessons in here? Why, there's hardly room for you, and no room at all for any lesson-books!'

And so she went on, taking first one side and then the other, and making quite a conversation of it altogether; but after a few minutes she heard a voice outside, and stopped to listen.

'Mary Ann! Mary Ann!' said the voice. 'Fetch me my gloves this moment!' Then came a little pattering of feet on the stairs. Alice knew it was the Rabbit coming to look for her, and she trembled till she shook the house, quite forgetting that she was now about a thousand times as large as the Rabbit, and had no reason to be afraid of it.

Presently the Rabbit came up to the door, and tried to open it; but, as the door opened inwards, and Alice's elbow was pressed hard against it, that attempt proved a failure. Alice heard it say to itself 'Then I'll go round and get in at the window.'

'That you won't' thought Alice, and, after waiting till she fancied she heard the Rabbit just under the window, she suddenly spread out her hand, and made a snatch in the air. She did not get hold of anything, but she heard a little shriek and a fall, and a crash of broken glass, from which she concluded that it was just possible it had fallen into a cucumber-frame, or something of the sort.

Next came an angry voice - the Rabbit's - 'Pat! Pat! Where are you?' And then a voice she had never heard before, 'Sure then I'm here! Digging for apples, your honour!'

'Digging for apples, indeed!' said the Rabbit angrily. 'Here! Come and help me out of this!' (Sounds of more broken glass.)

'Now tell me, Pat, what's that in the window?'

'Sure, it's an arm, your honour!'

'An arm, you goose! Who ever saw one that size? Why, it fills the whole window!'

'Sure, it does, your honour: but it's an arm for all that.'

31. Why didn't Alice leave the house when she noticed she was growing?
   A. She couldn't find her way out.
   B. She was already too big.
   C. She was hiding from the Rabbit.
   D. She was comfortable there.

32. As she grew, Alice had to
   A. keep changing position.
   B. break the roof of the house.
   C. be very gentle.
   D. climb up the chimney.

33. Alice had a long conversation with
   A. the Rabbit.
   B. herself.
   C. an old woman.
   D. Pat.

34. Mary Ann is most likely
   A. the name of the Rabbit.
   B. what the Rabbit calls Alice.
   C. Alice's little sister.
   D. Alice's friend.

35. Before the Rabbit called him, Pat was spending his time
   A. doing something secret.
   B. hiding from the Rabbit.
   C. doing something silly.
   D. growing food.

36. Why does the Rabbit argue about what they see in the window?
   A. He knows that Pat is foolish.
   B. He can't see it clearly.
   C. He can't believe his eyes.
   D. He is trying to trick Pat.

31. The correct answer is **B**. Paragraphs 1 and 2: "I hope I will not grow any more - as it is I can't get out at the door...Alas, it was too late to wish that! She went on growing and growing..." - Alice couldn't leave the house because she had grown so large she was not able to get out. For this reason answers A, C and D can't be correct.

32. The correct answer is **A**. Paragraph 2: "she tried the effect of lying down with one elbow against the door, and the other arm curled round her head. Still she went on growing, and, as a last resource, she put one arm out of the window, and one foot up the chimney". She tried her best to feel comfortable in the house, but it was impossible.

33. The correct answer is **B**. Paragraph 4: " 'It was much pleasanter at home,' thought poor Alice". Alice goes on to say how her life will be now that she is stuck in the house and what will happen to her. She carried on arguing each side of the conversation until the Rabbit turned up. For this reason the answer can't be A. There is no talk in the text about an old woman and Pat is the Rabbit's helper, so it can't be C or D.

34. The correct answer is **B**. Paragraph 8: "Mary Ann! Mary Ann!' said the voice...Alice knew it was the Rabbit coming to look for her." The Rabbit calls for Mary Ann and the text says that Alice trembled knowing that the Rabbit was in fact calling her. We can gather from this part of the text that A, C and D can't be correct.

35. The correct answer is **C**. Paragraph 11: " 'I'm here! Digging for apples, your honour!' 'Digging for apples, indeed!' said the Rabbit angrily." When you dig for something, you make a hole in the ground in order to uncover what is there. As we know apples grow on trees and aren't found in the ground; Pat's comment is therefore meant to be foolish. Pat doesn't make his actions secret, so A must be incorrect. Pat isn't hiding because he announces where he is when the Rabbit calls, so B is incorrect. And D is incorrect as Pat doesn't say he is growing food, but seems to be searching for it.

36. The correct answer is **C**. The last paragraph: "An arm, you goose! Who ever saw one that size? Why, it fills the whole window!" Normally an arm isn't the size of Alice's, so the Rabbit can't believe what he sees and he wants a second opinion.

Paper 1 Reading and Use of English **PART 6**

You are going to read a magazine article about one person's experience of being aware while she is dreaming, called lucid dreaming. Six sentences have been removed from the article. Choose from the sentences A-G the one which fits each gap 37-42. There is one extra sentence which you do not need to use.

Lucid Dreaming

The other night I experienced a lucid dream. In the dream I was sitting gazing into our fish aquarium. I peered in closely, examining our spotted suckerfish. I often gaze at him because he never moves much in the daytime. I watch him to see if he is OK. As I stared at him, suddenly I noticed there were two more suckerfish! They were identical to the original. **37 B** Then I wondered where they could have come from. As I pondered this I abruptly realised that I must be dreaming! **38 A** I jumped up and looked around. There were other people in this dream with me. I had a husband, a son and a dog. Before looking at the fish, I had been going along, living my daily life in a mundane fashion. The last thing I had remembered doing was feeding the dog and kissing my little boy on the head while he played on the kitchen floor.

As I looked at these people, I realised it wasn't my real husband or either of my real children - I excitedly blurted out at them that we were all dreaming. **39 E** I yelled again "WE ARE DREAMING!!!" As I became even more self-conscious, I announced that I could test my theory by flying.

If this really was a dream, I should be able to fly! So I jumped up and flew to the ceiling. I can still see the look on the man's face as he watched me float up to the ceiling. Unfortunately, as I watched the fear and doubt on his face, I began to fall. I sank all the way back down and landed with a hard thud on the floor. When that happened, I began to doubt my own perception and lost my awareness as I fell back into a regular dream state.

The above is an example of lucid dreaming. **40 G** You are aware that you are dreaming, while dreaming. If you have ever had it happen to you spontaneously, you understand how exciting it is, the heart races with excitement at your prospects.

Gazing at something in your home or on your body, such as your hands during your regular workday is a technique used by dream researchers to induce lucid dreaming. Another technique is to continually ask yourself throughout the day if you are dreaming. **41 F** On another occasion just before becoming lucid in a dream, I noticed that my kitchen cupboards were the wrong colour, which alerted me. The duplicated fish are another example.

Stephen LaBerge, the pioneer of lucid dreaming research, suggests that once you can become lucid, there is no limit to what your imagination can create in a dream. **42 C** You can even try out things you've always wanted to try and see what it is like. It has been discovered, and my experience supports this, that when you do become lucid, it is extremely difficult to stay that way. Research has shown though that the more you do it, the better at it you get and the better your control is. Often a few seconds of lucidity is all that is manageable. It is still a thrilling experience.

> A. "Of course!" I said; that explains this.
>
> B. At first I was startled and shocked, surprised that there were more.
>
> C. It truly is amazing, from flying, to inventing, to art.
>
> D. After waking from the dream and becoming lucid, I remember gazing at my hands and noticing that they were an odd shape.
>
> E. My husband looked at me, perplexed.
>
> F. If you develop these habits – if you happen to be in a dream state while looking at your hands – you will be tipped off when your hands look odd.
>
> G. Lucid dreaming is the state of being conscious in your dreams.

37. The correct choice is **B**. The text before the gap introduces the concept of a lucid dream, and begins to describe an experience, ending with the discovery of two fish. The gap begins a new paragraph, and following the gap we are told the writer's second reaction to the discovery of the fish. We would expect the gap to give the writer's first reaction. The only other possible reaction is choice A, which may be eliminated because the second reaction is to wonder, so the sense of understanding conveyed in A does not fit. B is appropriate; first she was shocked, then she started to wonder.

38. The correct choice is **A**. The writer is still trying to make sense of the extra fish. First, she is shocked, then she starts to wonder, then she realises she is dreaming and it all makes sense. As said in the Q.37 justification notes, A is also a reaction, but now it fits appropriately.

39. The correct choice is **E**. Since the sentence before mentions the writer's husband the correct answer must also include the same subject of husband and family. The writer spoke to her dream-family, and choice E shows the response of her husband.

40. The correct answer is **G**. The subject of the sentence before the gap is lucid dreaming, as is the subject of the sentence after the gap, so the correct answer must also refer to or involve this subject. The sentence before gives "an example of lucid dreaming" and choice G explains what this concept actually is.

41. The gap is best filled by choice **F**. Before the gap, we are told of two techniques to use to learn to induce lucid dreaming. Choice F refers to "these habits" meaning the two techniques. Also "tipped off" is used in sentence F and is also echoed in the following sentence through the phrase "...which alerted me". Choice D is wrong because it refers to noticing something odd while awake in a conscious state as opposed to while sleeping in a dream state.

42. The correct answer is **C**. The sentence before suggests that once you have mastered the ability to lucid dream, there are no limits on what your imagination can create. Choice C takes this idea further by suggesting some things which could be possible "from flying, to inventing, to art".

Paper 1 Reading and Use of English **PART 7**

You are going to read four accounts of people who have followed their dreams and travelled someplace amazing. For questions 43–52, choose from the people A–D. The people may be chosen more than once.

Which person:

interacted closely with wild animals?	43	A
was participating in a water sport?	44	A
did not think he/she would like the place so much?	45	D
was in relatively close proximity to dangerous animals?	46	C
refers to documenting their travel experiences?	47	B
appreciated the advantages of travelling alone?	48	D
spent time near places of worship?	49	B
told someone all about his/her experience?	50	B
compared the place he/she visited with other places?	51	D
was shown around by a professional?	52	C

Following a Dream

HARRY A

43

Just north of Fregate I met two manta rays. They were seven or eight feet wide with massive out-stretched fins that seemed like rubberized wings. The water was murky, rich with plankton that attracted the giant rays that filtered it through their wide mouths. They treated me with caution, maintaining a constant distance if I turned towards them, but were content to let me swim on a parallel course, as if I, too, was feed-ing on the plankton. For a few minutes we were companions, until, circling and shifting shape against the depths, they became faint black shadows in the gloom and were gone. The deep blue of the Indian Ocean has captured my heart and drawn me back again and again to these pure shores. On Praslin there were dolphins off-shore and a pair of octopus, sliding across the coral as they flashed signals to one another with changing skin tones as remarkable as – but much faster than – any chameleon. At Conception, close to Mahe, giant rocks formed an underwater cathedral beckoning me into its vaults where moray eels gaped at me, the strange visitor to their liquid world.

44 (left margin)
43 (right margin)

Gabriel B

And so my first real trip to Asia unfolded in what seemed a series of dream-panels - adven-tures and faces and events so far removed from my day-to-day experience that I could not con-vert them into any tongue I knew. I revisited them again and again, sleepless, in my memo-ries and notes and photographs, once home. Almost every day of the three-week trip was so vivid that, upon returning, I gave a friend a nine-hour account of every moment. The motorbike ride through Sukhothai; the first long lazy evening in an expat's teak house in Sunkumvhit; the flight into the otherworldly charm of Rangoon and the Strand Hotel, and the pulse of warm activity around the Sule Pagoda at night-fall. Long hot days in the silence, 5,000 temples on every side; slow trips at dawn along Inle lake, seeing a bird-faced boat being led through the quiet water; a frenzied morning back in Bangkok, writing an article while monsoon rains pounded on the windows all around me. **47**

50 (right margin)
49 (right margin)

MAYA C

As I stepped off the six-seater Cessna plane after a bumpy flight over the Okavango Delta and my feet touched the arid ground I knew this was what I'd been waiting for all my life – Africa. Our first day was at the Selinda Camp in one of the driest parts of the Delta and when we arrived I thought that nothing could possi-bly survive under the relentless sun. I was almost immediately proved wrong, as Selinda is near a small lagoon – home to a group of hip-pos. At night we could hear their bark-like call. Our guides warned us that although hippos may seem harmless, if threatened, they could easily kill a man! We went on to stay in various other camps that were situated in different habitats. Jacana Camp was surrounded entirely by water and only accessible by boat. But my favourite place was the Kalahari Desert. Our final camp was located just on the edge of the Makgadikgadi Salt Pans, which are home to many rare species of animal, such as the brown hyena.

52 (left margin)
46 (right margin)

TOM D

I'd been to New York three times in the past but not for long and I couldn't remember much of it.
This time I only had four days but I was on my own and this seems like a better way to get to know a city: less being sociable, more walking and visiting different places. Perfect. I liked New York even more than I expected and it's right up there on my list of foreign cities where I'd like to live. It's fighting for the top spot with San Francisco, with the next position occupied by Paris. I stayed at the Incentra Village House, which was lovely: reasonably priced, really friendly, comfortable rooms. I'd stay there again. I did a lot of walking and could easily have done a lot more. I rarely left Manhattan. One day I walked more than 12 miles, including the length of Central Park and on down Fifth Avenue. Fifth Avenue was the least pleasant place; it felt like London's Oxford Street. I also walked along the High Line, which is very nicely done, although rather shorter than Paris's Promenade Plantee.

48 (right margin)
45 (right margin)
51 (right margin)

Writing

Paper 2 WRITING   PART 1

*You **must** answer this question. Write your answer in **140-190** words in an appropriate style.*

1. You have watched a Youtube video about the problem of computer game addiction in children. Your English teacher has asked you to write an essay.

   Write an **essay** using **all** the notes and give reasons for your point of view.

   More and more young people spend most of their time playing computer games. How can we help children to overcome this addiction?

   Notes

   Write about:
   1. bad grades at school
   2. no social life
   3. .... (your own idea)

Paper 2 WRITING   PART 2

*Write an answer to **one** of the questions **2-4** in this part. Write your answer in **140-190** words in an appropriate style.*

2. You recently saw this notice in an English language magazine called "The Weekender".

   ### Reviews needed!

   Have you been to an exceptional restaurant lately?
   If so, tell us about it! Be sure to describe the type and quality of food, the atmosphere, the location, and say for what kinds of occasions you would recommend the restaurant.

   We will publish the best reviews in next month's issue.

   Write your **review**.

3. You follow a popular website covering wellness and you see an advertisement asking for writers to submit different articles with ideas about living a more healthy life.

   ### Writers Wanted

   Contribute wellness tips on how to exercise better, eat healthily or other lifestyle habits that give you more energy and a fuller life.

   Write your **article**.

4. Your pen friend wants to throw a party for her twelve-year-old sister's birthday, but she is not sure what to do. Write a **letter** giving her advice about where to have the party and what sort of activities they could do.

   Write your **letter**.

Practice Test 3

Listening

Paper 3 LISTENING **PART 1**

You will hear people talking in eight different situations. For questions **1-8**, *choose the best answer, A, B or C.*

1. You are in a supermarket when you hear this announcement about a lost child.
   Where did he last see his mother?
   A. in the butcher's area
   B. in the pet food area
   C. in the fruit and vegetable area

2. You are in an electrical shop when you overhear this woman speaking to the shop assistant.
   Why is she complaining?
   A. She was charged the wrong amount.
   B. The same item is cheaper elsewhere.
   C. The item was damaged.

3. You overhear a woman talking on the telephone. Next Thursday the woman is going to
   A. travel by coach.
   B. travel by plane.
   C. travel by train.

4. Listen to a policeman talking to a householder.
   What does the policeman want to do?
   A. speak to another member of the household
   B. speak to the householder
   C. speak to a neighbour

5. You are listening to the host of a radio phone-in programme speaking.
   Mary, the first caller, is
   A. a married woman with a child.
   B. a single woman with a child.
   C. a regular listener.

6. You have joined a four-day sailing course in Britain. Listen to your instructor giving some important information.
   What is he talking about?
   A. drinking water
   B. salt water
   C. running out of water

7. You overhear two people talking at a bus stop.
   The two speakers
   A. are both familiar with the war memorial.
   B. are taking different buses.
   C. are going to the same place.

8. You overhear a man chatting on the telephone about a form he has to fill in.
   The man is speaking to
   A. his wife.
   B. his mother.
   C. his daughter.

PART 1 - JUSTIFICATION OF THE ANSWERS

1. The correct answer is **C**. "When he last saw his mummy, he says, she was choosing some pears."

2. The correct answer is **B**. "...it's your price-beater guarantee ... I went into Lunthams and saw them there for only nine ninety-nine." Choice C is not correct because "...it works perfectly. That's not the problem at all."

3. The correct answer is **B**. "And the flight number...BA 893. And take-off time?" This suggests she's going by plane and not by train or coach.

4. The correct answer is **C**. The policeman says "...we would like to speak with him on a rather urgent matter." and is refering to "...a Mr Winston of number 43 just across the street there." Mr Winston is the man's neighbour.

5. The correct answer is **B**. "...we want to hear from any single parents out there who are listening and, in fact, we have one on the line right now. Hello, Mary..." Someone who is single is not married. Choice C is incorrect because there's no mention of the frequency with which Mary phones in.

6. The correct answer is **A**. "...we recommend you carry 10 gallons of bottled water." Choice B is not correct because he only mentions that you can't drink salt water and Choice C is incorrect because he is advising on how *not* to run out of water; not how to sell the bottled water.

7. The correct answer is **B**. One of the women says "Oh, look, here's your bus coming now." and the other woman says "And I hope you don't have to wait too long for yours." which shows that they are taking different buses. Choice A is not correct because the woman giving directions says "...you get out there in front of the war memorial. You can't miss it." If the other woman was familiar with it, she would not have needed this reassurance. Choice C is incorrect because they can't be going to the same place since they are taking different buses.

8. The correct answer is **A**. We may come to this conclusion by a process of elimination. B may be eliminated because he says "But why would they want to know mother's maiden name?" so he can't be speaking to his mother. C may be eliminated because he says "Sophie's grown up now. She's left home. It's not really any of my business..." so we can presume that Sophie is his daughter. Also, he mentions Sophie, so can't be talking directly to her. That leaves us with option A, his wife.

Paper 3 LISTENING | PART 2

You will hear part of a radio talk for young people about animals communicating with each other. For questions 9-18, complete the sentences with a word or short phrase.

Bees do a **9** | **special dance** to communicate where to find food.

Although parrots seem to speak, they are only **10** | **copying** the human sounds.

Primates can communicate a few **11** | **basic ideas** using simple sounds.

Monkeys have not been observed to use any kind of **12** | **grammar**.

Although dolphins can make vowel sounds, they cannot accurately imitate our **13** | **consonants**.

Amazingly, dolphins demonstrate an **14** | **awareness** of when to use phrases.

The sounds made by whales contain **15** | **more information** than human speech.

The songs of the bottle-nosed whale have many of the **16** | **characteristics** of human speech.

The unique grammatical nature of human language arose due to life in **17** | **large communities**.

Indeed, a young child needs enough **18** | **contact** with other people to develop speech.

PART 2 - JUSTIFICATION OF THE ANSWERS

9. "...several kinds of insect, including bees, have been observed performing a **special dance** to tell each other where they can find nectar and pollen..."
10. "Many people think that certain birds like parrots can speak...Such animals are only capable of **copying** the sounds of human speech but have no understanding..."
11. "...primates are capable of communicating a small number of **basic ideas** using a range of simple sounds..."
12. "...none of the groups of monkeys observed so far have developed any form of **grammar**..."
13. "They can manage the vowel sounds...and so on, but lack the necessary voice equipment to reproduce our **consonants**."
14. "But what makes these noises more amazing is that dolphins do show an **awareness** of when to use such phrases..."
15. "These are fast clicking and squeaking noises that whales make underwater and the sounds themselves actually contain **more information** than human speech."
16. "Of particular interest is a species called the bottle-nosed whale whose songs have many **of the characteristics** of human..."
17. "...we are the only species that has developed proper grammatical languages...because of the **large communities** that we live in."
18. "If, for any reason, a young child does not get **enough contact** with other people...he or she may never develop speech."

Paper 3 LISTENING | PART 3

You are going to hear five different people talking about their relationship with somebody. Match the speakers 1-5 with the letters A-H. Use the letters only once. There are three extra letters which you do not need to use.

A	She/He wants more freedom.	**Speaker 1**	**A** 19
B	She/He has a problem with her/his father.	**Speaker 2**	**D** 20
C	Her/His parents are divorced.	**Speaker 3**	**C** 21
D	She/He has a new baby.	**Speaker 4**	**F** 22
E	She/He has many brothers and sisters.	**Speaker 5**	**E** 23
F	She/He lives with her/his grandparents.		
G	She/He has problems with the babysitter.		
H	She/He has problems with an alcoholic parent.		

PART 3 - JUSTIFICATION OF THE ANSWERS

19. The correct answer is **A**. "I have to babysit...many jobs around the house ... difficult to get any spare time".

20. The correct answer is **D**. "he needs; feeding, changing, bathing etc."

21. The correct answer is **C**. "they were always fighting...noisiest house"...living in same house "now...he comes to visit sometimes" therefore living apart.

22. The correct answer is **F**. "three generations under one roof".

23. The correct answer is **E**. "enough of us to make a basketball team so we play as a family" therefore large family. "Two children would be enough for me though" therefore many children; brothers and sisters.

Listen to these two friends discussing the British national lottery. For questions 24-30, choose the best answer A, B or C.

24. How does the man feel about the lottery?

   A. It is silly but entertaining.

   B. There is nothing good about it.

   C. It is particularly bad for young people.

25. Who can play the national lottery?

   A. anyone older than 18

   B. only 20 million people

   C. anyone

26. Why was this week special for Tina?

   A. She felt lucky.

   B. She went to Camelot.

   C. She had money to spend.

27. What does Tina think the lottery company does with the money it makes?

   A. They keep it.

   B. They don't make any money.

   C. They give it to charity.

28. How often has Barry played the lottery?

   A. never

   B. one time only

   C. once in a while

29. What does Barry's dad's saying mean?

   A. Work for your money.

   B. Try to win the lottery.

   C. It is difficult to win the lottery.

30. What is Tina going to do next week?

   A. buy a lottery ticket

   B. work overtime

   C. not buy a lottery ticket

PART 4 - JUSTIFICATION OF THE ANSWERS

24. The correct answer is **B**. He says "It's enough to make anyone depressed. I haven't got a good word to say about it myself." Choice A is incorrect because he never says that it is entertaining - just silly. Choice C is incorrect because he says "...that's a good thing, otherwise all the kids would be spending all their pocket money on it." Young people can't play so it can't be bad for them.

25. The correct answer is **A**. "Over twenty million people entered last week, which is a lot if you consider that it's only open to people over eighteen."

26. The correct answer is **A**. She says "...this week was special. I just thought I was going to be lucky..." Choice B is incorrect because Camelot is the lottery company, and the money has gone there, not Tina.

27. The correct answer is **C**. Tina says "They don't keep the money, they give it all to charity and the arts." Choice A is incorrect because this is what the man says. Choice B is incorrect because it is the opposite of what Tina claims in the quote above.

28. The correct answer is **B**. He tells her he played "...just once. The lads and I at work did have a go when it started."

29. The correct answer is **A**. His dad says that "God helps those who help themselves." and he brings this up to support the idea that "I don't think it's right. Somebody getting all that money...for doing nothing." so choice B is not a good answer. Choice C is incorrect because Barry says the chances of winning are low but he has changed his topic by the time he brings up the quote from his dad.

30. The correct answer is **C**. She says "Well, I was thinking of giving it a miss next week, anyway. Maybe that's what I'll do."

Test 4

Paper 1 Reading and Use of English   PART 1

For questions **1-8**, read the text below and decide which word **A, B, C** or **D** best fits each space. There is an example at the beginning **(0)**.

Example:

0.   A. wonder   B. say   C. claim   D. know

| 0 | A | B | C | D |

Starting Your Own Business

At NatWest we **(0)**.......... how hard it is to get your business **(1)**.......... and running. Understanding your difficulties - and then helping you through them - has made us the number one bank for small businesses for each of the last 10 years, with more people turning to us for **(2)**......... than any other bank.

Our Start-Up service gives you the support you need to **(3)**....... up on your own. There are over 4000 Small Business Advisers (at least one in every high street branch) who **(4)**........ help, information and a wide **(5)**...... of services specifically designed to help things go that bit more **(6)**....... .

Since last year, we've offered 12 months' free banking **(7)**.......... you go overdrawn or stay in credit. We have also introduced another special scheme to help you keep your costs down for even longer. Provide us with a certificate from a NatWest recognised start-up training **(8)**......... that you have completed and there will be no account charges for the first 18 months.

1.	A. up	B. start	C. begin	D. on
2.	A. employment	B. performance	C. improvement	D. guidance
3.	A. make	B. turn	C. set	D. bring
4.	A. demand	B. provide	C. instruct	D. know
5.	A. range	B. stock	C. forecast	D. rate
6.	A. roughly	B. frankly	C. immediately	D. smoothly
7.	A. whether	B. whatever	C. however	D. although
8.	A. course	B. lesson	C. subject	D. chapter

Paper 1 Reading and Use of English   PART 2

For questions **9-16**, read the text below and think of the word which best fits each space. Use only **one** word in each space. There is an example at the beginning **(0)**.

Example: | 0 | except |

Christmas Eve

Christmas Eve had been a very tiring day for all the Bensons, **(0)** *except* Mr Benson. The head of the house usually got off lightly **(9)** at/around/over Christmas - lightly, that is, where personal effort was concerned. **(10)** Where money was involved, no; Mr Benson knew that Christmas was an expensive time of the **(11)** year . And later, when he got out his cheque book to give his usual presents, the expense would **(12)** be greater. But he could afford this. He could afford it better **(13)** this/that Christmas than at any other Christmas in the history **(14)** of his steadily increasing fortune. And he didn't need to think, he didn't have to choose. He just **(15)** had to look at a list and add one or two names, or remove one or two. There was something quite big to leave **(16)** out this year, though it didn't show on the list or in his cheque book.

If he felt like it, he would add the amount so saved to his children's cheques. Tim and Helen would then think that he was even more generous than he really was.

Paper 1 Reading and Use of English   **PART 3**

For questions 17-24, read the text below. Use the word given in capitals at the end of some lines to form a word that fits in the space in the same line. There is an example at the beginning (0).

Example: **0**   technological

New (0) ...*technological*.... advances are making life more difficult for	TECHNOLOGY
(17) ....**criminals**.......... as police are making progress on crime	CRIME
(18) ....**prevention**........ . Such is the level of expertise among detectives today	PREVENT
that a (19) ....**careless**........... thief is bound to be caught. There are also more	CARE
(20) ....**precautions**......... that can be taken by (21) ....**householders**...... to	CAUTION / HOUSE
ensure the safety and (22) ....**protection**......... of their homes. People can now	PROTECT
mark their belongings so that if they are stolen by an (23) ....**opportunist(ic)**....	OPPORTUNITY
thief they can later be identified. It is like having your (24) ......**signature**........	SIGN
on all your personal treasures.	

Paper 1 Reading and Use of English   **PART 4**

*For questions 25-30, complete the second sentence so that it has a similar meaning to the first sentence, using the word given. **Do not change the word given.** You must use between **two** and **five** words, including the word given. There is an example at the beginning (0).*

Example:

0 They think the owner of the house is in France.   thought

The owner of the house .... in France.

*The gap can be filled by the words "**is thought to be**" so you write:*   **0**   is thought to be

25. You need an hour to go to the city centre by train.   takes

The ....**train gets/takes you to the**........ city centre in an hour.

26. Writing on these walls is prohibited.   supposed

You ....**are not supposed to write**........ on these walls.

27. The bad weather conditions and the driver's carelessness caused the accident.   by

The accident ....**was caused by**........ the bad weather conditions

and the driver's carelessness.

28. The two boys are identical twins and they look exactly the same.   tell

I ....**cannot tell the difference**........ between the two boys.

29. Perhaps your family left early last night.   may

Your family ....**may have left early**........ last night.

30. It's a pity our teammate behaved like that.   wish

I ....**wish our teammate had not**........ behaved like that.

Practice Test 4

You are going to read an extract from a novel. For questions 31-36, choose the answer A, B, C or D which you think fits best according to the text.

"Good day!" said Monsieur Defarge, looking down at the white head that bent low over the shoemaking.

It was raised for a moment, and a very faint voice responded to the salutation, as if it were at a distance:

"Good day!"

"You are still hard at work, I see?"

After a long silence, the head was lifted for another moment, and the voice replied, "Yes, I am working." This time, a pair of haggard eyes had looked at the questioner, before the face had dropped again.

"I want," said Defarge, who had not removed his gaze from the shoemaker, "to let in a little more light here. You can bear a little more?"

The shoemaker stopped his work; looked, with a vacant air of listening, at the floor on one side of him; then similarly, at the floor on the other side of him; then, upward at the speaker.

"What did you say?"

"You can bear a little more light?"

"I must bear it, if you let it in."

The opened half-door was opened a little further, and secured at that angle for the time. A broad ray of light fell into the room, and showed the workman with an unfinished shoe upon his lap, pausing in his labour. His few common tools and various scraps of leather were at his feet and on his bench. He had a white beard, raggedly cut, but not very long, a hollow face and exceedingly bright eyes. The hollowness and thinness of his face would have caused them to look large, under his yet dark eyebrows and his confused white hair, even if they had been really otherwise; but, they were naturally large, and looked unnaturally so.

"Are you going to finish that pair of shoes today?" asked Defarge, motioning to Mr. Lorry to come forward.

"What did you say?"

"Do you mean to finish that pair of shoes today?"

"I can't say that I mean to. I suppose so. I don't know."

But, the question reminded him of his work, and he bent over it again.

Mr. Lorry came silently forward. When he had stood, for a minute or two, by the side of Defarge, the shoemaker looked up. He showed no surprise at seeing another figure, but the unsteady fingers of one of his hands strayed to his lips, and then the hand dropped to his work, and he once more bent over the shoe. The look and the action had occupied but an instant.

"You have a visitor, you see," said Monsieur Defarge.

"What did you say?"

"Here is a visitor."

The shoemaker looked up as before, but without removing a hand from his work.

"Come!" said Defarge. "Here is monsieur, who knows a well-made shoe when he sees one. Show him that shoe you are working at. Take it, monsieur."

Mr. Lorry took it in his hand.

"Tell monsieur what kind of shoe it is, and the maker's name."

There was a longer pause than usual, before the shoemaker replied:

"I forget what it was you asked me. What did you say?"

"I said, couldn't you describe the kind of shoe, for monsieur's information?"

"It is a lady's shoe. It is a young lady's walking-shoe. It is in the present style. I never saw the style. I have had a pattern in my hand." He glanced at the shoe with some little passing touch of pride.

"And the maker's name?" said Defarge.

Now that he had no work to hold, he laid the knuckles of the right hand in the hollow of the left, and then the knuckles of the left hand in the hollow of the right, and then passed a hand across his bearded chin, and so on in regular changes, without a moment's intermission.
"Did you ask me for my name?"

"Assuredly I did."

"One Hundred and Five, North Tower."

31. The place where the shoemaker was working
   A. was noisy and busy.
   B. was very small.
   C. needed to be cleaned.
   D. lacked light.

32. The most distinctive feature of the shoemaker was
   A. his short ragged beard.
   B. his white hair and dark eyebrows.
   C. his very large eyes.
   D. his thin hollow face.

33. How did the shoemaker feel about his work?
   A. He showed no emotion whatsoever.
   B. He felt ashamed of it.
   C. He was eager to promote it.
   D. He took some pride in it.

34. When questioned, the shoemaker
   A. was evasive.
   B. could not focus.
   C. refused to answer.
   D. was anxious.

35. The design for the shoe being made came from
   A. observations about what was in fashion at that time.
   B. written instructions.
   C. the shoemaker's imagination.
   D. a long line of traditions.

36. How could the shoemaker best be described?
   A. unfriendly and hostile
   B. lonely and painfully shy
   C. indifferent about his work
   D. unused to human interaction.

31. The correct answer is **D**. Column 1, lines 11-12 and lines 22-23: "I want...to let in a little more light here... A broad ray of light fell into the room...". When Monsieur Defarge first came into the workshop there was obviously not enough light as he asks the shoemaker if he can let some more in. The answer is not A as the text gives the impression that the place is silent and empty. The answers are not B or C, as these issues are not mentioned in the text.

32. The correct answer is **C**. Column 1, lines 26-28: "He had...exceedingly bright eyes." and "they were naturally large, and looked unnaturally so." His eyes are given a more lengthy description than his other features, indicating they were his most distinctive characteristic.

33. The correct answer is **D**. Column 2, lines 26-27: "He glanced at the shoe with some little passing touch of pride." The sentence suggests he showed some emotion when describing the kind of shoe he was making. His actions weren't overly enthusiastic but revealed his sense of satisfaction with the work. For this reason the answer isn't A or B. Monsieur Defarge had to encourage the shoemaker to describe the shoe to Mr. Lorry, so the answer is also not C as he didn't show eagerness to promote the shoe.

34. The correct answer is **B**. Column 2, line 21: "I forget what it was you asked me. What did you say?" The shoemaker was not able to focus on Monsieur Defarge's questions and his mind was clearly elsewhere. It is not A, which suggests he deliberately avoided giving an answer. Also it's not C, as he did eventually answer Monsieur Defarge's questions. And it is also not D as the shoemaker didn't give any indication of extra anxiety in response to the questions.

35. The correct answer is **B**. Column 2, lines 25-26: "I never saw the style. I have had a pattern in my hand." The text suggests that the shoemaker had never seen any women wearing the style, but had the pattern written down, which he then copied. The text also says the design was in the present style, meaning modern and not traditional. For these reasons the answer can only be B and not A, C or D.

36. The correct answer is **D**. Column 2, lines 34-36: "Did you ask me for my name?...Assuredly I did...One Hundred and Five, North Tower." As the story illustrates, the shoemaker was not very good at communicating. He was absorbed by his work and did not pay much attention to his company. He didn't seem used to being asked questions and even when he was asked his name he replied with his address. For this reason D is the most suitable answer; A, B and C are incorrect.

You are going to read a magazine article about debt. Six sentences have been removed from the article. Choose from the sentences A-G the one which fits each gap 37-42. There is one extra sentence which you do not need to use.

Debt and Poverty

Debt means owing money. Many of us have owed money, when we have borrowed it from our friends, parents, or from a bank. Many people borrow large amounts of money as a mortgage, to buy a house. Debt is not necessarily a bad thing - borrowing money enables us to do things that we would not otherwise be able to afford at the time.

When people borrow money they arrange a programme for repaying the money over a particular amount of time, plus interest that is added as a charge for borrowing the money. **37** **F** People may have taken on too much of a commitment, and be unable to afford the repayments that are due, or situations may change such as the rate of interest rising, or their income falling. When individuals become deeply indebted, we draw a line under the debt. **38** **A** Their debts are written off by law and they are allowed to start again, although it will be hard for them to borrow money again in the future.

Like individuals, countries may also take out loans to use for various purposes, such as large-scale projects or improvements to their infrastructure. However, when countries borrow money which they are then unable to repay there is no such thing as bankruptcy. Countries remain deeply indebted, diverting all of their resources to debt repayments to satisfy their lenders. A country will continue to become more and more damaged by unpayable debts. Public services suffer from a lack of investment and the poorest people go without their basic needs.

On average, debt payments cost many poor countries almost twice what they spend on education and more than three times the amount spent on the population's healthcare. Poor people suffer because of a lack of government investment in their country, such as better roads which would help them travel to market. **39** **B** And when the prices of basic foods go up, it is the poorest people again who can no longer afford to feed their families.

In 1982, when Mexico became the first country to admit it could not repay its debts, the International Monetary Fund (IMF) and the World Bank stepped in to help. **40** **D** In return they imposed a system known as 'structural adjustment' on these countries. The aim was literally to alter the structure of how money in each country was spent. These programmes consisted of strict measures designed to help a country repay its debts by earning more hard currency through increasing its exports and reducing its imports. **41** **G** Governments were forced to spend their money on debt repayments, rather than public services for the population. Farmers had to grow cash crops for export, rather than food to feed their families. The exported cash crops being sold were cheap, but imported processed goods were costly. The prices of goods went up, and people struggled to survive.

In 1996 the World Bank and the IMF launched a new international debt relief scheme known as the Heavily Indebted Poor Countries Initiative (HIPC). The initiative called for the reduction of external debt through write-offs by official donors. As of January 2012, 39 countries were receiving debt relief under HIPC.

The HIPC, unfortunately, has not solved the problem. There are still many countries which are not receiving help, because they do not fulfil the HIPC criteria. **42** **E**

A. That line is called bankruptcy.

B. It is the poorest people who are unable to afford to start paying for schools when fees are introduced, so their children miss out.

C. Some people claim debt cancellation would just allow corrupt leaders to have more money for themselves, rather than benefiting the poorest people.

D. They lent money to help Mexico, and other struggling countries, repay their old loans.

E. It is clear that more needs to be done to deal with the growing debt crisis.

F. Problems arise when the amount of debt accumulated is unpayable.

G. Structural Adjustment programmes, however, actually led to a decline in living standards and deepened poverty.

37. The correct answer is **F**. The sentence before refers to borrowing and repaying money. Sentence F then introduces a problem, and after the gap, we are told reasons why problems might arise and why people who borrow money might not be able to repay it.

38. The correct answer is **A**. The topic of the paragraph is *debt and what happens when people become too heavily indebted*. The sentence before uses the phrase 'draw a line', and choice A follows on from this term and explains what it means. Similarly, the sentence that follows the gap briefly explains the meaning of bankruptcy.

39. The choice that best fits the gap is **B**. The topic of the paragraph is how poor people are affected by debt. It therefore makes sense to fill the gap with B which goes on to explain how poor people can be affected.

40. The correct choice for the gap is **D**. The previous sentence mentions the role of the IMF in the case of 1982 with Mexico and its debt. It says that it stepped in to help. Choice D continues this theme by describing exactly how the IMF helped. It also introduces "other struggling countries" which is necessary so that the phrase "these countries" in the following sentence has something to refer back to.

41. The correct answer is **G**. The gap is in the position of the topic sentence of the paragraph, and the following sentences support the concept of declining standards of living. Importantly, choice G uses the word 'however' to transition from the idea of help in the previous paragraph. The programme, which may have begun positively, actually produced worse effects as choice G indicates.

42. The correct answer is **E**. The previous sentence speaks about HIPC; the IMF's new programme to help poor countries, that unfortunately doesn't seem to work. Choice E concludes that more needs to be done about the growing debt crisis. It is also a fitting closing sentence for the piece.

Paper 1 Reading and Use of English   PART 7

You are going to read four people's reviews of the book "Who Elected the Bankers?" by Louis Pauly. For questions 43–52, choose from the people A–D. The people may be chosen more than once.

Which person:

says the author's former job gave him insight?   **43** **B**

says why the IMF was started?   **44** **A**

thinks the book should be read by many people?   **45** **D**

mentions an event in a particular decade?   **46** **B**

thinks the author wanted to surprise people?   **47** **A**

does not offer a personal opinion on the book?   **48** **A**

says the book was pleasant to read?   **49** **D**

mentions what has influenced today's global markets?   **50** **C**

states the specific time frames covered in the book?   **51** **C**

says the book would interest those studying political systems and how they will evolve in the future?   **52** **D**

Book Reviews

JANE MORRISON A

48 - by process of elimination - no personal opinion offered here

47 Louis Pauly obviously wanted to startle people when he set out to write the story of the International Monetary Fund, a group that he believes is credited with wielding far more power than it really has. In a discussion of the failings of the League of Nations, Pauly details how industrialized nations moved to create the **44** IMF in the midst of World War II in the belief that an organisation that balances international monetary policy would help prevent future wars. He shows how the IMF has become intertwined with the political foundations of today's global economy.

INGRID BRYAN B

As a former staff member of the IMF, Pauly is in a unique position to give a fresh perspective. **43** He traces the development of the IMF from its roots in the League of Nations and gives an excellent account of how it redefined its role after the demise of fixed exchange rates in the **46** 1970s.

JACQUES DE LAROSI C

51
Pauly has, with remarkable clarity, described the evolution of the international markets over the past fifty years. He skillfully describes the evolution of international monetary cooperation from the League of Nations in the early 1920s to the International Monetary Fund in the 1990s, **51** stressing the continuities and changes over the past seventy-five years. *Who Elected the Bankers?* is, in my view, one of the first attempts to show how the global markets of today have been shaped by central banks, the IMF, the G-7, and the policymakers of the world. **50**

ERIC HELLEINER D

49
This very interesting and readable book examines the relationship between global finance, democracy and international institutions in the context of OECD countries. Its arguments are important and innovative not just for those studying the political economy of global finance, a field in which Pauly has been a leading figure over the last decade. They are also highly significant to anyone interested in broader debates about globalisation and the **52** future of democracy in advanced industrial states. *Who Elected the Bankers?* will be seen by all as a very welcome and major contribution to debates on the political economy of global finance, the history of international financial policy making and analysis of the relationship between politics and globalisation. It deserves a wide audience. **45**

Writing

Paper 2 WRITING   PART 1

*You **must** answer this question. Write your answer in **140-190** words in an appropriate style.*

1. In your English class you have been talking about endangered species, animals or plants that will likely become extinct. Your English teacher has asked you to write an essay.

   Write an **essay** using **all** the notes and give reasons for your point of view.

> Around the world many wildlife species are in danger of extinction. How can we protect endangered animals?
>
> **Notes**
>
> Write about:
> 1. pollution
> 2. hunting wild animals
> 3. .... (your own idea)

Paper 2 WRITING   PART 2

*Write an answer to **one** of the questions 2-4 in this part. Write your answer in **140-190** words in an appropriate style.*

2. You have seen this announcement in an international magazine.

> **A SPECIAL DAY**
> Tell us about a very special day that you spent.
> Why was it special?
> What did you do?
> We will publish the three best articles next month.

Write your **article**.

3. The Mayor of your town is concerned that there is not enough for young people to do. He has asked you to write a **report** about what sort of leisure facilities are available to young people in your area, and what new facilities you and the people that you know would most like to have. Recommend what you think could be done to improve the situation.

   Write your **report**.

4. You walk by a bulletin board at the library and see the following advertisement:

> **Computer Repair Service**
> Call us with all of your Mac and PC issues. We promise quick service at great rates.
> Check our website and Twitter page for testimonials from our past clients!

You used this company recently and they did a great job of fixing your printer and Mac desktop computer.
Write a **review** of the company to post on their website expressing your experience with it and why you have a positive point of view.

Write your **review**.

Listening

Paper 3 LISTENING PART 1

You will hear people talking in eight different situations. For questions 1-8, choose the best answer, A, B or C.

1. You are visiting a friend when you hear him answer the telephone.
   The caller
   A. agrees to sell something.
   B. agrees to buy something from the speaker.
   C. changes his/her mind.

2. You are sitting in an aeroplane when you hear this announcement.
   When will your flight be arriving?
   A. late
   B. on time
   C. early

3. You have visited an English doctor because of a skin problem.
   For a quick recovery you should
   A. travel by car.
   B. not go out in the daytime.
   C. be careful when you are outside.

4. While waiting to check in your luggage at an airport, you hear this conversation.
   On the flight, what are you normally allowed?
   A. 15 kg of luggage
   B. 16 kg of luggage
   C. 30 kg of luggage

5. You are watching the weather forecast for Britain on TV. Tomorrow the weather in north-eastern Britain will
   A. not change.
   B. be getting much brighter.
   C. be different to all other regions.

6. Listen to this answerphone message for a business.
   The company
   A. arranges surprise parties.
   B. sells office supplies.
   C. are office cleaners.

7. You overhear two people talking in an office.
   What does the man want the woman to do?
   A. speak to Jack about Colin
   B. sack Jack
   C. speak to Colin about Jack

8. You hear a parent asking a child to go to the newsagent's and buy a newspaper.
   The parent wants
   A. today's *Andover Gazette*.
   B. *Today* and the *Gazette*.
   C. yesterday's *Gazette*.

PART 1 - JUSTIFICATION OF THE ANSWERS

1. The correct answer is **B**. The person who answered the phone says "...I had intended to stick with the original price but let's say 75 pounds." and so must be selling the item. Choice A is incorrect because the caller is enquiring about the item and so must be interested in buying it, however we are not told if the caller makes any decision so choice C is not a good answer.

2. The correct answer is **C**. "...we should still be arriving in Malaga five minutes ahead of schedule."

3. The correct answer is **C**. The doctor says "...if you do decide to go out at all - I mean, out of the house - in the open air, especially in the daytime, just...er...take good care...."

4. The correct answer is **A**. "...these bags weigh 32 kilograms. That's more than twice the normal baggage allowance for this flight."

5. The correct answer is **A**. "But, I'm afraid there will be no improvement in north-eastern England and Scotland for a day or so." Choice B is incorrect because it is the east Midlands that should get much brighter. Choice C is not correct because most of the country is rainy as is the north east.

6. The correct answer is **B**. We have to assume they sell office supplies, since they used to sell office cleaning supplies. Choice C is incorrect because they aren't office cleaners, but used to sell cleaning supplies. Choice A is not a good answer because they sell items from a catalogue. No mention is made of organising parties.

7. The correct answer is **C**. We are told that Jack is "...getting the sack..." which means he is being fired. We are also told that "...Colin's being too hard on him." Finally, the man says "Couldn't you have a word? I mean, he listens to you." which means he wants the woman to have a word with Colin about Jack.

8. The correct answer is **A**. "Oh, good. Then you can get a copy of today's 'Andover Gazette'." Choice B is not correct because the speaker says: "...if they haven't got one, get us a copy of 'Today'..." (which also renders choice C wrong).

Paper 3 LISTENING | PART 2

You will hear part of an international radio broadcast on the subject of Guy Fawkes Night, an annual public celebration in Great Britain. For questions 9-18, complete the sentences with a word or short phrase.

On Guy Fawkes Night people burn a **9** **life-sized model** of a man called 'Guy'.

The models are made only for the **10** **purpose** of being burned.

On this night pets are usually **11** **terrified** because it is very noisy.

Years ago, a Protestant king made life difficult for Britain's **12** **Catholics**.

A group of important men decided that King James I and his supporters **13** **must die**.

The conspirators bought a house that had **14** **a tunnel** in its basement.

The conspirators put barrels of highly **15** **explosive gunpowder** under the government building.

Guy Fawkes' job was to keep a lookout for and tell the others about any **16** **approaching danger**.

Guy Fawkes is the most well-known conspirator because he was **17** **caught first**.

Nowadays Catholics and Protestants get along so the celebration is mostly **18** **harmless fun**.

PART 2 - JUSTIFICATION OF THE ANSWERS

9. "...people celebrate Guy Fawkes Night. The celebration centres around the burning of a **life-sized model** of a man, with a black hat and beard, called 'Guy'."
10. "The model has been specially made for this **purpose**."
11. "...but not so much fun for cats and dogs, which are usually **terrified** by sounds of exploding fireworks and skyrockets."
12. "In 1605, the king, James I, and his government, were Protestants and they made life rather difficult for the country's **Catholics**..."
13. "...a group of prominent Catholics met secretly and decided that the king and his government **must die**."
14. "...the conspirators bought a house beside the parliament building, which already had **a tunnel** going into the Houses of Parliament from its cellar."
15. "...Catesby and his companions moved huge barrels of highly **explosive gunpowder** along the tunnel and placed them... under the government building."
16. "Guy Fawkes had the important job of watching the street outside the conspirators' house and warning the others of any **approaching danger**."
17. "...but Guy Fawkes has remained the most famous, probably on account of his being **caught first**."
18. "...Catholics and Protestants have learned to live together in peace and so the celebration itself is mostly **harmless fun**."

Paper 3 LISTENING | PART 3

You will hear five different people describing five different recipes for desserts. For questions 19-23, choose from the list A-H which speaker's recipe fits the description given. Use the letters only once. There are three extra letters which you do not need to use.

A   It is not suitable for vegetarians.
B   It cannot be made with fresh ingredients at Christmas.
C   It is from an ancient recipe.
D   It involves no cooking.
E   It is the easiest to make.
F   It is rather expensive.
G   It is her least favourite.
H   It uses 50 grams of ground almonds.

Speaker 1   **D**   19
Speaker 2   **A**   20
Speaker 3   **B**   21
Speaker 4   **E**   22
Speaker 5   **F**   23

PART 3 - JUSTIFICATION OF THE ANSWERS

19. The correct answer is **D**. The recipe only involves putting ingredients together. There is no cooking.
20. The correct answer is **A**. "...gelatin is made from the hooves of cows, so, unfortunately, some people won't be too keen on this." Vegetarians would not eat gelatin.
21. The correct answer is **B**. "...you will only really be able to make this recipe from May to early July; after that, raspberries can be used instead up to late August."
22. The correct answer is **E**. "...indeed it has such a simple method that they could even make it themselves."
23. The correct answer is **F**. "Now, these are about one pound fifty for a fifty gram packet, so you'll not want to waste any."

Paper 3 LISTENING   PART 4

You will hear a woman and a man speaking together on a train. For questions 24-30, choose the best answer A, B or C.

24. Why can't the woman complete her phone conversation?

A. noise

B. another passenger is bothering her

C. the reception is bad

25. Where does the man want to go?

A. Salisbury

B. Brighton

C. Redhill

26. How does the man feel when he hears he is on the wrong train?

A. He can't believe it.

B. He is angry at the woman.

C. He is frightened.

27. What is the problem with the man's ticket?

A. He doesn't have one.

B. It is not valid for the train he is on.

C. It is made of plastic.

28. What is the next stop?

A. Balcombe

B. Three Bridges

C. Brighton

29. Where is the woman going?

A. Balcombe

B. Brighton

C. Lewes

30. What does the man ask the woman to do?

A. take him to his station

B. make a call for him

C. talk to the guard for him

PART 4 - JUSTIFICATION OF THE ANSWERS

24. The correct answer is **C**. "I'm talking to you on my mobile and the train keeps going into tunnels and we get cut off." Choice B is not correct because another passenger speaks to her, but he does so after her phone call has ended.

25. The correct answer is **A**. He asks, "Isn't this the train to Salisbury?" Choice B is not correct because the train they are on goes to Brighton. Choice C is not correct because the train divided at Redhill.

26. The correct answer is **A**. He says "...but that's impossible..." and "I can't believe this is happening."

27. The correct answer is **B**. "...if this is the Brighton train, I haven"t got the right ticket." Choice C is incorrect because the man's bank card is the thing that is plastic.

28. The correct answer is **A**. "...we should be arriving in Balcombe in just a minute." Choice B is incorrect because the last (previous) stop was Three Bridges. Choice C is incorrect because the final stop is Brighton.

29. The correct answer is **C**. She says "...I'll be taking the connecting service to Lewes..."

30. The correct answer is **B**. She says "...I could phone through to central enquiries and make sure." and he responds "If it wouldn't be too much trouble."

Test 5

Paper 1 Reading and Use of English | PART 1

*For questions **1-8**, read the text below and decide which word A, B, C or D best fits each space. There is an example at the beginning (0).*

Example:

0.   A. oneself   B. itself   C. alone   D. unique

| 0 | A | B | C | D |

The Roman City of Verulamium

Verulamium has established (0)............ as one of the most popular museums of Roman Life in the country. Since it was redisplayed in 1991 the number of visitors has (1)............ to 90,000 a year. The redisplay was the first phase of a strategy to ensure that the Museum was in a fit state to (2)............ the challenges of the new century.

Key to this was the provision of the facilities which our visitors deserve; namely a new (3)............ with cloakrooms, a larger shop, a baby changing room, toilets, disabled facilities and a lift.

In addition, the Museum wants to develop new ways of (4)............ visitors to access the collections, through new (5)............ and computer technology.

For the past four years Museum (6)............ have worked with architects and engineers to produce a solution. The result is the Verulamium Project; an exciting new (7)............ to extend the Museum, providing a new entrance, improved displays and facilities. An artist's impression of the new entrance can be (8)............ by all visitors.

1.	A. lifted	B. recreated	C. been	**D. risen**
2.	A. argue	**B. face**	C. deal	D. compete
3.	A. opening	B. window	C. ceiling	**D. entrance**
4.	A. making	**B. enabling**	C. forcing	D. suggesting
5.	**A. displays**	B. shelves	C. windows	D. cases
6.	A. pupils	B. tourists	**C. staff**	D. players
7.	A. deal	**B. plan**	C. map	D. instruction
8.	A. explored	B. proposed	**C. viewed**	D. visited

Paper 1 Reading and Use of English | PART 2

*For questions **9-16**, read the text below and think of the word which best fits each space. Use only **one** word in each space. There is an example at the beginning (0).*

Example: | 0 | o f |

Romance in the country

The country house (0) ...*of*... of Mr. John Jackson was a delightful place. (9) ....**It**.......... had broad, smooth lawns and green, towering oak trees; there were charming shady woods, and a pretty brook with a little wooden bridge over it. There were fruits and flowers, pleasant people, games to (10) ......**play**........ indoors and out, rides, walks and fishing. These were great attractions, but they would not (11) ....**have**........ held me at the house for very long. What really kept me (12) ..**there**.. , more than the fine fishing, the brook and the scenery, (13) ....**was**.......... the girl I saw walking in these places - my Cecilia.

She was not really my Cecilia. I had never in any sense acquired her. Nor (14) ......**did**.......... she know that I wanted to. But the dream of winning her was what kept me alive, and in my dreams I called her (15) ......**mine**...... . You might say that if I had confessed my feelings to her, I might have been allowed to (16) ......**call**........ her "my Cecilia" aloud. But I was unwilling to say anything, because she might refuse me .

Paper 1 Reading and Use of English   PART 3

For questions 17-24, read the text below. Use the word given in capitals at the end of some lines to form a word that fits in the space in the same line. There is an example at the beginning (0).

Example: | 0 | traditionally |

The Olympic Games are (0)......**traditionally**...... a time when	TRADITION
(17)......**competitors**...... from all over the world - from cities and	COMPETE
(18)......**provincial**...... areas - compete (19)......**peacefully**...... against each	PROVINCE / PEACE
other. The athletes are representatives of their countries and they all (20)**specialise**	SPECIAL
in a particular sport. Most of them have an (21)......**obsession**...... with their	OBSESS
sport and it is (22)......**dreadful**...... for some of them if they do not win a	DREAD
medal.	
When a medal is won there is usually (23)......**thunderous**...... applause	THUNDER
from the audience.	
The Games have been commercialised by wealthy companies, though, and the	
(24)......**innocence**...... of the Games has, in a way, been destroyed.	INNOCENT

Paper 1 Reading and Use of English   PART 4

*For questions 25-30, complete the second sentence so that it has a similar meaning to the first sentence, using the word given. **Do not change the word given.** You must use between **two** and **five** words, including the word given. There is an example at the beginning (0).*

Example:

0 They think the owner of the house is in France.   thought

    The owner of the house .... in France.

*The gap can be filled by the words "**is thought to be**" so you write:* | 0 | is thought to be |

25. We paid 100 pounds for his new trainers.   **us**

    His new trainers ......**cost us**...... 100 pounds.

26. The expert had no idea that the painting was not genuine.   **know**

    Little ......**did the expert know**...... that the painting was not genuine.

27. Mary and her mother both dislike Italian food.   **nor**

    Neither ......**Mary nor her mother like**...... Italian food.

28. Helen has never seen such beautiful houses.   **most**

    These are ......**the most beautiful houses Helen**...... has ever seen.

29. I am sure they lied to you.   **have**

    They ......**must have lied**...... to you.

30. The neighbours took care of her cat while she was in Poland.   **after**

    The neighbours ......**looked after her cat**...... while she was in Poland.

Paper 1 Reading and Use of English **PART 5**

You are going to read an extract from a magazine article about a mountain lodge in Sweden - an ideal destination to view the Aurora Borealis, also called the Northern Lights, which appears in the night sky in Arctic regions. For questions 31-36, choose the answer A, B, C or D which you think fits best according to the text.

When I step out onto the deck there's no mistaking the intensity of the Arctic chill. That's not surprising. I'm a good hundred miles inside the Arctic Circle; in fact you can't get much farther north and still be in Sweden. This is Abisko Mountain Station, perhaps the crown jewel of the Swedish mountain lodges. I'm back for a second time to this remote, scenic spot under the landmark Lapporten mountain, the gateway into the wilds of Lapland.

When an early, heavy snowstorm last autumn pinned me down in my tent for days and eventually chased me from the backcountry back to the station and its comforts, I was to discover a different side to Abisko. People come here for many reasons - some to hike, some to climb, some to bird-watch, some to cross-country ski in the winter. But there's yet another entirely different attraction here. For proof, all I have to do is look up from the station's expansive deck into the night sky above the huge lake called the Tornetrask. Bright, undulating waves of light, tinged with subtle shades of green and red, ripple across the sky. The Northern Lights display tonight varies from subdued flashes to outrageously intense surges of ghostly lights rolling across the dark expanse of night sky. A new moon accentuates the mind-blowing show.

The Aurora may be old hat to those who live this far north, but for the rest of us it is an unforgettable experience. For travellers from afar it's a spectacle that has us shivering on the deck, bundled up in all the cold-weather gear we've brought. The lights here are so mesmerizing we quickly forget the discomfort of the cold.

One of the factors that makes Abisko a prime location for viewing the Aurora is the Tornetrask itself. The huge lake, which sprawls more than 70 kilometres long just north of the station, creates an unusual weather phenomenon that keeps the skies above the station clear even when fog or clouds blanket most of northern Sweden. This is the famed "blue hole of Abisko", a perennial patch of sky kept mostly clear by the climatological effects of this inland sea and its valley.

When this quirk of weather is combined with the comforts of the station, the package adds up to one of the best options anywhere for viewing the Aurora. Much more elaborate than many wilderness huts, the Abisko mountain stations feature restaurants, hot showers and other comforts. Abisko is the only one of these stations located on a highway, so the range of accommodations and level of service here is in a class by itself.

In addition to the lodge itself, however, it's Abisko's remote location and its unique infrastructure that make it such a prime vantage point to view a heavenly phenomenon. It is dark; Abisko is far from any city lights that might dim the show. The station operates a ski lift to the top of Nuolja Peak, more than 3,000 feet high. For the first time this year, a cafe at the top of the mountain has been turned into a viewing platform for the Northern Lights, called the Aurora Sky Station. Also, the station posts "forecasts" each night of expected Aurora activity, gleaned from scientific observations arriving via computer, so visitors may choose the best viewing time.

31. What is true of the author's first visit to the lodge?

    A. He went there in search of the Aurora.

    B. He was camping there.

    C. He was forced there by the weather.

    D. He was not very impressed with the experience.

32. What is meant by the phrase "old hat" in the first line of paragraph 3?

    A. poor

    B. familiar and unexciting

    C. strange and shocking

    D. in very bad taste

33. The travellers viewing the Aurora

    A. are distracted by the cold.

    B. are in awe of what they see.

    C. needn't dress warmly.

    D. can only see it before midnight.

34. What does 'quirk' mean in paragraph 5, line 1?

    A. an unusual feature

    B. a flaw

    C. a very pleasant surprise

    D. a fast change

35. What is NOT said to help make a good viewing of the Aurora at Abisko more likely for visitors there?

    A. There is a mountain viewing platform.

    B. Weather forecasts are available.

    C. It is located near a highway.

    D. There are no city lights nearby.

36. The author's overall opinion of Abisko is that

    A. it's an exceptional place.

    B. the primitive conditions are made worthwhile by the experience.

    C. it is not as popular as it deserves to be.

    D. it could be improved.

31. The correct answer is **C**. "When an early, heavy snowstorm last autumn...eventually chased me from the backcountry back to the station and its comforts [the station being referred to is Abisko]"

32. The correct answer is **B**. "The Aurora may be old hat to those who live this far north, but for the rest of us it is an unforgettable experience." The "but" signals a contradiction will be made, so, both "old hat" and the correct answer must contradict "an unforgettable experience", as choice B does.

33. The correct answer is **B**. "For travellers from afar it's a spectacle that has us shivering on the deck...The lights here are so mesmerizing we quickly forget the discomfort of the cold." - "the lights" is another name for the aurora.

34. The correct answer is **A**. "this quirk of weather" refers to the always-clear skies around lake Abisko, and a quirk is an unusual happening or aspect of someone's character, so in this case, an "unusual feature" of the weather is the best choice.

35. The correct answer is **C**. "it's Abisko's remote location, and its unique infrastructure that make it such a prime vantage point...It is dark; Abisko is far from any city lights that might dim the show. The station operates a ski lift to the top of Nuolja Peak...a cafe at the top of the mountain has been turned into a viewing platform for the Northern Lights, called the Aurora Sky Station. Also, the station posts "forecasts each night", therefore A, B and D are incorrect. The highway makes the station exceptional for its comfort, service and ease of access, but none of these factors will help to ensure a good viewing or make one more likely.

36. The correct answer is **A**. Early on in the text the author calls Abisko "the crown jewel of the Swedish mountain lodges" and "I'm back for a second time" so clearly the impression is positive, and praise for the place continues throughout the text. B is incorrect because it is "Much more elaborate than many wilderness huts". C and D are not mentioned.

You are going to read an article about the illegal international trade of whale meat. SIX sentences have been removed from the article. Choose from the sentences A-G the one which fits each gap 37-42. There is one extra sentence which you do not need to use.

Eating Endangered Species?

The International Whaling Commission was established in 1946 to manage dwindling stocks of whales. Quotas were set to limit the number of whales that could be killed each year for commercial use, but these were often ignored and whale numbers continued to decrease. In 1975, the Convention on International Trade in Endangered Species of Wild Flora and Fauna (CITES) gave full protection to several species including the blue, grey, humpback and right whales. International pressure on the IWC continued and in 1986 it finally put a limit on commercial whaling.

37 D This is achieved by issuing scientific research permits, as killing whales for research is not forbidden. The stated aim of the Japanese research programme is to establish sustainable whaling in the Antarctic Ocean. Both Japan and South Korea are also permitted to trade, within their own countries, whale meat from animals killed as an incidental result of other fishing. **38 B** Also, in an attempt to control hunting, individual whales are logged on a DNA register so that they can be identified.

The value of "lethal sampling", that is, the practice of killing whales in order to study them, is a highly contentious issue. **39 E** On the other hand, opponents say this information is not strictly necessary, and moreover, there are better ways to get it. The selling of whale meat from the lethal sampling to fish markets is purportedly to help fund the research. This claim, however, is disputed by opponents as being a cover for illegal whaling. Now there is evidence to support their views.

A team of scientists, led by Professor Scott Baker, have used DNA to analyse samples of sushi from restaurants in Los Angeles and Seoul. **40 G** The results of the study were handed over to local and national authorities and have since resulted in criminal proceedings against the Los Angeles restaurant.

The researchers used DNA sequencing to identify the species of whale and then used DNA profiling – the same technique used to identify human individuals in criminal forensics – to identify the source of the meat. **41 A** In addition, some of the meat purchased in Seoul came from Antarctic minke whales, a species which is not local to South Korea and must have therefore also been traded illegally.

Although Japanese authorities keep a DNA register of each whale destined to be sold commercially, this information is not available for monitoring purposes. **42 C** As the authors state, "The illegal trade of products from protected species of whales, presumably taken under a national permit for scientific research, is a timely reminder of the need for independent, transparent and robust monitoring of any future whaling".

A. The DNA results showed that the whale meat in the Los Angeles restaurant had almost certainly originated in Japanese 'scientific' whale hunts.

B. However, the export of any whale meat from these countries to the U.S.A. is strictly prohibited.

C. The researchers suggest that urgent action is needed in making this information available to scientists so further monitoring and analysis of commercially available whale meat can take place.

D. Despite the 1986 ban, Japan has continued to hunt whales legally.

E. Some claim that it is required in order to learn about the eating habits and lifespan of whales.

F. Since the 1986 international moratorium, it has been assumed that there is no international trade in whale products, but this does not seem to be the case.

G. The sushi was found to be made from the illegally-traded meat of protected whale species.

37. The correct answer is **D**. The gap must be filled by something that could be achieved with a scientific research permit. Because it is ok to kill whales for research, this would allow Japan to hunt them legally.
38. The correct answer is **B**. We are told, in the sentence before the gap, that trade within Japan and Korea is allowed. Using "However" to indicate a contrast in meaning, choice B follows this information with the fact that they may not trade internationally.
39. The correct answer is **E**. Because of "on the other hand" located immediately after the gap, we would expect some information that gives an idea that is in contrast with the idea in this sentence - that opponents say "lethal sampling" is not necessary. Choice E informs us of reasons some people think that "lethal sampling" is required.
40. The correct answer is **G**. "samples of sushi" from the previous sentence tie in with "the sushi" in choice G. And "illegally traded" in choice G ties in with "criminal proceedings" in the sentence following the gap. Choice A might also appear to fit, as the two choices are very similar, but the emphasis in A is where, geographically, the meat came from, while the emphasis in choice G is whether or not the sushi was legal.
41. The correct answer is **A**. This paragraph is about the source of the meat. Also, the mentioning of the DNA results link Sentence A with the sentence before gap 41. Choice G may seem to work, but it is not the best choice; see Q.40 above for discussion.
42. The correct answer is **C**. Before the gap we are told that information is not available, and choice C says that scientists urgently need the same information.

Paper 1 Reading and Use of English   **PART 7**

You are going to read some extracts about four people's favourite buildings from around the world. For questions **43–52***, choose from the people* **A–D***. The people may be chosen more than once.*

Which person:

originally visited it only because it was famous?	**43**	A
implies that his/her favourite building could change?	**44**	B
likes a building that is no longer in use?	**45**	D
mentions a building designed using a novel tool?	**46**	B
does not mention who designed the building?	**47**	D
describes a special place to see a movie?	**48**	B
seems to value personal freedom of expression?	**49**	C
mentions the incorporation of a natural feature into a building?	**50**	C
talks about a place with limited public access?	**51**	D
would like to visit the building again for a specific reason?	**52**	A

Buildings from around the world

KEIRA   A

There is no contest! The Taj Mahal in India, definitely! I visited it while travelling recently, <u>not because I knew anything about it, just because it's considered one of the seven wonders of the world, you know.</u> **43** But it was completely breathtaking. The great white domes of the mausoleum, standing out against the sky, and mirrored in the reflecting pool. I've never seen anything like it. It's decorated very simply, with geometric shapes, following what the Islamic religion believes is appropriate for places of burial.

It's an amazingly romantic building. It was built by the grief-sticken emperor, Shah Jahan, after the death of his third wife, as an expression of his sorrow. <u>I would love to get married there one day;</u> **52** I can't think of a better place for a wedding, although I suspect it would be very very costly. Oh well, it doesn't hurt to dream.

DYLAN   B

My favourite building, this year at least, is **44** the Experience Music Project Museum in Seattle. It was designed by Canadian architect Frank Gehry and his client was Paul Allen of Microsoft fame. <u>Gehry was the first person to use a computer modelling system</u> **46** <u>called CATIA</u> – which was used in the aerospace industry. As he said, "we did a building by computer for a computer guy"!

The building is formed from 400 tons of steel. It is covered by 21,000 aluminium and stainless steel shingles. At the heart of the structure is <u>the Sky Church – a high-tech cinema with a 70 ft high ceiling and the</u> **48** <u>world's largest LED screen</u>. It is an amazing place.

I think this is truly a design where art and architecture merge. It is challenging, the colours are amazing and the wow factor is high! I'll admit I had mixed views about the exhibits that were inside the building – but that doesn't take away from the building itself!

GEORGIA   C

My favourite building? Anything designed by the Austrian architect, Hundertwasser! I can't choose just one. He was <u>a real character</u> **49** <u>and his buildings are all so creative and progressive;</u> they stand out wherever they are located and make an impression on everyone.

To give you an idea about what he believed in, he proposed something called the "Window Right". He said a person in a rented apartment must be able to lean out of his window and scrape off the masonry within arm's reach. And he must be allowed to take a long brush and paint everything outside within arm's reach, so that it will be visible from afar to everyone in the street that someone lives there who is different from the imprisoned, enslaved, standardised man who lives next door.

Hundertwasser condemned the sterile grid system of conventional architecture. He rejected rationalism, the straight line and functional architecture, and demanded instead creative freedom of building, and the right to create individual structures. His designs included <u>forested roofs,</u> **50** the spiral house, the eye-slit house, <u>the high-rise meadow house</u> and even an inaudible Green Motorway.

AARON   D

First of all, I have many favourite outdoor places here in the UK; Golitha Falls on Bodmin Moor - a very special one; in fact, most of Bodmin Moor is very special. I love being outdoors in a natural environment at any time of day or night.

A favourite building? That's more difficult; there is a tiny chapel on top of St Ives Island <u>that used to</u> **45** <u>be used by fishermen</u>. I have spent many nights walking round St Ives Island and always wanted to look inside this little building that <u>was kept closed</u> **51** <u>to the public.</u>

One day I was lucky to find a cleaner working there, giving the place a clean, so I couldn't resist. I asked him nicely if I could have a look inside, he didn't seem to mind. There was nothing in there but a huge Bible and a window looking out to sea. It had a rather mysterious, rather sad atmosphere. I have been back there many times but, as usual, the place is always locked up. I'm so pleased I managed to go inside and look around at least once.

47 - no mention is made in text D of a designer; the building is very old so it is most likely unknown.

Paper 2 WRITING PART 1

*You **must** answer this question. Write your answer in **140-190** words in an appropriate style.*

1. You have listened to a radio programme about deforestation, the cutting down of trees in many wild areas around the world. Now, your English teacher has asked you to write an essay.

   Write an **essay** using **all** the notes and give reasons for your point of view.

   > Many forests around the world are being destroyed for agricultural, commercial, or housing use without allowing time for the forests to regenerate themselves. What can be done to improve the situation?
   >
   > **Notes**
   >
   > Write about:
   > 1. what contributes to the greenhouse effect
   > 2. floods
   > 3. .... (your own idea)

Paper 2 WRITING PART 2

*Write an answer to **one** of the questions **2-4** in this part. Write your answer in **140-190** words in an appropriate style.*

2. You saw this notice in an entertainment magazine:

   > ## Reviews Wanted
   >
   > Have you visited a wonderful or awful cafe recently?
   > Now is your chance to write about it. We are looking for reviews of cafes.
   >
   > Describe your experience at the cafe that you visited.
   > Say why you were satisfied or dissatisfied with it.
   >
   > We will publish the most interesting reviews.

Write your **review**.

3. Your class has been discussing environmental issues, including the problems associated with the presence of too many cars on the roads and the benefits of using more responsible means of transport. As a follow up, your teacher has asked you to write a **report** about the public transportation services available in your area. You should mention what is available, what is not available, and give recommendations for improving your local public transport facilities.

Write your **report**.

4. You see the following notice in a lifestyle magazine, and decide to submit an **article**.

   > ## Living in 2080
   > We invite our readers to write an article on the topic *"Living in 2080"*.
   > What will life be like?
   > The writer of the best article will win an MP3 player.

Write your **article**.

Practice Test 5

Listening

Paper 3 LISTENING   PART 1

You will hear people talking in eight different situations. For questions 1-8, choose the best answer, A, B or C.

1. You are watching TV and you hear this advertisement.
   What is the speaker encouraging you to do?
   A. to maintain your car's tyres
   B. to watch out for children crossing
   C. not to drink and drive

2. You overhear these two people discussing a football match.
   The speakers
   A. support different teams.
   B. both support Manchester United.
   C. both support Liverpool.

3. You are out shopping when you pass a man in the street selling something.
   The item he is selling is
   A. not available elsewhere.
   B. cheaper than elsewhere.
   C. cheaper because it is damaged.

4. You are at a wedding reception when a man starts to make a speech.
   Who is the speaker?
   A. the best friend of the groom
   B. the father of the bride
   C. the groom

5. Listen to this person speaking about a recent holiday.
   What is the speaker complaining about?
   A. the holiday company
   B. the country she visited
   C. the whole holiday

6. You are in an office when you hear a woman making this telephone call.
   The speaker complains about
   A. being given the wrong supplies.
   B. the lateness of the delivery.
   C. having paid too much.

7. You hear a friend telephoning a sandwich delivery company.
   What is the speaker ordering?
   A. 2 sandwiches
   B. 3 sandwiches
   C. 4 sandwiches

8. You are watching the evening news on TV when you hear this item about Dino the dog.
   Dino
   A. went to find his owners.
   B. travelled to his original home.
   C. got lost.

PART 1 - JUSTIFICATION OF THE ANSWERS

1. The correct answer is **A**. "...a good set of tyres with at least five millimetres of tread can and will save your life." Choice B is not correct because "Whether it be another vehicle, a child crossing, or an unexpected bend in the road..."; children crossing are just one of many things to watch out for. Choice C is incorrect because there could be problems "...even if you never touch a drop of alcohol...".

2. The correct answer is **B**. "Look, I've been supporting this team longer than you have." They both support the same team, therefore choice A is incorrect. Choice C is incorrect because the pronoun 'we' is used with Man. United, which indicates their support.

3. The correct answer is **B**. "...you won't find it anywhere at this...bargain basement price..." Choice A is incorrect because "...you've all seen it before on TV anyway..." and choice C is incorrect because it is "...exactly the same quality as all the others..."

4. The correct answer is **A**. "...ever since we were at school together..." Choice B is incorrect because the speaker and the groom are the same age; see above. Choice C is incorrect because George is the groom, not the speaker.

5. The correct answer is **A**. "...I've got a mind to write to Tomlinson's right now and tell them just what I think of them." Tomlinson's is the name of a tour provider. Choice B is incorrect because "...the scenery was nice and some of the local people were friendly" so the country had some positives. Choice C is incorrect because "it wasn't a total disaster".

6. The correct answer is **C**. "...you have overcharged us by $14." Choice A is incorrect because "...everything was supplied as ordered..." and choice B is incorrect because "...No, it was for this morning, so that's fine...".

7. The correct answer is **B**. The clue is that one list of fillings is requested on brown bread, then other fillings are requested "both" on white bread. "both" indicates 2 (two white sandwiches and one brown; therefore, 3 in all).

8. The correct answer is **B**. "...a letter arrived from a former neighbour in Naples where Dino had turned up..." Choice A is incorrect because his owners were in Germany, which he left. Choice C is incorrect because he was described as "streetwise" because he managed to find his way all the way home to Italy from Germany.

Practice Test 5

Paper 3 LISTENING | PART 2

You will hear a psychologist speaking on British radio on the subject of astrology. For questions 9-18, complete the sentences with a word or short phrase.

Over 60% of [9 | **British adults**] admit to being interested in astrology.

Less than 3% of people would consult the stars before making [10 | **business decisions**] .

Psychologists now believe that time of birth can affect a person's [11 | **character**] development.

Time of birth is not the only factor, but it is the [12 | **foundation / base**] for future changes.

To test his idea, the speaker decided to compare people's [13 | **choice of career**] and zodiac sign.

An amazing number of [14 | **artists and entertainers**] were born around mid July to mid August.

Other connections found by the study were [15 | **less obvious**] .

A fair number of serious sports players were born in the [16 | **winter**] months.

The speaker thinks that the lack of professions dominated by mostly one star sign is a little
[17 | **disappointing**] .

The connections may be weak because people are removed from the [18 | **effects of nature**] .

PART 2 - JUSTIFICATION OF THE ANSWERS

9. "An incredible 62% of **British adults** say that the stars are of some interest to them..."
10. "...only 3.5% would use them to choose a husband or wife and only 2.9% of people would refer to them in making **business decisions**."
11. "Psychologists now widely agree that both early life experiences and time of birth are a great influence on the development of a person's **character**."
12. "...this does not make the whole of a person's character, but rather the **foundation or base** on which later changes are made."
13. "...made a statistical comparison between people's **choice of career** and their zodiac sign."

14. "An astonishing 20% of **artists and entertainers** were born in the period between the 12th of July and the 20th of August."
15. "This, in fact, is the most positive connection we have found so far. But there have been others although they have been **less obvious**."
16. "We looked at keen sports players...and found a sizable number were born in the **winter** months..."
17. "...so far, we haven't found any professions containing large percentages of one particular star sign, which is a little **disappointing**..."
18. "...because our modern technological world has removed us further and further from the **effects of nature**."

Paper 3 LISTENING | PART 3

You will hear five different people talking about pets. For questions 19-23, choose from the list A-H which pet each one has at home. Use the letters only once. There are three extra letters which you do not need to use.

A cat	**Speaker 1**	H	19
B dog	**Speaker 2**	C	20
C parrot			
D fish	**Speaker 3**	B	21
E tortoise			
F spider	**Speaker 4**	F	22
G canary			
H mice	**Speaker 5**	D	23

PART 3 - JUSTIFICATION OF THE ANSWERS

19. The correct answer is **H**. "...all cuddled up together. Makes me wonder how some people can hate them so much..." People often hate mice and spiders, however spiders don't cuddle.

20. The correct answer is **C**. "He squawked every so often..." a squawk is a loud noise made by a bird. Also, parrots are the only pet listed here sometimes known to talk.

21. The correct answer is **B**. "...yapping and barking..." are sounds made by a dog.

22. The correct answer is **F**. "He's not a bit like you'd imagine...if you are brave enough to hold him, he's actually quite soft and furry and really quite warm." One might not expect a fish or spider to be warm, but the fish may be eliminated because it would not be furry.

23. The correct answer is **D**. "I can spend hours in front of the tank..."; only fish are kept in tanks and come in lots of colours.

Paper 3 LISTENING   PART 4

You will hear a conversation which takes place in a busy restaurant between a couple, Ivan and Hannah Smythe, and a young waiter, Joel. For questions 24-30, choose the best answer A, B or C.

24. Why does Hannah tell her husband not to speak so loud?
    A. He is disturbing others.
    B. She can't hear him.
    C. The waiter is next to him.

25. How would the manager probably react to an order of two starters?
    A. He would not be agreeable.
    B. He would be happy to oblige.
    C. It wouldn't matter to him.

26. What did Joel use to be?
    A. a waiter
    B. a customer
    C. a vegetarian

27. Why does Ivan complain about the numbers?
    A. They are confusing.
    B. He doesn't like the idea of using numbers on a menu.
    C. He can't see them.

28. What does Ivan want with his Banana Split?
    A. lemon sauce
    B. additional cream
    C. nuts

29. Why can't meals be changed?
    A. They are pre-prepared.
    B. The meals are assembled off-site.
    C. The waiter is busy.

30. What is Ivan's mood at the end of the conversation?
    A. angry
    B. annoyed
    C. impressed

PART 4 - JUSTIFICATION OF THE ANSWERS

24. The correct answer is **A**. "Not so loud, darling - people are looking." He is speaking so loudly that the other people can hear him and are looking to see what the fuss is about.

25. The correct answer is **A**. "...I don't think he'd be too happy." Choice B has the opposite meaning and so is incorrect. It would matter - he wouldn't like it - so choice C is incorrect.

26. The correct answer is **C**. Joel says "...I used to be a vegetarian..." Choice A is incorrect because Joel is a waiter now.

27. The correct answer is **C**. "...you could try writing the numbers a bit more clearly. Er, can you deal with this, dear? I've left my reading glasses in the car." Although he blames the numbers, the fact that he needs his glasses and his wife can see them indicates that the problem is with his vision and not with the numbers so choice A is not a good answer.

28. The correct answer is **B**. "...and one banana split." then "...and don't forget the extra cream."

29. The correct answer is **A**. "...all our meals are assembled in advance and nothing extra can be added - or removed."

30. The correct answer is **C**. He says "My word, that's very efficient. Even the officer's canteen in Stanbroke isn't that fast." Although his attitude for most of the exchange could be described as one of annoyance or perhaps even anger, at the end his attitude changes completely.

Test 6

Paper 1 Reading and Use of English PART 1

For questions 1-8, read the text below and decide which word A, B, C or D best fits each space. There is an example at the beginning (0).

Example:

0. A. bustling   B. deserted   C. foreign   D. permanent

The Town of Aylesbury

Aylesbury is a (0).......... market town (1).......... modern shopping facilities include the recently opened Friars Square shopping centre. The market has been an (2).......... part of Aylesbury life since the early 13th century. Nowadays, regular markets are held on Wednesdays, Fridays and Saturdays.

The town has a (3).......... and varied history, many clues to which can be seen in the (4).......... area to the north of the market square. In this area (5).......... the 15th century *King's Head* Public House which over the years has played host to many famous names. These have included King Henry VIII, who regularly visited the Inn whilst courting Anne Boleyn and Oliver Cromwell, on his visit to Aylesbury in 1651.

(6).......... a National Trust property, the *King's Head* is at present undergoing extensive refurbishments to (7).......... the building to its former glory and is expected to re-open in the autumn. Other (8).......... buildings in the conservation area include the Saxon Church of St Mary and the Buckinghamshire County Museum.

1.	A. what	B. which	C. whose	D. with
2.	A. essential	B. expensive	C. unexpected	D. impossible
3.	A. poor	B. perfect	C. rich	D. nearby
4.	A. pollution	B. conservation	C. environment	D. maintenance
5.	A. lives	B. happens	C. stands	D. shows
6.	A. Since	B. Now	C. Even	D. Despite
7.	A. refresh	B. recall	C. restore	D. remind
8.	A. reliable	B. annual	C. excitable	D. notable

Paper 1 Reading and Use of English PART 2

For questions 9-16, read the text below and think of the word which best fits each space. Use only one word in each space. There is an example at the beginning (0).

Example: | 0 | When |

The Waterloo Station Mystery

(0) ....When........ the girl returned, she was much calmer. Mike realised that (9) ....she......... must think she had made herself look rather foolish and had (10) ....given........ more importance to the happening than it deserved. Mike realised that the girl felt awkward, and that at Waterloo Station she would be glad to (11) ......say/wave....... good-bye to him and forget the event.

When they (12) ......reached...... the station, he took her to find a taxi. The man who had frightened her must be (13) ......somewhere...... in the crowd, and it was (14) ......possible...... that he might trouble her again. But they did not see him.

The (15) ....girl.......... gave the driver an address in Kensington and stepped into the taxi. "Thank you," she said. "Thank you very much." The taxi moved off. Mike stepped forward to wave, and (16) ....was.......... nearly knocked down by another taxi, which was behind.

Paper 1 Reading and Use of English **PART 3**

*For questions **17-24**, read the text below. Use the word given in capitals at the end of some lines to form a word that fits in the space in the same line. There is an example at the beginning (0).*

Example: **0**   r e l a x a t i o n

Holidays are meant to be a time of (0)...*relaxation*... and fun but unfortunately this isn't always the case. There are some (17)....**(un)predictable**.... problems such as delayed flights and the usual (18)....**frustration(s)**....... of waiting at airports.	RELAX PREDICT FRUSTRATE
However the (19)....**anticipation**.... of spending two or three (20)....**wonderful**.... weeks in the sun on an (21)....**unspoilt / unspoiled**.... island is enough to make most people think the delays are worth it. It's best to make a reservation at a hotel so that you can leave home (22)....**confident(ly)**...., knowing that at least your (23)....**accommodation**.... is secure. Finally it's best to travel with a friend to avoid (24)....**homesickness**...... and loneliness.	ANTICIPATE WONDER / SPOIL CONFIDENCE ACCOMMODATE HOMESICK

Paper 1 Reading and Use of English **PART 4**

*For questions **25-30**, complete the second sentence so that it has a similar meaning to the first sentence, using the word given. **Do not change the word given.** You must use between **two** and **five** words, including the word given. There is an example at the beginning (0).*

Example:

0 They think the owner of the house is in France.   thought

   The owner of the house .... in France.

*The gap can be filled by the words "**is thought to be**" so you write:*   **0**   is thought to be

25. She made her children wash the dishes.   were

    Her children ....**were made to wash**........ the dishes.

26. "Let's play chess", he said.   playing

    He ....**suggested playing**........ chess.

27. I'm sure they didn't show up here last night.   shown

    They ....**can't/couldn't have shown up**........ here last night.

28. Her parents don't want her to smoke at home.   object

    Her parents ....**object to her smoking**........ at home.

29. The last time Tim went to France was four years ago.   been

    Tim ....**hasn't been to France**........ for four years.

30. The local council will build a new car park.   be

    A new car park ....**will be built by**........ the local council.

Paper 1 Reading and Use of English **PART 5**

You are going to read an extract from a magazine article about attitudes towards reality TV. For questions 31-36, choose the answer A, B, C or D which you think fits best according to the text.

Today's university students have none of the fear of "Big Brother" that marked their parents' generation. In fact, their fascination with the notion of watching and being watched has fuelled a dramatic shift in entertainment programming and ushered in the era of Reality Television.

Mark Andrejevic, an assistant professor of communication studies, says a number of factors including technology and economy paved the way for the rise of reality television, but none so much as a transformation of Americans' attitudes towards surveillance.

As a graduate student at the University of Colorado in the mid- to late 1990s, he studied the ways in which new technology allowed viewers to move from the role of passive media consumers to active participants. "I was interested in the ways that the promise of participation also became a means of monitoring people," he says. "All over the Internet people were providing information about themselves that could be used by marketers. Being watched became more and more economically productive."

Andrejevic believes that the interactivity of the Internet paved the way for reality TV mania. He interviewed producers of early reality programmes such as MTV's *The Real World* who said that they initially had a hard time finding people willing to have their lives taped nearly 24 hours a day for several months. That was 1992. Now they hold auditions in college towns and thousands of young people form queues snaking for blocks just for the chance to audition. "There are now more people applying to *The Real World* each year than to Harvard," Andrejevic says.

The key to that success is connected to people's increasing comfort with levels of surveillance that were once hated in American society. Andrejevic has attempted to think about the ways in which reality TV reconfigures public attitudes about surveillance. He says: "We're trained to make a split between private and public surveillance - to be worried about government surveillance but not private, which is entertainment or gathering information to serve us better. We're moving into a period where that distinction starts to dissolve. Private surveillance is becoming so pervasive that it's time to start worrying about it as a form of social control."

That viewers of reality programming don't worry about surveillance or social control is testament to the power of television as a messenger. Andrejevic points out that "The cast members on these shows are constantly talking about how great the experience is and how much they have grown personally because of it. It connotes honesty - you can't hide anything about yourself if you're on camera all day every day. It becomes a form of therapy or almost a kind of extreme sport - how long can you withstand allowing yourself to be videotaped?"

Viewers believe in the benefits cast members describe and crave that opportunity for themselves. In this way, each programme becomes a kind of advertisement for itself. Millions of university students watched *The Real World* and then began clamouring for the opportunity to participate. The same is true for newer programmes including *Survivor, American Idol, Fear Factor* and the like.

Andrejevic says he encourages his students to look beyond the characters and the surface glamour of reality television and consider the broader issues of surveillance, privacy, democracy and technology that the shows present.

"I try to cure my students of the habit of watching reality TV uncritically," he says. "The challenge of teaching popular culture is that students are trained to separate the world of academics from the world of popular culture. They tend not to think of that part of life using theories they have learned in class. There's a tendency with students to say 'you're reading too much into it'. But TV is so powerful in conveying messages about the world precisely because people don't think it's doing that. There's something so vital about reality TV as a cultural form," he continues. "It's always changing, moving so fast, continuously reinventing itself. It reflects cultural trends. It's a good place to examine and inspect our culture."

31. What does the phrase 'paved the way' mean in paragraph 2?

    A. invented

    B. slowed down the progress of

    C. got things ready for

    D. were influenced by

32. New technologies helped viewers to

    A. passively enjoy the media.

    B. be economically productive.

    C. become active participants.

    D. consume more.

33. People consider public and private surveillance to be

    A. different things.

    B. equally harmless.

    C. carried out by the government.

    D. a cause for concern.

34. Which of the following is NOT something that makes participation in reality shows a good experience (according to the shows' participants)?

    A. It makes honesty unavoidable.

    B. It can be a sort of therapy.

    C. It is an opportunity to advertise.

    D. It is like an extreme sport.

35. Students tend to

    A. ignore what their studies have taught them when watching reality TV.

    B. read too much into reality TV.

    C. see beyond the glamour of reality TV.

    D. not want to participate in reality shows themselves.

36. What is Andrejevic's attitude towards television?

    A. It is a harmless and entertaining aspect of popular culture.

    B. It is secretly controlled by the government.

    C. It can provide an experience that everyone would benefit from.

    D. It can teach us about our culture but we should use it cautiously.

31. The correct answer is **C**. To pave a road means to cover it with flat blocks of stone or concrete, so that it is easy to travel on, so, to "pave the way" for something means to prepare things so that something may happen more easily.

32. The correct answer is **C**. "new technology allowed viewers to move from the role of passive media consumers to active participants."

33. The correct answer is **A**. "We're trained to make a split between private and public surveillance". Choices C and D, both apply to public surveillance only, and B is incorrect because while people are not worried about private surveillance, they don't like the idea of public surveillance at all.

34. The correct answer is **C**. "The cast members on these shows are constantly talking about how great the experience is and how much they have grown personally because of it. It connotes honesty…It becomes a form of therapy or almost a kind of extreme sport …". Advertising is not mentioned.

35. The correct answer is **A**. "students are trained to separate the world of academics from the world of popular culture. They tend not to think of that part of life using theories they have learned in class." Choice B is not correct because this is what students accuse others of doing. Choice C is incorrect because while "Andrejevic says he encourages his students to look beyond the characters and the surface glamour of reality television" this does not mean that they do. D is incorrect because this was true in the past, but today "young people form lines snaking for blocks" in their efforts to get on reality shows.

36. The correct answer is **D**. He says "it's time to start worrying about it as a form of social control" and that he "encourages his students to look beyond the characters and the surface glamour of reality television and consider the broader issues of surveillance, privacy, democracy and technology", he also says that "it's a good place to examine and inspect our culture".

You are going to read a magazine article about Susan Boyle who was on Britain's Got Talent, and quickly became a celebrity. Six sentences have been removed from the article. Choose from the sentences A-G the one which fits each gap 37-42. There is one extra sentence which you do not need to use.

Reality TV Stars
and Serial Killers

What could the Britain's Got Talent star, Susan Boyle, have in common with one of America's most notorious serial killers? More than you might think. **37** **F** But after her appearance on Britain's Got Talent she was catapulted to fame and splashed across all the front pages.

What is interesting about Susan Boyle from a sociological point of view is that her rapid rise to fame marks a significant milestone in the evolution of contemporary celebrity. Reality TV stars tend to become very famous for five minutes before plunging quickly back into obscurity, but Boyle's "career" is an order of magnitude above your average Big Brother favourite. **38** **G** Boyle's celebrity is born of a synergy between the old and the 'new' media. Her debut TV appearance turned her into an overnight YouTube sensation (65 million views and counting), which spiralled into a news story flashed across all the 24-hour rolling news networks. She piqued the interest of A-List celebrities (Demi Moore, Oprah Winfrey) who helped spread the word, and as a consequence Boyle is a household name *Over There*, in the US, too.

The fascination with Boyle is simple. In the age of superficiality the media people regularly impose impossible to achieve beauty standards on our entertainment. For example, it's common practice for dance music videos to replace powerful but "aesthetically dubious" female vocalists with lip-synching dancers and models. So ubiquitous has the management of celebrity appearance become that it is accepted as given. **39** **A** Her frumpy non-sculptured looks lured them into thinking they were in for a comedy or joke performance. But their expectations were utterly confounded. Her soaring voice surprised and immediately won over everyone who was watching. She reminds us talent triumphs over looks, which immediately casts her as an underdog in comparison with the weight of standardised products churned out by the culture industries.

40 **C** Prolific murderers like Fred West, John Wayne Gacy, Jeffrey Dahmer, Harold Shipman and Ted Bundy inspire horror and fascination in equal measure, and command massive media interest. The more gruesome the murders, the higher the body count, the greater the level of fame. Their crimes spawn countless books, movies and merchandise. Serial killer artefacts, such as John Wayne Gacy's art, are much sought after by collectors. And their effect on popular culture has been profound.

The instantaneous celebrity that attaches to them is not even matched by acts of mass murder, such as school shootings. Hungerford, Columbine, Dunblane and Virginia Tech are burned deeply into popular consciousness, but the names of the people responsible are less well-known and this is despite at least one killer pursuing a post-spree media strategy. **41** **D**

Boyle's pattern of fame so far maps onto that of the Dahmers and the Gacys - but will it last? Her brush with the acute pressures and strains of being suddenly thrust into the limelight might convince her to retire into private life. But with talk of record contracts and lucrative tours here and in the US, it is possible her celebrity could be as long-lived as that of the inglorious pioneers of instant fame. **42** **B**

A. Just look at the audience and panel's faces before Boyle started singing.

B. Boyle's significance lies in her not having to kill anyone for it.

C. Only one group of people have travelled the path to instant fame as quickly: serial killers.

D. So far instant and lasting fame and notoriety has exclusively attached itself to serial killers, at least until now.

E. After losing out to an urban dance troupe, Boyle was sent to The Priory amid rumours of stress and backstage meltdowns.

F. Eight weeks ago Boyle was completely unknown.

G. No other celebrity has travelled the road from nowhere to global fame as fast.

37. The correct answer is **F**. The "but" after the gap indicates that we must expect two contrasting statements. Choice F tells us that she was completely unknown, while after the gap we learn that she rapidly became very famous. Although choice G may seem promising, it does not set up the contrast required by the "but".

38. The correct answer is **G**. The topic sentence basically says her rapid rise to fame is something new; choice G builds on this statement, and the sentences after the gap explain the reasons why her rise to fame was so fast.

39. The correct answer is **A**. The sentence after the gap contains an un-introduced "them" who had expectations about what Boyle's performance would be like. Choice A provides us with an appropriate subject for the "them" to reference - "the audience and panel". This choice might not be immediately obviously because it does not mention the subject of the paragraph - appearance and fame - directly, but in context, it does have to share this subject.

40. The correct answer is **C**. Now, in this paragraph we are introduced to the subject of serial killers. The gap is placed so that it must contain the paragraph's topic sentence. Each sentence in the paragraphs supports the idea that serial killers become famous. Only choice C can fulfil the role of topic sentence for this subject. B and D also share the subject of serial killers, but both compare them with something else, which is not done in this paragraph.

41. The correct answer is **D**. This paragraph gives examples of how no one else can match serial killers' fame; choice D sums the paragraph up, and ties in nicely to the subject of Boyle's exceptional fame in the next paragraph with the phrase "at least until now".

42. The correct answer is **B**. Much of this paragraph compares Boyle's fame with that of serial killers, as does choice B, which also provides an appropriate ending for the text.

Paper 1 Reading and Use of English   **PART 7**

You are going to read some reviews that four people have written about movies that they saw. For questions 43–52, choose from the people A–D. The people may be chosen more than once.

Which person:

disliked almost everything about the film?	43	B
says you must keep alert?	44	A
refers to the film as a product of commercialism?	45	B
indicates exactly when the film had its first release?	46	D
had mixed feelings about the film?	47	C
commented on the amazing special effects?	48	C
says that the film is not able to make a point?	49	B
thinks the film has an irresponsible story line?	50	C
says the movie can appeal to different generations?	51	D
thinks that secrets are part of the subject matter?	52	A

Film Reviews

IVAN   A

Every scene in *Miller's Crossing* is essential so that all the pieces fall into place in the last shot. But there's actually one very brief earlier scene that off-handedly sets up the entire picture. It seems like a throwaway, a chance encounter, but so much information is packed into this brief exchange that the mind boggles in retrospect. Don't blink or you'll miss it! **44**

In this perversely funny, moving and intelligent masterwork, everyone has his or her secret rea- **52** sons for what they do. But the wisdom of *Miller's Crossing* is that it understands that the human heart sometimes keeps those reasons a mystery - not only from others, but occasionally from itself as well.

One of the characters, Bernie, has blatantly chosen to violate the rules. Therefore, according to the gangster's code, Bernie deserves to die. However, for personal reasons, permission for this to go ahead is not granted. And that's when the gangsters' warped but precariously maintained moral/ethical structure begins to collapse. *Miller's Crossing* is an indelible film about betrayal and self-destruction and perhaps the first great movie of the '90s.

GLORIA   B   **43** - nothing at all positive is said

Pretty Woman sells itself as a contemporary Hollywood fairy tale; and the fairy tale aspect of the picture almost works, thanks to a few snappy one-liners and Garry Marshall's sitcom-style direction, which tries, but in the end finally fails, to bleach out the movie's darker implications about America's culture of greed.

In this heavily processed and polished Disney product, it's not clear what has actu- **45** ally made the unconvincing difference in the characters' lives: love or money. Finally, all the movie really says is that nothing else matters as long as you look like you live in Beverly Hills, then people will respect you and it won't matter how you get your money, just as long as you spend lots of it. Of course, it is beyond the scope, or intention, of the movie to sharpen this into an ironic or satirical **49** point. The bleak notion is just there on the screen, acknowledged and reinforced, but never questioned.

BILL   C

To begin with, yes, this is the epic visual masterpiece that you've all been waiting for and it succeeds in everything it tries to do, visually at least. The overall look is stunning beyond belief, the special effects **48** are impeccable.

In allowing everything to be part of a greater whole, Director James Cameron truly created a world of his own. To both the actors' and director's credit, the performances also came through extremely well. It's amazing how much of the actors' emotions you could see through their *Avatar* characters. Cameron got me to shed a tear and sit on the edge of my seat, but the film isn't flawless, **47** not by a long shot.

This brings me to one of the things I really didn't like about the movie; the plot. A white man comes in, learns the ways of a more primitive people, then destroys their world, has a change of heart, and comes back and uses their own ignorance and belief system to make himself a hero. Although this is an old story that we've seen many times before and I can't blame Cameron for coming up with it, is this really a message we want to be spreading, and more so, promoting? What about taking responsibility **50** for yourself?

JACK   D

A tarnished NO TRESPASSING sign is the first thing we see in Orson Welles' *Citizen Kane*, an opening sequence that's still as electrifying as any in the history of movies.

The thrills of Welles' breathtakingly exciting **46** debut film, from 1941, are many. For one thing, there's the exhilaration of watching the cocky 25-year-old director genius explore the possibilities of the medium, playing with the properties of film as if he'd been doing it all his life. *Kane* is as stunning and sophisticated as any movie ever made, yet it moves at a **51** pace that can keep the MTV generation riveted to the screen.

Then there's the thrill of watching the exuberant young actors, among the finest ever to work in front of a movie camera, having the time of their lives. Their fresh performances still bristle with spontaneity and an edge that few contemporary actors can match.

And, behind that NO TRESPASSING sign, there's the thrill of the forbidden. For *Citizen Kane* takes us behind that barrier, erected to keep out the public, for an intimate look at a great and powerful man who got everything he ever wanted and then lost it.

Paper 2 WRITING | PART 1

*You **must** answer this question. Write your answer in **140-190** words in an appropriate style.*

1. You have watched a video on a non-profit organisation working to stop the use of animals for testing medicines used by human beings. Now, your professor has asked you to write an essay.

   Write an **essay** using **all** the notes and give reasons for your point of view.

> Testing on animals is a standard in scientific research.
> What is the best way to deal with this problem?
>
> **Notes**
>
> Write about:
> 1. animals suffer
> 2. outdated form of research
> 3. .... (your own idea)

Paper 2 WRITING | PART 2

*Write an answer to **one** of the questions **2-4** in this part. Write your answer in **140-190** words in an appropriate style.*

2. You work part-time at your local gym, which has decided to invest £20,000 in new equipment and facilities. Your manager has asked you to write a **report** about the gym's existing facilities and say where you think the money should be spent.

Write your **report**.

3. You are looking through some of your favourite websites and notice the following ad:

> **Write on Innovation Trends**
>
> Submit reviews of your favourite trends and devices like the new version of iTunes or the latest mobile apps to our web forum. We are looking for new voices with fresh perspectives on the latest tech advances!

You just got a new mobile phone that you are very pleased to have. Write a **review** discussing the terrific user experience, speed and other aspects that have impressed you.

Write your **review**.

4. You've been enjoying a long Christmas holiday at your favourite beach in the Caribbean and want to share your experience with your family back home. Write a **letter** that you'll send by e-mail describing how you've been spending your time. Mention the people you've met, the food you've had, where you've visited and any other information you'd like to share.

Write your **letter**.

Listening

You will hear people talking in eight different situations. For questions 1-8, choose the best answer, A, B or C.

1. You are at a college lecture when you hear this student interrupting the lecturer.
   What does the student want the lecturer to do?
   A. repeat a particular word
   B. explain something
   C. repeat an important point

2. You hear this politician being interviewed on TV.
   What is his political party called?
   A. Social Liberal Democrats
   B. Liberal Democratic Party
   C. Christian Democratic Alliance

3. You overhear a hotel receptionist speaking on the telephone with a customer.
   Why is the hotel unable to provide the customer with rooms?
   A. there aren't enough rooms
   B. the facilities are inadequate
   C. the customer wants better service

4. You overhear this woman talking to her child in a shop.
   She is
   A. warning the child about something.
   B. explaining something to the child.
   C. telling the child off.

5. You overhear this woman talking about a problem she had with a CD player.
   Now the woman is
   A. angry.
   B. worried.
   C. satisfied.

6. You are at a pay phone in a hotel when you hear this man ordering a taxi to take him home.
   Where does the man live?
   A. 269, Radleigh Road
   B. 69, Rudleigh Road
   C. the Half-way Hotel

7. You are on a train when you overhear this man talking about the prices of railway tickets.
   How much has he just paid?
   A. £6.50
   B. £16.50
   C. £5.60

8. You hear this man on the radio introducing a song.
   The man
   A. likes the song very much.
   B. never liked the song.
   C. is less keen on the song now.

PART 1 JUSTIFICATION OF THE ANSWERS

1. The correct answer is **C**. "You said something very important about the core laws and I was just wondering...Could you possibly go back over this?" Choice A is incorrect because although the student misunderstood a word, it is not what the student was asking. Choice B is not correct because "I missed some of what you said; it was very fast." This means the student didn't have time to write it down, not that the student didn't understand.

2. The correct answer is **B**. "...we in the L.D.P. believe" - the personal pronoun 'we' is the clue; it shows affiliation. Also you must extrapolate from the abbreviation because we are not told the exact name of the party. The correct answer choice is the only one that shares the same initials. Choices A and C are incorrect because these parties are mentioned but criticised; they are opponents.

3. The correct answer is **A**. "They have over twice the number of rooms we have..." Choices B and C are incorrect because the other hotels "...offer very much the same facilities and standards".

4. The correct answer is **C**. "How many times have I told you not to touch things that don't belong to you?"; her tone is angry. Choice A is incorrect because the child's safety is not a concern here, as far as we know and choice B is incorrect because there is no explanation given, just orders.

5. The correct answer is **C**. "...they were wonderful...fixed it right there in front of me, and I didn't have to pay a penny." Choices A an B are incorrect because she "was worried" and she "was furious" but the problem was solved.

6. The correct answer is **A**. "I want to go to Radleigh Road number two-six-nine..."

7. The correct answer is **B**. "...but with the card it's only six fifty" and "I did also have to pay ten pounds to buy the card".

8. The correct answer is **C**. He says "...the song that everyone loved when they first heard it, but I think we're all ready for a new number 1, aren't we?" He is speaking for everyone, but also for himself.

Practice Test 6

Paper 3 LISTENING | PART 2

You will hear a programme about roller-coasters. For questions 9-18, complete the sentences with a word or short phrase.

You can't control a car in a roller-coaster because it has no **9** **brakes** on it.

The roller-coasters are made at **10** **Great Salt Lake** in Utah.

The designers don't want to make people feel **11** **sick** .

The **12** **track** is the most difficult part of the ride to design.

The roller-coaster gets its energy from **13** **gravity** .

The fastest roller-coaster travels at **14** **85 m/p/h** .

If you know what's happening when you are on a roller-coaster you feel more **15** **scared/fear** .

The Grand Slam Canyon coaster travels at **16** **40 m/p/h** .

In the future, coasters may have **17** **virtual reality** helmets.

A roller-coaster travels faster if the atmosphere is **18** **warm but dry** .

PART 2 - JUSTIFICATION OF THE ANSWERS
9. "no **brakes** on board".
10. "the minds that come up with" (ie think of) "all this... the shores of Utah's **Great Salt Lake**."
11. "can make you **sick** but they won't... we won't do that we refuse".
12. "the cars are easy ... the real art comes in designing the **track**" therefore most difficult.
13. "uses **gravity**".
14. "maximum speed...record is **85 mph**".
15. "you're able to comprehend...there's a lot more kind of **fear**".
16. "**40 plus (+) mile** an hour screamer"
17. "the next generation ... maybe a coaster with a **virtual reality** helmet".
18. "coaster will go faster when the air is **warm but dry**".

Paper 3 LISTENING | PART 3

You will hear five different people being interviewed on the radio about Christmas. For questions 19-23, choose from the list A-H which words best describe their feelings about this celebration. Use the letters only once. There are three extra letters which you do not need to use.

A	enthusiastic	Speaker 1 — **D** 19
B	bored with it	Speaker 2 — **F** 20
C	upset by it	Speaker 3 — **A** 21
D	unappreciated	Speaker 4 — **B** 22
E	satisfied	Speaker 5 — **C** 23
F	happier than expected	
G	lonely	
H	frightened	

PART 3 JUSTIFICATION OF THE ANSWERS
19. The correct answer is **D**. "I don't seem to remember a single person actually saying thank you and really meaning it."
20. The correct answer is **F**. "I was all set to have another unexciting Christmas" and "...they'd noticed that I was going to be alone that day and would I like to join them. And of course, I had a wonderful time."
21. The correct answer is **A**. "It isn't over yet. I mean we've had the actual festivities on the 25th, but there's so much more to Christmas than that."
22. The correct answer is **B**. "It wasn't as good as it's been in the past. For a start the telly was pretty disappointing" and "there's been nothing to watch all Christmas."
23. The correct answer is **C**. "But what's most distressing is..."

Paper 3 LISTENING PART 4

*You will hear an extract from a radio programme. For questions **24-30**, decide which of the choices **A, B** or **C** is the correct answer.*

24. "Say it like it is"

   A. is always about the weather.

   B. is directed by members of the public.

   C. gives people a chance to express their opinions.

25. Mrs Kent

   A. is an expert on the weather.

   B. is worried about the weather in the near future.

   C. thinks there is going to be another Ice Age.

26. According to Tom Sheridan,

   A. food is always a good topic of conversation.

   B. everyone likes to talk about the weather.

   C. people don't talk about the weather any more.

27. Paul Spenser

   A. does the production of a cookery programme.

   B. enjoys listening to the cookery programme.

   C. thinks the cookery programme should be more difficult.

28. Jane

   A. uses the library often.

   B. thinks students should be given free books.

   C. thinks that libraries should charge.

29. An elderly listener

   A. doesn't think young people should have to pay in the discos.

   B. doesn't like going to the pub.

   C. thinks that people should pay in the library.

30. Most listeners to the programme seem

   A. to have something to complain about.

   B. to have a personal problem.

   C. to be worried about money.

PART 4 - JUSTIFICATION OF THE ANSWERS

24. The correct answer is **C**: "Jim Adams: Hi, this is "Say it like it is", the programme in which your comments about what's been on Radio One for the last week are read." Choice B is wrong: the programme is not direct it by the audience. Choice A is also wrong: "based on weather this time" therefore NOT always.

25. The correct answer is **B**. Mrs Kent says: "I'm more concerned about the present day situation...should...focus on short-term weather forecasts". She is is worried about the weather. Choice A is wrong. Mrs Kent says: "Some experts may tell us what the weather may be like in the next century but I'm more concerned..." therefore she is not an expert herself. Choice C is also wrong: Ice Age information was from the previous speaker - John Holmes.

26. The correct answer is **B**. "all those conversations about the weather would disappear" said as a negative point. Choice A is wrong: Tom does not mention food at all (Jim Adams says "food...seems to be a favourite to introduce the next readers". Choice C is also wrong: Tom Sheridan: "...would disappear" therefore are still talking about the weather.

27. The correct answer is **A**. "the producer of our cookery show here today, Mr Paul Spenser". Choice B is wrong: he's the producer of the show - not a listener. Choice C is also wrong: says it has to be easy for the beginners - it will get more difficult.

28. The correct answer is **A**. Jane says: "...we depend on libraries for our books". Choice B is wrong: "...too expensive to buy...depend on libraries" therefore she thinks borrowing books should be free. Choice C is also wrong: "...20p is too much" so she is against the idea that libraries should charge.

29. The correct answer is **C**. An elderly listener: "Why shouldn't others pay...they pay in...Discos...why not at libraries". Choice B is wrong: No mention of not liking pubs. Choice A is also wrong: "Why shouldn't others pay...they pay in ...Discos...why not at libraries".

30. The correct answer is **A**. Most letters read out were complaints i.e. negative reactions. Choice B is wrong: There are not any real personal problems mentioned. Choice C is also wrong: There is no mention of money worries except paying for library books which is, at present, a rumour i.e. don't have to pay yet.

Test 7

For questions 1-8, read the text below and decide which word A, B, C or D best fits each space. There is an example at the beginning (0).

Example:

0.   A. seminar   B. exhibition C. discussion D. conference

The Art of Patrick Heron

This summer the Tate Gallery presents a major retrospective (0)........... of paintings by Patrick Heron, one of the leading (1)........... in twentieth-century British art.

Heron (2)............. the early years of his (3)........... in Cornwall, an influence that has remained with him. In 1956 he returned to a house at Zennor, (4)........... Eagles Nest, with an extraordinary garden. Here the beauty of his surroundings inspired his work and he produced a series of garden paintings in (5)........... forms are shown with colour, light and texture.

Heron moved into pure abstraction in 1956 with a group of impressive, (6)........... coloured canvases, including stripe paintings. He became a leader of the major development of abstract art which was then taking place in Britain and which flowered in (7)........... painting and sculpture in the 1960s.

In the 1980s Heron's art entered a new phase in which his inspiration seemed to be once more drawn (8)........... from his natural surroundings.

1.	A. figures	B. actors	C. politicians	D. authors
2.	A. lost	B. saw	C. took	D. spent
3.	A. childishness	B. kindergarten	C. childhood	D. infantry
4.	A. replied	B. written	C. known	D. called
5.	A. what	B. which	C. were	D. every
6.	A. probably	B. certainly	C. intensely	D. rarely
7.	A. addition	B. advance	C. progress	D. both
8.	A. directly	B. likely	C. timely	D. commercially

*For questions 9-16, read the text below and think of the word which best fits each space. Use only **one** word in each space. There is an example at the beginning (0).*

Example: 0   of

Murder in London

I was full (0) ......*of*........ hate. I forgot all danger and rushed at him. I hit him twice and the second (9) ....**time**....... I cut his face. In his surprise he did not (10) ....**hit**.......... me back. This saved my life. It was my (11) ....**last/final**....... desperate effort. I moved back and went down on one knee. "He will ride at me now," I thought. "This will be the end (12) ....**of/for**....... me, or perhaps both of us."

At that moment (13) ....**there**........... was a shout. I looked round. A man was riding hard, with a revolver in his hand. It was my dear friend Jack. Nelson saw him, and stopped his rush at me. But he did not hurry away. He said, (14) ....**with**........... a smile: "We shall meet again!" And (15) ....**then/so**......... he left the farm girl and me with easy ceremony.

His wound did not trouble him. He smiled, and happily (16) ......**raised/waved**...... his hand to Jack. Jack fired at him, and the bullet hit his sword. He dropped his sword and rode away fast.

Paper 1 Reading and Use of English   PART 3

For questions **17-24**, read the text below. Use the word given in capitals at the end of some lines to form a word that fits in the space in the same line. There is an example at the beginning (0).

Example: | 0 | carefully |

Nowadays some people are (0)......*carefully*........ preparing themselves for   CARE

(17)......**retirement**......... a long time before they actually reach it. Some people   RETIRE

prefer to retire early. Early retirement is usually (18)......**optional**............ and   OPT

most companies don't have any objection to it. However, once the

(19)......**formalities**........ are over and a person finds himself at home,   FORMAL

projects such as home (20)......**maintenance**........ become a new speciality,   MAINTAIN

especially for men although their (21)......**enthusiasm**........ may not match   ENTHUSE

their (22)......**performance**...... . Often accidents are caused by someone's   PERFORM

(23)......**eagerness**........ to save money as their lack of (24)......**expertise**......   EAGER / EXPERT

causes more problems than it solves.

Paper 1 Reading and Use of English   PART 4

For questions **25-30**, complete the second sentence so that it has a similar meaning to the first sentence, using the word given. **Do not change the word given.** You must use between **two** and **five** words, including the word given. There is an example at the beginning (0).

Example:

0 They think the owner of the house is in France.　　　　　　thought

   The owner of the house .... in France.

The gap can be filled by the words "**is thought to be**" so you write: | 0 | is thought to be |

25. "There is no reason to be alarmed", Joe said   cause

    There was no ......**cause for alarm**...................... according to Joe.

26. We all thought that man was George's father.   for

    We ......**all (mis)took that man for**.............. George's father.

27. The vet examined my brother's pet dog last week.   had

    My brother ......**had his pet dog examined**............ last week.

28. "You both lied to my husband", Jane said to her parents.   lying

    Jane ......**accused her parents of lying**............ to her husband.

29. This is the village where we were born.   in

    This is the ......**village in which we were**............ born.

30. Peter likes to participate in team sports.   part

    Peter likes ......**to take part in**................ team sports.

You are going to read a newspaper article about developments of global importance in the last century. For questions 31-36, choose the answer A, B, C or D which you think fits best according to the text.

A Century of Change

The 20th century was a time of remarkable change. In less than one hundred years, the population of our planet went from around 2 billion people to close to 6 - that's right; almost treble the number of people live in the world today as did ten or so decades ago. And not only have our numbers exploded, but our lives have become more intertwined than ever before. For most of human history, the different communities which existed lived in their own very small worlds – worlds inside a bigger world they knew little about. The only world that mattered was the one you could see in your immediate surroundings. Compare that situation with today, when even the poorest parts of sub-Saharan Africa can boast 43 television sets per thousand people. The world view is no longer limited to the horizon; it stretches across the planet. The global village is here. Now, let's see how it came about.

The lessons of two world wars in quick succession signalled the dawning of a new age. Statesmen and women saw that the way forward lay in bringing the world closer together. World War Three was to be avoided at all costs, they said. It was believed that by making nations more interdependent the risk of conflict would be lessened as it would be in nobody's interest to go to war then.

That desire to see the nations of the world united gave birth to the U.N. – the United Nations. The idea of the U.N. was to share power, responsibility and decision making for world affairs equally between all the members of the new global village, so it is the nearest thing we have ever had to a world government. The U.N. brings together officials from 193 member states. Their task is to preserve world peace and prevent conflict, but the dream never quite became a reality as this body has very little 'real' power - it just does a lot of talking.

Not long after the United Nations was founded, Europe started to play with the idea of uniting its own continent. After all, it was internal conflict there that had been the main cause of both world wars. Then, in 1957, the idea took shape; it started as the European Coal and Steel Community with six member states. Today, we know it as the E.U. or the European Union – 28 countries, called member states, united in one large free trade area and committed to supporting each other in order to make Europe a safer, more secure and more prosperous place. 15 of those members have since gone a step further and created a single currency. The system is hardly perfect, but at least the members are working together and not trying to destroy each other anymore. Today, the Eurozone has 18 members.

But, for all the political movement that took place in the last century, there was a revolution more powerful, and yet more simple, that changed the world as we know it forever – and that was the dawn of the information age. First the television brought people from opposite sides of the globe into contact; then the internet made the world our living room. Technology was the most powerful tool for uniting people in the last century, and the first to create a truly global community.

Now we can communicate with people from different 'tribes' in an instant; debate with them; learn from them; understand them; just chat with them if that's all we want. But for all the change, have we made the world any better? There's still a huge gap between the richest and the poorest nations; there's still misunderstanding and conflict. We may be closer; we may live in a global village; maybe we're getting there, but there's still a lot more to do.

31. What does the writer mean by saying communities used to live in worlds inside a bigger world?

   A. In the past people knew little about faraway places.

   B. In the past people only cared about themselves.

   C. Most people didn't travel very much in the past.

   D. Most people cared about what was happening in the bigger world.

32. What changed after the experience of two world wars?

   A. Politicians felt determined to prevent another world war.

   B. Information technology brought the world closer together.

   C. Nobody was interested in conflict anymore.

   D. Nations wanted to become more independent.

33. What is suggested about the United Nations?

   A. It keeps the world peaceful and conflict-free.

   B. It will become a global government.

   C. It doesn't have a lot of meaningful influence.

   D. It is controlled by a few big powers.

34. What does the phrase 'took shape' mean in the context of paragraph 4, line 42?

   A. succeeded

   B. developed

   C. concluded

   D. changed

35. The arrival of new technology and the information age

   A. seemed unimportant compared to the political changes taking place.

   B. had a strong impact on the opposite side of the globe.

   C. brought people together in a way that politicians could not.

   D. saw people use the internet a lot in their living rooms.

36. What does the writer's tone in the final paragraph suggest?

   A. He is satisfied with what has been achieved.

   B. He is critical and pessimistic about the future.

   C. He is confused and upset.

   D. He is realistic about the situation.

31. The correct answer is **A**. "...worlds inside a bigger world they knew little about. The only world that mattered was the one that you could see in your immediate surroundings." While C may seem likely to be true, it is not actually mentioned, so is not a good answer choice.

32. The correct answer is **A**. "Statesmen and women saw that the way forward lay in bringing the world closer together. World War Three was to be avoided at all costs, they said." B is incorrect because this happens much later. C is not correct because they wanted to prevent it, which is a form of interest -they were interested in preventing conflict if you like. D is incorrect because they were becoming more "interdependent" which is the opposite of independent.

33. The correct answer is **C**. "Their task is to preserve world peace and prevent conflict, but the dream never quite became a reality as this body has very little 'real' power - it just does a lot of talking." A is incorrect because, although this is the dream, it didn't quite happen. B is incorrect, because "the nearest thing we have ever had to a world government" implies that it might be close but it isn't quite world government. D is incorrect because "the U.N. was to share power, responsibility and decision making for world affairs equally between all the members of the new global village".

34. The correct answer is **B**. To "take shape" means something develops or begins to appear in its final form.

35. The correct answer is **C**. "Technology was the most powerful tool for uniting people in the last century, and the first to create a truly global community."

36. The correct answer is **D**. "We may be closer; we may live in a global village; maybe we're getting there, but there's still a lot more to do." This is neither very positive nor very negative. It is balanced and realistic.

You are going to read an article about winter sport in Scotland. Six sentences have been removed from the article. Choose from the sentences A-G the one which fits each gap 37-42. There is one extra sentence which you do not need to use.

Hope and Sadness

There's often a sense of the hopeless romantic associated with those who trek to the Highlands in search (more in hope than expectation) of the white stuff. More often than not, these ski and snowboard fanatics are met with disappointment. Either a thaw has set in and the rocks are visible or it's a total whiteout as gales blow and blizzards blast the poor expectant hopefuls. The Highlands, you see, is a tale of extremes; it's all or nothing up there.

37 A But those patient folk – those old romantics whose sense of loyalty and optimism seems to know no bounds – are having the last laugh this winter. Picture this: fresh powder everywhere; 180cm of accumulated snow at the base of the resort; more falls forecast for later in the week; clear blue skies and a blazing sun. No, this isn't some upmarket French alpine retreat full of five-star chalets and bulging wallets. This is humble little Cairngorm, pride of Scotland. This is real, old-style skiing without the gloss. There's an infectious passion and enthusiasm here today. **38 D**

Despite all the talk of global warming spelling the end for Scotland's long-suffering winter sport industry, Cairngorm and its four sister resorts; the Lecht, Glenshee, Glencoe and the Nevis Range aren't about to go down without a fight. And, finally, nature has lent them a helping hand. As I am about to hop onto the chairlift, I can't resist the urge to pause and admire the scene around me; the Highlands at its best. **39 C** Back then, these slopes were crowded with thousands of skiers all season long; full to capacity – just as they are once again today. The cafes are overflowing with people enjoying their apres ski. You can see skiers of all sorts; beginners, wannabes and the real deal – the masters – don't get in their way! And all of them have one thing in common. They are all wearing big smiles on their faces.

If this is a freak winter, as the Meteorology Office would have us believe, and all the snow will have gone in a few years, then I am saddened. **40 E** And on the rare occasions when the snow base left us wanting, we'd pull out the sled and toboggan to our little hearts' content. Sure they'd take a battering on the rocks and stones, but those wooden sleds could handle it – they were tough! And I'm angered by the idea that my kids won't get to enjoy the same innocent sense of delight that I once did. **41 B** It isn't fair.

So instead of booking that package deal to Europe this winter, come home to Scotland; do your pocket and the planet a favour. Why waste money on expensive flights that will only add to our environmental woes? They're not Les Trois Vallees; they're not Courcheval; some would say they're not even close, but Scotland's small ensemble of ski resorts have had a bumper season, so don't be too quick to write them off. There's life in the old dog yet! He just needs your help.

42 F Well, I guess I'm one of them. And I hope that the Highlands continue to defy the odds and that nature confounds us all and brings a little joy to our children's hearts for many a winter to come. Snow, bonnie Scotland! Snow right up to the start of May! I'll be here waiting when you do.

A. The more we begin to feel the effects of global warming, the more it seems to be nothing instead of all.

B. Why have we wrecked this planet for future generations?

C. It's like going back in time to the glory days of the 1960s and 70s.

D. These people have waited a long time!

E. All of my happiest memories of winters growing up as a child were spent flying down the slopes.

F. Do you remember those hopeless romantics I described before?

G. But sadly there isn't the snow base to satisfy their passion or desire.

37. The correct answer is **A**. The sentence before the gap ends with "it's all or nothing up there" and A echoes this with "...it seems to be nothing instead of all".

38. The correct answer is **D**. We would expect the gap to be filled by an explanation of the reason for the enthusiasm referred to and the paragraph is about "those patient folk" so it would make sense that they "waited a long time" and something they wanted (they wanted snow) finally happened.

39. The correct answer is **C**. The gap is followed by "Back then...", so the missing sentence must be about the past which eliminates all but choices C and E. Choice E is not a good choice because it talks about childhood memories, which do not fit so well with crowded shops and overflowing cafes. The "glory days" of skiing would be a time when skiing was very popular, which fits better with the description after the gap.

40. The correct answer is **E**. We would expect the gap to give a reason why the author would be saddened by a lack of snow, and because the sentences following the gap speak of a time in the past, the gap must as well. E satisfies these requirements, and also fits nicely with the subject of the author's children not having an opportunity to enjoy snow which is mentioned later in the paragraph.

41. The correct answer is **B**. Before the gap, the author tells us that his children might not have the "same innocent sense of delight that I once did" and after the gap says that "it isn't fair". The unfair thing that caused the previously mentioned loss, is explained in choice B.

42. The correct answer is **F**. "One of them" refers to "those hopeless romantics". The author is not ready to give up hope for winter sports in Scotland.

Practice Test 7

You are going to read the transcripts of four interviews conducted as part of a research project on culture. For questions 43–52, choose from the people A–D. The people may be chosen more than once.

Which person:

is glad their nation is made up of people from lots of different backgrounds?	43	B
is proud that their country has kept a particular political system?	44	B
mentions something which attracts a lot of people to their country?	45	D
believes money has had an effect on something?	46	C
thinks their country has an unfair reputation?	47	D
believes their country has progressed very fast?	48	C
believes geography has influenced their country's culture?	49	A
feels their nation's identity is threatened by something?	50	B
wishes their country was as successful as it once was?	51	A
sees evidence of the work and achievements of their ancestors around them today?	52	A

A research project on culture

Andreas: The Greek   **A**

For me, Greeks are a unique people, and our culture is quite distinct from any other I've experienced in my extensive travels. You see, we are perched on the edge of the European continent. We are certainly European - there's no mistaking that - but being in such close proximity to both Africa and the Middle East has given us a unique perspective. **49** Maybe we've been influenced to some degree by both those regions and that is part of what has given us our unique identity. Then, of course, there's also our history. I am no different to any other Greek; immensely proud of my people's achievements. The Ancient Greeks after all gave a lot to the rest of the world; think democracy, philosophy and so on. And history is everywhere you go here, too; it's alive. I mean, **52** there are ancient ruins, thousands of years old, all around you. It's really quite inspiring. There are reminders of the achievements of my forefathers everywhere. It's just a shame the present isn't quite as glorious as the past. **51**

Linda: The Briton   **B**

What I admire about my people is their diversity. **43** I suppose that stems from our past. Britain, after all, once colonised nearly half the world, so it's not surprising. And it's not just the fact that all sorts of different people live here, it's also because they manage to live in harmony; well, most of the time. No matter whether you are a Briton of one generation or ten, so long as you consider yourself British everyone else will. I'm also quite proud of the monarchy. So many countries have abandoned the **44** monarchical system, and I think that's sad. We are one of the last in Europe. I hope we never go down the route of getting rid of the Queen. The one thing I'm sceptical of is Europe. I am afraid that the more involved **50** we become in the European Union, the less distinct we are as a nation. I, for one, was very happy we didn't join the Euro.

Tae-Hee: The Korean   **C**

Korea has one of the richest and longest histories of all the nations in the world. Very few people are aware of that because, traditionally, Korea has kept itself isolated. We used to be known as 'the Hermit Kingdom', but that is all changing now. What I am most proud of is how far we have come in such a short space of **48** time. In the half a century or so South Korea has existed as an independent state, it has turned itself from one of the poorest nations in the world into one of the biggest and fastest-growing economies. We're no longer an agriculture-based society, now we export high-technology products all over the world. Recently, we hosted a G20 summit. That was a very proud moment for me. It was a sign that my country is now quite influential and can take its place alongside the other great nations. Of course, as we have become wealthier, our lifestyles have changed, **46** too. We really enjoy social drinking these days – some people call us 'the Irish of Asia'! I guess they like their drink, too!

Gamu: The South African   **D**

Maybe my country has a chequered history, but it's sad to think this is all the rest of the world knows **47** about us. Besides, although the situation is by no means perfect yet, my people are more united than ever before. But what I am most proud of perhaps is our natural beauty. Our coastal waters are second-to-none for studying and viewing marine life. And don't forget the huge variety of native land species, too. People from all over the world come **45** to visit our wildlife reserves and marvel at the amazing creatures we have in abundance. The World Cup was a real coming of age moment for us I have to say. It put South Africa on the map and showed a better side of our country to the rest of the world. My people did themselves proud by hosting a really successful tournament. We showed the world that we understand the meaning of sportsmanship and fair play, and I hope we proved that we can't forever be associated with the corruption and wrongdoing of the past.

Writing

Paper 2 WRITING PART 1

*You **must** answer this question. Write your answer in **140-190** words in an appropriate style.*

1. You have listened to a radio programme about the problem of widespread starvation in many parts of Africa. Your English teacher has asked you to write an essay.

   Write an **essay** using **all** the notes and give reasons for your point of view.

   > In many parts of Africa people are dying of starvation and lack of fresh water. Can these problems be solved?
   >
   > **Notes**
   >
   > Write about:
   > 1. war
   > 2. lack of organised farming
   > 3. .... (your own idea)

Paper 2 WRITING PART 2

*Write an answer to **one** of the questions **2-4** in this part. Write your answer in **140-190** words in an appropriate style.*

2. You see this announcement on a English-language computer magazine:

   > **Articles wanted**
   > **New City breaks**
   >
   > Write an article telling us which city you want to visit and why? Why would you recommend this city to others?

   Write your **article**.

3. Your teacher wants you and your classmates to improve your critical-thinking skills. She asks you to write a **review** of your favourite film. Discuss the plot of the movie, the director's style in telling the story, the development of the characters and what you find interesting as well as lacking. Mention if and how you would change the production in any way.

   Write your **review**.

4. You have seen this advertisement for a job in the UK in an international magazine.

   > **UK Winter Camps**
   >
   > Can you speak English? Are you cheerful, energetic and hard-working?
   > If the answer to both questions is yes, then you are the person we are looking for. We provide food and accommodation, and your airfare is reimbursed at the end of the contract.
   >
   > You will:
   > - look after children aged 6-10
   > - help organise activities and events
   > - work as part of a team of ten camp entertainers
   >
   > Send letters of application to Mr. Michaels, camp director.

   Write a **letter**.

Listening

Paper 3 LISTENING   PART 1

You will hear people talking in eight different situations. For questions 1-8, choose the best answer, A, B or C.

1. You are in a large electrical shop when you overhear this man describing a washing machine.
   What is the advantage of this machine?
   A. it is cheaper to buy
   B. it washes better
   C. it costs less to use

2. You hear a man on TV talking about a programme on Tuesday night.
   The programme *Just Penelope* is
   A. a chat show.
   B. a comedy series.
   C. a detective series.

3. You are in a supermarket when you hear this couple arguing.
   What are they arguing about?
   A. which brand of coffee to buy
   B. which tin of soup to buy
   C. which brand of fruit juice to buy

4. You dial a number to find out about night classes.
   You hear this recorded message.
   None of the cookery courses are
   A. for more than six weeks.
   B. in English cooking.
   C. only at weekends.

5. You overhear this man talking about a book.
   The man
   A. did not like the book very much.
   B. found it completely useless.
   C. benefited a lot from buying it.

6. You overhear a woman on the telephone inviting a friend to dinner.
   The friend cannot come because
   A. he will be away.
   B. he is unwell.
   C. of his work.

7. You ask a policeman for directions to the bus station.
   Where is the bus station?
   A. at the top of a hill
   B. by the river
   C. at the bottom of a hill

8. You are watching a repeat of a British TV sitcom called *Teacher's Always Right*.
   What does the teacher want the girl to do?
   A. stop misbehaving in lessons
   B. stop missing lessons
   C. bring the right books

PART 1 JUSTIFICATION OF THE ANSWERS

1. The correct answer is **C**. "...it will cut a substantial slice off your family's electricity and water bills...economical with both water and energy making running costs a third less..." Choice A is incorrect because it is "...a more expensive model..." and choice B is incorrect because "...it has the same features as all our other models and does the job just as well."

2. The correct answer is **C**. "Penelope Parchment has a particularly difficult case to solve..." Detectives solve cases. Choice A is incorrect because "Alvin Major's guests tonight include..." Alvin has the talk show, not Penelope. Choice B is incorrect because no mention is made of comedy show.

3. The correct answer is **A**. "...it makes more than fifty cups..." Cups go with coffee. Choice B is incorrect because bowls would go with soup and choice C is incorrect because glasses would go with juice.

4. The correct answer is **B**. "Cookery courses for the new year are in Chinese, South American and Indian cuisine..." Choice A is incorrect because the Indian cookery class will "...last an extra 2 weeks beyond the usual 5 week duration". Choice C is incorrect because "...Indian cookery course on Mondays, Wednesdays and Saturdays..."

5. The correct answer is **A**. "I think it made a lot of things unnecessarily difficult" He did not find it completely useless: "Mind you, it does have some useful diagrams that helped me pick up the fingering", so choice B is incorrect. Choice C is not a good answer because he suggests "...if I were you, I'd spend my money on having some actual lessons".

6. The correct answer is **A**. When he says he can't come she responds "Still, you deserve a break..." and "Will you be going abroad?" Choice B is not correct because: "You've been quite run down recently - and we don't want you getting ill." While 'run down' is not exactly well, it is not serious enough to be considered 'unwell'. Choice C is incorrect because he has been working a lot but that's not the reason he can't come to the dinner; see above.

7. The correct answer is **C**. "...you go all the way up St Mark's Hill, over the top and right down..." Choice B is incorrect because "...if you get to the river, you know that you've gone too far".

8. The correct answer is **B**. The teacher says "...haven't you been missing your classes quite a lot recently?" Choices A and C are incorrect because when the student says "...I promise I'll try to pay more attention and bring the right books next time..." he responds: "...that's not the problem...".

Practice Test 7

Paper 3 LISTENING | PART 2

You will hear part of a talk from a television programme about dealing with broken bones. For questions 9-18, complete the sentences with a word or short phrase.

The word 'fracture' is a technical word for **9** | **broken bones** .

Bones are vital for the body because they **10** | **support** and protect it.

Bones are composed of a **11** | **hardened** outer layer and a soft centre.

Bone marrow is important because it makes **12** | **(new) blood** cells.

Bones do not always break; sometimes they actually **13** | **bend** .

It is important to try to find any fractures before trying to **14** | **move** a victim.

Moving an injured person can cause **15** | **multiple** fractures.

If the injured party is conscious, they can inform you of the **16** | **position** of any fractures.

Part of the procedure for treating an unconscious victim has been discussed in **17** | **previous programmes** .

If someone is unconscious, carefully check each major bone for any **18** | **change in shape** .

PART 2 JUSTIFICATION OF THE ANSWERS

9. "...that of fractures - or to put it more simply - **broken bones**."
10. "... performing the two vital functions of **support** for the body and protection for the internal parts of the body ..."
11. "Bones are ... made up of a **hardened** outer layer of cells around a soft material in the centre ..."
12. "The bone marrow, incidentally, performs the equally vital function of producing **new blood cells**."
13. "Bones do not break easily." and "the bones ... can actually **bend** to a surprising degree..."
14. "...locate any fractures before attempting to **move** the victim."

15. "further movement of the damaged area will result in '**multiple fractures**' - in other words - many small breaks..."
16. "If the victim is conscious ... he or she will be able to tell you the **position** of any fractures"
17. "But, in the case of an unconscious victim, a different procedure should be followed. After checking...as described in **previous programmes**, the next step..."
18. "... in the case of an unconscious victim ... methodically feel each major bone in the body noting any **change in shape** that would indicate the presence of a break."

Paper 3 LISTENING | PART 3

You will hear five different people talking about jobs that they have done around the house. For questions 19-23, choose from the list A-H which job each speaker is describing. Use the letters only once. There are three extra letters which you do not need to use.

A	mending a leaking tap	Speaker 1	**F**	19
B	doing the washing	Speaker 2	**B**	20
C	cleaning the windows	Speaker 3	**A**	21
D	washing-up	Speaker 4	**C**	22
E	decorating	Speaker 5	**E**	23
F	ironing			
G	lighting a fire in the fireplace			
H	fixing the roof			

PART 3 JUSTIFICATION OF THE ANSWERS

19. The correct answer is **F**. "The fabric was too wet and I just couldn't get things to come out without creases..."
20. The correct answer is **B**. Clues include "...rather than send everything to the laundry..." and "hanging everything out afterwards."
21. The correct answer is **A**. "In the end, we did end up having to call a professional plumber out..."; plumbers fix leaking taps.

22. The correct answer is **C**. "You rub and rub until you think you've finished and then ten minutes later, when you go outside, you see a bit you've missed."
23. The correct answer is **E**. "...wallpapering is so much easier than it looks..."; wallpapering is included within decorating.

Paper 3 LISTENING | **PART 4**

You will hear a conversation which takes place in an open market between three people, Bob and Andrea Jones, and Bob's friend Carl. For questions 24-30, choose the best answer A, B or C.

24. When Bob spots his old colleague he
A. is thrilled to see him again.
B. does not want to talk to him.
C. is unsure about who he is.

25. How does Bob feel about Irish folk music?
A. He hates it.
B. He is indifferent towards it.
C. He doesn't mind it.

26. What does the stall sell?
A. different kinds of music
B. Irish folk music
C. country music

27. How did Carl think of starting the stall?
A. It was suggested to him.
B. He wanted to sell his collection.
C. He had always wanted to try it.

28. What happened to *Acres the Bakers*?
A. It was shut down.
B. It expanded its business.
C. It is under new ownership.

29. How did Bob spend most of his redundancy money?
A. on a car
B. on a holiday
C. he hasn't yet

30. When Andrea suggests that Bob sell his silverware he seems
A. reluctant.
B. enthusiastic.
C. surprised.

PART 4 - JUSTIFICATION OF THE ANSWERS

24. The correct answer is **B**. He says "Quick, pretend we haven't seen him." and therefore choice A is not a good answer. Choice C is incorrect because he says "...hang on...hey! That's Carl." He recognises him fairly quickly.

25. The correct answer is **A**. When Andrea mentions it he says "Oh, God." which indicates he dislikes even the thought of it and when Carl says "it didn't seem to sell too well" Bob replies "I'm not surprised".

26. The correct answer is **C**. Carl asks "Are you interested in country music?" and Andrea responds "Is that what all this is? All country music?" and Carl does not contradict her so we can assume her assumption is true.

27. The correct answer is **A**. "...then one day, I got talking to my claims officer...er...about my collection...and he suggested that I did

this..." Choice B is incorrect because although he was talking about his collection, no mention is made of him selling it or wanting to sell it.

28. The correct answer is **A**. "After 'Acres' closed down..." and "pays even less than 'Acres' did." Acres is referred to in the past tense, therefore it no longer exists.

29. The correct answer is **B**. "Oh, I spent my redundancy money on a holiday." and "Well, yeah, yeah, it didn't quite cover the car." In other words, he spent some of the money on the car, but most of it was already gone.

30. The correct answer is **A**. Bob says "Oh, er...I don't know about that. I'm not sure all that standing around in the cold would be good for my poor circulation." He does not really like the idea.

Test 8

Paper 1 Reading and Use of English   PART 1

For questions **1-8**, read the text below and decide which word **A, B, C** or **D** best fits each space. There is an example at the beginning **(0)**.

Example:

0.   A. expensive   B. affordable   C. costly   D. priceless

| 0 | A | B | C | D |

Bargain Rail Travel

Local rail travel is now much more **(0)**..........., thanks to the **(1)**.......... by Anglia Railways of the Anglia Plus range of tickets.

With an Anglia Plus ticket you can enjoy **(2)**.......... rail travel within Norfolk and Suffolk for an unbeatable price. In addition, Anglia Plus offers you free travel on buses from Ipswich station to the town centre or any **(3)**.......... within the town served directly by Ipswich Busses.

For days **(4)**.......... with the family, visiting friends or relatives, even for **(5)**.......... to work, Anglia Plus is just the ticket, providing you with the exceptional standard of Anglia service and comfort at a reduced cost. Its flexibility offers you all sorts of **(6)**.......... for discovering more of this **(7)**.......... region.

There are three types of Anglia Plus ticket available. The One Day Pass and the Three Day Pass are ideal for travelling around the region during your leisure time, whilst the Seven Day Pass is an excellent low-cost option for daily commuters which also **(8)**.......... you to travel on other routes after work or at weekends.

1.	A. beginning	B. introduction	C. encouragement	D. courage
2.	A. applicable	B. exterior	C. worthless	D. unlimited
3.	A. destination	B. information	C. application	D. situation
4.	A. outing	B. out	C. work	D. in
5.	A. communicating	B. commuting	C. consuming	D. conducting
6.	A. limits	B. needs	C. options	D. changes
7.	A. unsightly	B. ruined	C. terrifying	D. unspoiled
8.	A. allows	B. admits	C. lets	D. enjoys

Paper 1 Reading and Use of English   PART 2

For questions **9-16**, read the text below and think of the word which best fits each space. Use only **one** word in each space. There is an example at the beginning **(0)**.

Example: | 0 | best |

Revenge is sweet

I had suffered, as **(0)** .....*best*..... I could, the thousand wrongs that Henry had done to me, but when he began to become insulting I swore to avenge myself. I did not, of **(9)** ......*course*......, threaten him. I waited for my chance patiently. I wanted to avoid the risk of failure; and if **(10)** .....*one/punishment*..... is to succeed, two conditions are necessary. The wrong-doer must know that he is being punished, and by **(11)** ......*whom*......; and it must be impossible for him to hit back.

I continued to **(12)** ....*treat*........ Henry kindly and to smile at his face. He did **(13)** ....*not*.... realise that my smile was at the thought of how I would sacrifice him.

On the **(14)** ......*whole*......, Henry was a man to be respected and, if you were his enemy, even feared. Henry had only **(15)** ....*one*......... weakness - his love of wine. He was very proud **(16)** ....*of*........ his knowledge of the subject. In other respects, he merely pretended to be wise, but on the subject of wine he was sincere.

Paper 1   Reading and Use of English   PART 3

For questions 17-24, read the text below. Use the word given in capitals at the end of some lines to form a word that fits in the space in the same line. There is an example at the beginning (0).

Example: **0**   p r e d i c t i o n

An accurate (0) *prediction* of the weather used to (17)..........**primarily**........   PREDICT / PRIMARY

be a case of intelligent estimates that consistently turned out to be wrong. Now

the (18)..........**reputation**.......... of weather forecasters has improved and there   REPUTE

is a (19)............**tendency**........ for them to be taken more seriously.   TEND

(20)..........**Disturbances**............ in the weather caused by pollution and global   DISTURB

warming have worrying (21)...........**implications**..........., though. The weather has   IMPLICATE

become (22)..........**unpredictable**...... with cold days in summer and hot days in   PREDICT

winter. These (23)...........**variations**.......... in the temperature act as a   VARY

(24)..........**distraction**........ from other world problems such as war but this   DISTRACT

makes them no less of concern.

Paper 1   Reading and Use of English   PART 4

*For questions 25-30, complete the second sentence so that it has a similar meaning to the first sentence, using the word given. **Do not change the word given.** You must use between **two** and **five** words, including the word given. There is an example at the beginning (0).*

Example:

0   They think the owner of the house is in France.   thought

     The owner of the house .... in France.

*The gap can be filled by the words "**is thought to be**" so you write:*   **0**   is thought to be

25. "Don't park near the bank!" the policeman said to us.   not

     The policeman ....**told us not to park**.................... near the bank.

26. He tried really hard to recover from his wife's death.   over

     He tried really hard ....**to get over his**........................ wife's death.

27. We must make a decision now.   high

     It's ....**high time we made**........................ a decision.

28. They say the boss will be leaving the company soon.   said

     The boss ....**is said to be leaving**........................ the company soon.

29. There wasn't much we could do to help him.   little

     There ....**was little we could do**........................ to help him.

30. We ate everything except the salad.   eat

     The only thing ....**we didn't eat was**........................ the salad.

You are going to read a newspaper article about different approaches to education. For questions 31-36, choose the answer A, B, C or D which you think fits best according to the text.

Getting the best out of our children

There is a strange paradox to the success of the Asian education model. On the one hand, class sizes are huge by Western standards with between 30 and 40 students per class, on average, in countries like Japan and Korea. On the other hand, school children in developed Asian economies rank among the highest in the world for academic achievement in the areas of science and mathematics, especially on standardised tests. Meanwhile, British secondary school students fail to shine in conditions most educational researchers would say are far more likely to help them succeed.

Why do Asian students seem to perform so well then? Is it their legendary discipline? Certainly, classroom management seems to be a whole lot easier in places like Korea, and perhaps lessons are more effective as a direct consequence. After all, we are only too aware of the decline in discipline standards in our own schools; belligerent and disrespectful students appear to be the norm these days. Teachers in Britain seem powerless to control what happens anymore. Surely this situation cannot create a very effective learning environment, so perhaps the number of students is far less relevant than is the manner in which they conduct themselves.

But there are other factors to consider, too. Korean students spend a lot more time with their teachers. It seems logical to suggest, therefore, that they might form stronger bonds and greater trust, and that Korean teachers, in understanding their pupils better, might be able to offer them a more effective learning programme. Of course, trust and understanding leads to greater respect as well, so Korean students are probably less likely to ignore their teachers' advice.

Then there is the home environment. The traditional family unit still remains relatively intact in Korea. Few children come from broken homes, so there is a sense of security, safety and trust both at home and at school. In Britain meanwhile, one in every two marriages fails and divorce rates are sky high. Perhaps children struggle to cope with unstable family conditions and their only way to express their frustration is by misbehaving at school. Maybe all this delinquent behaviour we are complaining about is just a cry for help and a plea for attention.

But while the Japanese, Korean and Asian models generally do seem to produce excellent results, the statistics don't tell the whole truth. You see, behind those great maths and science scores, there is a quite remarkable work ethic. Asian students tend to put their education before literally everything else. They do very few extracurricular activities and devote far more time to their studies than their British peers. And this begs the question; is all that extra effort justified for a few extra percentage points in some meaningless international student performance survey? So Asian students are on average 3-5% better at maths than Britons – big deal! What is their quality of life like? Remember; school days are supposed to be the best, are they not?

There has been a lot of attention and praise given to these Asian models and their 'impressive' statistics of late. And without question, some of this praise is justified, but it seems to be a case of two extremes in operation here. At one end, there is the discipline and unbelievably hard work ethic of the Asian students – success in education before all else. At the other end, British students at times appear careless and extremely undisciplined by comparison, but at least they DO have the free time to enjoy their youth and explore their interests. Is either system better outright? Or is it perhaps about time we stopped comparing and started trying to combine the best bits of both, so that we can finally offer our students a balanced, worthwhile education? We are not just dealing with statistics; never forget that every statistic is a little human being somewhere who desperately needs our help and guidance – who deserves it.

31. What does the writer mean when he says there is a 'paradox'
    in the Asian education model?

    A. There are too many students in each class.

    B. You would expect larger classes to get poorer results but they do not.

    C. Class sizes are much smaller in other parts of the world.

    D. Asian students outperform their peers in other countries.

32. British secondary school students

    A. have larger class sizes.

    B. fail at school more than they succeed.

    C. do better on standardised tests.

    D. enjoy better classroom conditions.

33. What does the writer suggest might make lessons in Korean schools
    more successful than in Britain?

    A. better teachers

    B. better school Boards of Management

    C. more effective lesson planning

    D. better discipline

34. The traditional family unit

    A. is more common in Korea than in Britain.

    B. is disappearing in Korea due to high divorce rates.

    C. is bad for children that come from broken homes.

    D. is unstable in Korea due to conditions in the home.

35. According to the writer, Asian students

    A. focus too much on recreational activities.

    B. don't have as good a work ethic as British ones.

    C. don't allow themselves much time to relax and have fun.

    D. make a big deal of their good results.

36. Based on what you have read, what do you think is the writer's opinion
    of the two educational systems discussed?

    A. The Asian system is clearly better.

    B. The British system is too strict.

    C. Neither system is perfect.

    D. Both systems are quite satisfactory for different reasons.

31. The correct answer is **B**. A "paradox" involves two facts that contradict each other. Choice B is the only choice that has two such facts.

32. The correct answer is **D**. British students have "conditions most educational researchers would say are far more likely to help them succeed."

33. The correct answer is **D**. "classroom management seems to be a whole lot easier in places like Korea,...belligerent and disrespectful students appear to be the norm these days. Teachers in Britain seem powerless to control what happens anymore."

34. The correct answer is **A**. "The traditional family unit still remains relatively intact in Korea. Few children come from broken homes," while in Britain "one in every two marriages fails and divorce rates are sky high".

35. The correct answer is **C**. "Asian students tend to put their education before literally everything else. They do very few extracurricular activities and devote far more time to their studies than their British peers".

36. The correct answer is **C**. The author says "is it perhaps about time we stopped comparing and started trying to combine the best bits of both"; this implies that both could be improved.

You are going to read an extract from the journal of an ornithologist about the Lyrebird, a type of bird with unique vocal skills native to Australia and Tasmania. Six sentences have been removed from the article. Choose from the sentences A-G the one which fits each gap 37-42. There is one extra sentence which you do not need to use.

The Master Mimic

My first introduction to this unique and quite remarkable creature came by way of a BBC nature series narrated by the one and only David Attenborough. Sitting on my sofa, feet up, I switched on the television and was immediately dumbstruck by what I saw. A male Lyrebird had begun his mating ritual in what, to me, seemed a most extraordinary fashion. The sound of a chainsaw, trees falling, then a camera shutter – this medley of peculiar noises was but a brief illustration of the impressive vocal range of the Superb Lyrebird, one of two species of Lyrebird native to the rainforests of Australia and Tasmania.

An ornithologist by trade, I just couldn't resist the temptation to use my upcoming holidays to take the opportunity to see this incredible creature up close for myself. **37** **E** Having studied the indigenous birdlife of the British Isles for over twenty years, I could hardly contain my excitement at finally having the opportunity to examine some more exotic birds. I landed in Sydney at 8 a.m. local time, and, not wanting to waste a moment, jumped straight from the terminal into a waiting rental jeep and headed for the Illawarra region, south of Sydney.

I had enlisted the help of local wildlife expert, Mark Mathews, and once we'd set up camp in one of the few open areas of the forest and secured our belongings, Mark showed me some of his favourite spots for observing the Lyrebird. **38** **G**

No sooner had we got ourselves in position, hidden in the undergrowth on the forest floor, than an unsuspecting male appeared as if from nowhere. It was a Superb; this much I could tell, even from 25 yards away. The larger of the two species, the Superb male is close to one metre long. It also has the more spectacular plumage, making it instantly recognisable from the other species, the Albert's Lyrebird. **39** **D** But, though I hadn't sensed it yet, Mark, being the more experienced of the two of us, seemed to know we were in for something very special. And sure enough there followed a two-hour display quite the like of which I had never seen before (and may never again). First, he spread his feathers wide, revealing them in all their glory; then began the vocal performance. I ducked for cover, almost betraying our presence. Mark couldn't contain his amusement at my reaction and let out a quiet chuckle. But still we remained undetected. **40** **A**

Why had I risked giving us away? Well, as far as I could tell, we had just been shot at. Or, at least, by the sounds of it, rifle-shots seemed to be firing in all directions. **41** **B** And it finally dawned on me that we'd just witnessed act one of this remarkable creature's theatrical performance. And though I had seen and heard this before on the television, nothing could prepare me for the quite astonishing powers of mimicry this bird possessed, and which I was now observing firsthand.

Acts two and three didn't fail to impress either. And then, to top it all, there appeared a female, clearly as captivated by this extraordinary exhibition as we were, if not more. **42** **F** This was the single most important moment of my career so far – and it was still only day one!

A. This male had other things on his mind.

B. Mark whispered, still chuckling a little; "He fooled you with that one!"

C. The female must have sensed our presence, though, as she hastily departed the scene.

D. Indeed, the sight of his bright, colourful feathers alone would have been enough to make my long journey seem worthwhile.

E. So, a few days later, I was on a plane to Sydney for a two-week vacation that I was sure I would never forget.

F. I couldn't believe my good fortune; it is extremely rare to see Lyrebirds mating in the wild.

G. And I didn't have to wait long to catch my first glimpse.

37. The correct answer is **E**. The sentence before the gap mentions "upcoming holidays", choice E describes the writer on the way to Sidney, and, after the gap, the author describes the excitement of finally being there. So, choice E fits nicely in the sequence of the narration.

38. The correct answer is **G**. Choice G ties the paragraph which it completes to the first sentence of the next paragraph, which repeats the same idea while adding more detail. "No sooner" in the following sentence means immediately, which is certainly not long to wait.

39. The correct answer is **D**. The sentence before the gap mentions the Lyrebird's "spectacular plumage" which means amazing feathers. Choice D continues on the same topic - the bird's "bright, colourful feathers". The author says the feathers by themselves would have made the journey worthwhile, and the sentence after the gap indicates that, in spite of this, things were going to get even better.

40. The correct answer is **A**. A reason is given for why they remained undetected. The male Lyrebird was completely absorbed in his performance and so didn't notice them.

41. The correct answer is **B**. Here, Mark tells the author that the bird has fooled him with its song, which, as we learn after the gap, leads him to realise that what he was hearing was the bird and he was not actually being shot at.

42. The correct answer is **F**. It makes sense that witnessing something extremely rare would be a very important moment in the author's career which is what the following sentence confirms.

Paper 1 Reading and Use of English   PART 7

You are going to read weather reports for four different countries. For questions 43–52, choose the correct report A–D. The reports may be chosen more than once.

In which weather report is the following stated?

people going outside should wear extra clothes to stay warm	43	A
it would be wise to wear sunscreen if you spend a lot of time outdoors	44	C
nights will be cold due to lack of cloud cover	45	A
there may be a serious danger of water levels rising	46	B
there will be a very significant temperature drop	47	A
there is an increased risk of stormy weather at this time of year	48	D
there is a possibility of snow over high ground	49	D
the prospects for a certain type of winter activity look poor	50	B
different weather may be experienced inland and near the sea	51	B
record-high temperatures were experienced recently	52	C

Weather Reports

JAPAN A

We have come to the end of the monsoon season now and, indeed, winter is fast approaching. Right on cue, we can expect a band of Arctic air to sweep down over the country from Siberia. It's a little early in the season yet for snow, but expect the next few days to be **47** markedly colder than recent weeks. Daytime temperatures could fall by as much as 10 degrees, so do make sure you put on an extra **43** layer if you are going out. This will be especially important in the late evening as the clear skies will see night-time temperatures plummet below **45** freezing and we may experience our first frosts of the year, so care on the roads is also advised. Towards the latter half of the week, however, a warm front will encroach from the south, so southerly regions can expect increased levels of precipitation towards the weekend. The warmer air will nudge its way slowly upwards and begin to dominate weather patterns, so we are likely to see a return to milder weather for the whole country by the end of the week.

CANADA B

50 The signs are not good for the winter sports industry, which took a battering last season. It will continue wet and windy, but temperatures will remain at or above normal, so there is little chance of an early dusting of snow on the mountains. Unfortunately, all our long-range forecasts seem to suggest a mild winter, so there is not much cause for optimism, it would seem. Getting back to the week ahead, we will have a break from the rain midweek when high pressure moves in from the west. By Thursday, most of central Canada will be **51** dry, though the coastal regions can still expect to experience some light showers from time to time. Newfoundland will be the exception; as the depression holds on here, so islanders can expect to see a continuation of the miserable wet weather they've had up to now. In **46** fact, a flood warning is in place as the rain is expected to be heavy and persistent and there is a high risk of the already swollen rivers breaking their banks.

SCOTLAND C

The British Isles are having an unusually good spell of weather at the moment, and there doesn't seem to be any sign that you should pack away those swimming trunks yet. In fact, our weather model for the next ten days shows continued fine weather. It would be too much to ask for the temperatures to remain at their record highs; however, it will stay **52** dry and calm, and unseasonably mild. Top daytime temperatures will reach about twenty-one degrees and the temperature won't fall any lower than fourteen or fifteen at night. Of course, we'd like to remind everyone that the UV Index is still quite high, so please ensure that you apply protection to your skin if you are going to go outside during the **44** day for any significant length of time.

AUSTRALIA D

Spring is finally upon us in the Southern Hemisphere and we can look forward to some good weather towards the start of the week. However, remember that with the warmer **48** temperatures comes an increased risk of tropical storms and we are heading into the typhoon season. There are signs that a depression lying to the south of Melbourne could intensify and develop into something more sinister towards the end of the week. We are therefore monitoring the situation carefully, but no weather warnings are being issued for the moment. It is clear, however, that the fine weather will be interrupted midweek by a band of heavy rain sweeping over the country from the south. This **49** could fall as snow over the mountains and prolong the bumper season for you lucky winter sports enthusiasts out there – you've really been spoilt this year!

Writing

Paper 2 WRITING   PART 1

*You **must** answer this question. Write your answer in **140-190** words in an appropriate style.*

1. In your education class, you have listened to a lecture on the importance of teaching foreign languages in school. Your teacher has asked you to write an essay.

   Write an **essay** using **all** the notes and give reasons for your point of view.

> Learning a foreign language helps students develop a set of important skills. Why should foreign languages be taught in schools?
>
> **Notes**
>
> Write about:
> 1. new cultures
> 2. employment
> 3. .... (your own idea)

Paper 2 WRITING   PART 2

*Write an answer to **one** of the questions 2-4 in this part. Write your answer in **140-190** words in an appropriate style.*

2. You are looking through a job database online and see a position you are interested in for managing a local tutoring service.

   > Person needed to manage a group of tutors. Have skills in administration and education as well as possess excellent communication abilities. Please e-mail a letter of interest and your CV to manager@tutoringpros.co.uk. Describe in your cover letter why you are interested in the position and any relevant experience and skills you possess.

Write your **letter**.

3. The local council is opening a new community centre for youths. Basketball, music lessons and cookery have all been suggested as possible activities for the centre. Mr. Jones, who is a member of the council, has asked you to talk to your friends and then write a **report** to the council about how popular each activity would be and then make a recommendation about which activities should be offered.

Write your **report**.

4. You saw this notice in a travel magazine:

   > ### Reviews wanted
   >
   > Have you stayed in a good or bad hotel?
   > Now is your chance to write about it.
   > We are looking for reviews of hotels anywhere in the world.
   > We will publish the most interesting reviews.

Describe the hotel and say why you did or didn't enjoy your stay.

Write your **review**.

Listening

Paper 3 LISTENING | PART 1

You will hear people talking in eight different situations. For questions 1-8, choose the best answer, A, B or C.

1. You switch on the radio and hear this exchange in progress.
   What are you listening to?
   A. a phone-in programme
   B. a talent contest
   C. a general knowledge quiz

2. You overhear this man talking about a restaurant.
   In his opinion, the restaurant
   A. has improved.
   B. isn't as good as it used to be.
   C. is too expensive.

3. Listen to a woman interviewing a man on a TV chat show.
   What is the man?
   A. a famous criminal
   B. a detective
   C. a crime writer

4. You are travelling by train when you overhear this exchange.
   The woman
   A. has never met the man before.
   B. is a good friend of the man.
   C. is a distant relative.

5. Listen to this teacher giving a lesson.
   What is the teacher's subject?
   A. politics
   B. literature
   C. geography

6. You hear this announcement being made in a railway station.
   The 7:15 train to London
   A. has been cancelled.
   B. will leave from a different platform.
   C. has been delayed.

7. You overhear this man answering a telephone in a record shop.
   The man is
   A. polite.
   B. impatient.
   C. bored.

8. You are staying in the home of a British family when you hear this exchange between the husband and wife.
   What does the wife want her husband to do?
   A. make less noise at night
   B. complain to the neighbours
   C. fit new windows in another room

PART 1 - JUSTIFICATION OF THE ANSWERS

1. The correct answer is **C**. "...I can't give you a point for that..." Points are given on quiz shows. Choice A is incorrect because no mention is made of phoning in. Choice B is incorrect because knowledge is being demonstrated, not talent.

2. The correct answer is **B**. "It really isn't the same any more...you do have to wait longer for everything and there isn't the same selection as before - especially the desserts..." and therefore A is incorrect. Choice C is incorrect because "it's still good value".

3. The correct answer is **A**. "life on the outside" and "the day I got out" indicate he was in jail, so he must be a criminal and he calls himself "a celebrity" so he is famous for some reason. Choice B is incorrect because no mention is made of a detective, only a "...detective writer", which means the same thing as crime writer; and Sam Beesly is the "...detective writer".

4. The correct answer is **A**. "So, how did you know that I was his daughter?" indicates they have never met, otherwise it would not be surprising if he knew who she was. Choices B and C are incorrect because actually the man was the woman's father's "arithmetic and geometry" teacher.

5. The correct answer is **C**. "If you open your books to page 62, you will see two contrasting maps of the region." Geography includes the study of maps, demography and land usage.

6. The correct answer is **C**. "This service is now running about 7 minutes late and will now depart at 7:22..." Choice B is incorrect because the train "...will now depart at 7:22 from platform 3 as advertised"; 'as advertised' means there is no change of platform.

7. The correct answer is **B**. "Yes, I know it was advertised on television but the distributor...Well, I'm sorry, too"; The caller clearly wants the disc right now. Choice A is incorrect because although the speaker is trying to be polite, the response of "Well, you'll just have to do that, won't you?" indicates that the caller probably said something that was not very polite.

8. The correct answer is **B**. "Well, if you don't go round there and talk to them, ...I will." Choice A is incorrect because it is the students next door making noise, not the husband. Choice C is incorrect because she wants him to "...go straight to the source of the trouble" [in other words, confront the problem directly].

Practice Test 8

You will hear part of a scientific television programme for young people in which the speaker explains what 'meteors' are. For questions 9-18, complete the sentences with a word or short phrase.

'Meteors' is another name for **9** **shooting stars** .

To help explain meteors, planet Earth is compared to a **10** **car** .

You can think of meteors as a group of **11** **insects** .

In reality, meteors are very small chunks of **12** **iron** .

The circular path the Earth travels around the Sun is called its **13** **orbit** .

When Earth comes close to a meteor, the meteor is pulled **14** **downwards** by gravity.

A meteor travels very fast - a hundred times faster than **15** **a jet plane** .

Due to the speed it travels through the air, the meteor becomes **16** **hotter and hotter** .

Because of the heat, the meteor becomes less hard, **17** **melts** and then burns.

We are lucky that most meteors burn up and never **18** **reach the ground** .

PART 2 JUSTIFICATION OF THE ANSWERS

9. "...a shower of meteors or **shooting stars**."
10. "To imagine what is happening, it helps us to imagine a car driving fast along the road. In a way, our planet Earth is like that **car**."
11. "In many ways, the meteors are similar to the swarm of **insects**..."
12. "In fact, meteors are mostly tiny pieces of **iron** that look like little stones."
13. "...the Earth...does follow the same circular route around the sun once every year. This enormous circular path is called the Earth's '**orbit**'."
14. "...when the earth approaches one of these stones, it is **pulled downwards** towards our planet by a strong force called gravity."
15. "This is about a hundred times faster than **a jet plane**."
16. "Now, because it is going through the air so fast, the shooting star starts to become **hotter and hotter**..."
17. "...the outside of this piece of iron gets very hot indeed and as a result, it gets soft and **melts** and then starts to burn."
18. "...fortunately for us, most meteors are so small that they have completely burned up, long before they could ever **reach the ground**..."

You will hear five different people talking about journeys they have made. For questions 19-23, choose from the list A-H the correct word or phrase that describes how each person completed their journey. Use the letters only once. There are three extra letters which you do not need to use.

A	by plane	**Speaker 1**	**G** 19
B	by train	**Speaker 2**	**B** 20
C	as the driver of a car	**Speaker 3**	**E** 21
D	by bus	**Speaker 4**	**F** 22
E	on foot	**Speaker 5**	**A** 23
F	on a bicycle		
G	as a passenger in a car		
H	by taxi		

PART 3 JUSTIFICATION OF THE ANSWERS

19. The correct answer is **G**. "... and Sally braked..." so Sally was the driver of the car, not the speaker.
20. The correct answer is **B**. "...going from carriage to carriage ..." Carriages are unique to trains.
21. The correct answer is **E**. "... in the end, I had no choice but to set off on a four-mile march ..." To 'march' means to walk somewhere quickly, in a determined way, so the speaker went on foot.
22. The correct answer is **F**. "... the chain had come off..." Bicycles have chains.
23. The correct answer is **A**. "We'd taxied to the end of the runway ...". A runway is where a plane takes off and lands.

Paper 3 LISTENING | PART 4

You will hear a scene from a radio soap opera called Willowdale Green, in which a couple, Charles Miller and Daphne Jameson, are speaking with the barman Bill Dexter in a village pub. For questions 24-30, choose the best answer A, B or C.

24. The man working at the bar presumes that Charles and Daphne
    A. are locals.
    B. are married.
    C. live at Draycott farm.

25. How well did Charles know Andy Draycott?
    A. He never met him.
    B. They were close relatives.
    C. He didn't know him well.

26. What happened to the previous owner of the farm?
    A. He died.
    B. He sold it.
    C. He left.

27. Bill says the couple should not have the farm because
    A. they are not from Willowdale.
    B. the owner committed suicide.
    C. they are not frank.

28. What have people been saying, according to Bill?
    A. Charles and Daphne are bad people.
    B. The farm will not be maintained as a farm going forward.
    C. Charles and Daphne did not inherit the farm.

29. What motivated Charles and Daphne to move to the country?
    A. a healthier life
    B. Charles' work
    C. the local services

30. How does Bill's attitude change at the end of the conversation?
    A. He becomes suspicious.
    B. He regrets his previous attitude.
    C. He becomes more positive.

PART 4 JUSTIFICATION OF THE ANSWERS

24. The correct answer is **B**. After Charles introduces himself, the bartender says: "What can I get you then, Mrs Miller?" Choices A and C are incorrect because: "The farm - I know very well ... but you, I don't." He knows they are not locals and he is surprised to hear they live at Draycott farm.

25. The correct answer is **C**. Charles says "Of course, I did actually meet the poor man once - worked there on summer picking strawberries."

26. The correct answer is **A**. "About the suicide you mean? Yes. What a terrible tragedy". The owner killed himself.

27. The correct answer is **A**. "...and he would have wanted the farm to go to someone from Willowdale...which you are not." While choice B is true, this is not the reason that Bill thinks they shouldn't have the farm. Choice C is incorrect because Bill says that he is being frank, which means that he is stating things in an open and honest way.

28. The correct answer is **B**. Charles says "...that Draycott farm won't be a farm any more and ..." and Bill replies "...That is what people have been saying". Choice C is incorrect because, although Bill says " ... and he would have wanted the

farm to go to someone from Willowdale ... which you are not." this only means he does not think the farm was taken over by the right people, NOT that Charles and Daphne didn't actually take it over. Clearly, they did. They have a "fancy estate agent", after all.

29. The correct answer is **A**. "So we wanted to get away from the city and make a healthier life." Choice B is not correct because Charles' work is flexible; he can work wherever he is so it's not a reason they needed to move to the country. Choice C is incorrect because they have "...every intention of using the shops and the local services." In other words, since they live there, they will support the local community but this does not mean they moved there for the purpose of doing so.

30. The correct answer is **C**. After he hears about the high salary, Bill says "Well, that is rather generous" which, is the first positive thing he has said. Choice A is incorrect because he expresses suspicion from the start and choice B is incorrect because, although he changes his attitude, he does not indicate that he is sorry for his previous negativity.

Test 9

Paper 1 Reading and Use of English   PART 1

For questions **1-8**, read the text below and decide which word A, B, C or D best fits each space. There is an example at the beginning (0).

Example:

0.   A. hostel   B. whole   C. association   D. city

[0] [A] [B] [**C**] [D]

Oxford University

Oxford University is a(n) (0)........... of over 35 colleges, varying in (1)............ of foundation from medieval to more recent times. The colleges also vary in wealth, in character and in architecture.

Some (2).......... imposing buildings and grounds, (3).......... are almost intimate in their scale. Most colleges can boast well-known former students - Oxford is the place where (4).......... as diverse as Margaret Thatcher, Mrs Gandhi, Michael Palin and Evelyn Waugh were educated.

Most visitors will want to see a college and one or more of the University buildings, such as the Bodleian Library or the Ashmolean Museum.

The University has supported the (5).......... of The Oxford Story Exhibition, in Broad Street - now recognised as the best short (6).......... to Oxford University. Here, during an entertaining ride through recreated (7).......... and events, Magnus Magnusson offers an informed view of Oxford's past and present. Special materials for children and foreign (8).............. commentaries are also available.

1.	A. place	B. date	C. manner	D. form
2.	A. live	B. reside	C. exist	D. occupy
3.	A. rest	B. else	C. those	D. others
4.	A. characters	B. cartoons	C. caricatures	D. participants
5.	A. discovery	B. creation	C. expectation	D. education
6.	A. history	B. beginning	C. introduction	D. past
7.	A. postcards	B. maps	C. paintings	D. scenes
8.	A. custom	B. currency	C. phrase	D. language

Paper 1 Reading and Use of English   PART 2

For questions **9-16**, read the text below and think of the word which best fits each space. Use only **one** word in each space. There is an example at the beginning (0).

Example: [0] [for]

"Hidden Dangers"

You are always ready (0) ....*for*....... danger, but you don't think of (9) ....**it**........ very much. The real dangers are (10) ....**not**.............. from living things. They are the small, quiet things - a knot in the air-line, a cut safety-rope. Taylor knew this (11) ....**part/area**.......... of the sea bed well: it was grey and flat and familiar. But today, for the first time, it held a surprise. Taylor stopped when he saw the new shape.

At first he (12) ....**thought**.......... it was an aircraft. But it was the wrong shape, and it was too small; only seven metres long and three metres wide. Here and (13) ....**there**........... were round doors. The metal body seemed to be undamaged. But one end was black, perhaps (14) ....**as**.......... a result of strong heat. From the other (15) ....**end**.............. grew a small forest of metal posts. Almost all of them were broken or pushed flat, perhaps when it hit the water. Now they (16) ....**looked/were**...... like the legs of a great insect.

Paper 1 Reading and Use of English PART 3

For questions 17-24, read the text below. Use the word given in capitals at the end of some lines to form a word that fits in the space in the same line. There is an example at the beginning (0).

Example: **0**   e f f e c t i v e

Most people don't make (0)......*effective*...... use of their local pharmacy and go	**EFFECT**
straight to their doctor for (17)......**treatment**...... as soon as they get any	**TREAT**
kind of (18)......**illness**...... . You should trust your pharmacist though	**ILL**
and not be (19)......**suspicious**...... of his or her abilities. Pharmacists can	**SUSPECT**
help with many problems from (20)......**inflammation(s)**...... of various parts of	**INFLAME**
the body to swollen ankles. Some people would prefer to leave these problems	
(21)......**untreated**...... but depending on the (22)......**severity**...... of	**TREAT / SEVERE**
the condition a quick visit to the pharmacy is usually the only (23)......**assistance**......	**ASSIST**
that you'll need and it will cause the minimum (24)......**disruption**...... to	**DISRUPT**
your day.	

Paper 1 Reading and Use of English PART 4

*For questions 25-30, complete the second sentence so that it has a similar meaning to the first sentence, using the word given. **Do not change the word given.** You must use between **two** and **five** words, including the word given. There is an example at the beginning (0).*

Example:

0 They think the owner of the house is in France.   thought

   The owner of the house .... in France.

*The gap can be filled by the words "**is thought to be**" so you write:*   **0**   i s   t h o u g h t   t o   b e

25. I haven't written to Bob since he left for Canada.   last

    The ......**last time I wrote to**...... Bob was before he left for Canada.

26. The doctors told her to reduce the amount of fat she eats.   down

    She was told by the doctors ......**to cut down on**...... the amount of fat she eats.

27. Michael is not usually rude.   like

    It is ......**not like Michael to be**...... rude.

28. You can play football, but you must do your homework first.   long

    You can play football ......**as/so long as you do**...... your homework first.

29. My brother is as old as Sam's.   same

    Sam's brother ......**is the same age as**...... mine.

30. It is possible that the teachers didn't see you cheating on the test.   may

    The teachers ......**may not have seen you**...... cheating on the test.

*You are going to read an article reviewing the website RealAge. For questions **31-36**, choose the answer **A, B, C** or **D** which you think fits best according to the text.*

RealAge, Inc. is an American media corporation that provides health information to consumers, primarily through a website also called RealAge. The company's stated mission is to encourage consumers to maximize their health and wellness by making their RealAge younger.

The basic concept of RealAge is that a person's true biological age is not the same as his or her chronological age. In other words, you may be 35 years old but your body may work like a 25-year-old's or a 50-year-old's depending on a number of factors. The heart of RealAge is a website offering a test that asks 132 questions about family history and lifestyle to determine a person's RealAge by adjusting their current age based on how they answer the questions. In the RealAge test, for example, smoking increases your age by 8 years, but taking an aspirin every day will make you 2.2-2.9 years younger.

RealAge has undeniably been profitable for its founder, Dr. Michael Roizen. It was sold for an estimated $60-$70 million in 2007, and as of 2009, was still reporting a profit. In spite of the sale, RealAge.com serves as the official online home for both Dr. Michael Roizen and Mehmet Oz, MD., co-authors of the best-selling *YOU* book series. Indeed, the RealAge website has fuelled five New York Times number 1 best-selling books, including *RealAge: Are You as Young as You Can Be?*, which has been promoted by Oprah Winfrey. The test has been taken by more than 27 million people since 1999.

RealAge is clearly a very popular website, but is the RealAge it generates real? That is less clear. Longevity science is challenging. The RealAge test is based on life expectancy research; Michael Roizen claims that he has pored over more than 33,000 medical studies, but that claim is rather hard to believe. If he spent one hour per medical study for 8 hours a day, it would take him over 11 years to finish. And even if he had, researchers cannot do studies to prove that John Doe would

have lived 8 years longer if he quit smoking. Either he quit or he didn't. We don't have two John Does to compare. Researchers must rely on statistics like averages to determine the impact of lifestyle behaviours, which gets very complicated. In short, we can't really know the impact of all the lifestyle factors in the level of detail presented in RealAge. Each lifestyle factor interacts with other factors in a complex way. RealAge does try to address this, adjusting some of the factors for age (for example aspirin reduces age by 2.2 years at 55 and 2.9 years at 70). The bottom line, however, is that we cannot know our RealAge with the precision suggested by the test.

On top of this, RealAge, unfortunately, is not transparent about how it uses information from the tests. Users' health histories, which they provide while taking the test, are used by the website to generate personalized content, including health tips, but also including highly targeted advertisements and marketing messages which are sent to members by e-mail. As a result, the website generates a great deal of revenue from pharmaceutical companies paying to advertise their drugs to individuals who have taken the test and become members. This is not specified to those who become members, and critics say that this amounts to a clever way of skirting the strict regulation of pharmaceutical advertising.

So is it a moneymaking scam, or does it offer something worthwhile? The test can be a fun way for people to learn about the benefits and dangers of various lifestyle choices, and by linking behaviours to increasing or decreasing age, the approach lets people compare different lifestyle factors and prioritise their effort. If they adopt some of the lifestyle suggestions, they will probably be healthier and better off for it. They just need to watch out for advertising, be careful about what boxes they check if they don't want to receive e-mails, and certainly talk to a doctor before taking any sort of pills or supplements the site might recommend.

31. A person's RealAge is determined by

A. various unknown factors.

B. lifestyle choices.

C. family history and lifestyle.

D. current age.

32. We may conclude, from the information in paragraph 3, that

A. RealAge is a media scam.

B. RealAge is becoming more and more profitable.

C. RealAge is a passing trend.

D. people are interested in RealAge.

33. RealAge addresses the complexity of interacting factors by

A. going into great detail.

B. using statistics.

C. clearly stating its limitations.

D. adjusting some factors for age.

34. In paragraph 6, the author implies that

A. the website does not fully inform its users.

B. the website has hidden costs.

C. although the website profits from users, they are warned.

D. the website is run by pharmaceutical companies.

35. Users of the website are likely to receive

A. random health tips.

B. advertisements for treatments for their health problems.

C. more attention from medical professionals.

D. information about the latest pharmaceutical products.

36. Overall, the author's opinion of RealAge is

A. completely negative.

B. very sceptical.

C. somewhat positive.

D. approving.

31. The correct answer is **C**. "...questions about family history and lifestyle to determine a person's RealAge".

32. The correct answer is **D**. If people are buying the books, and taking the test, and it has even been on Oprah's show, then people must be interested. A is not correct, because in this paragraph no value judgement is made. B is incorrect because while we know about current profits, no mention is made of past or future profits. C is not correct because the future is not mentioned at all; we don't know how things will develop nor is it speculated about.

33. The correct answer is **D**. "Each lifestyle factor interacts with other factors in a complex way. RealAge does try to address this, adjusting some of the factors for age..."

34. The correct answer is **A**. "RealAge, unfortunately, is not transparent about how it uses information..." and "This is not specified to those who become members..." "Transparent" means clear, open, and easily understood, and "specified" means explained.

35. The correct answer is **B**. "Users' health histories, which they provide while taking the test, are used by the website to generate personalized content, including health tips, but also including highly targeted advertisements." "Personalized" and "highly targeted" are key words here that mean something is individualized to cater to the needs or tastes of a particular person. This eliminates A because the tips contain 'personalized content' and are therefore not random. D is wrong because the website does not provide 'information' about products but rather advertises them.

36. The correct answer is **C**. Overall, the review would not be regarded as very positive (ruling out D). That said, the writer has some positive comments to make in the final paragraph (ruling out A) and, although he expresses his doubts or scepticism about the test in said paragraph, his criticism isn't very strong and he doesn't emphasise these doubts. Therefore, while he may be slightly sceptical or doubting, he is not very much so (ruling out B). If anything, he is 'somewhat positive', ceding that 'the test can be...fun' and that people who use it 'will probably be healthier and better off for it'. This is not a comment filled with lots of doubt; indeed, it is fairly committal, bordering on a mild endorsement, and is followed not by warnings but a caveat to simply take the usual and obvious precautions as with any service of this kind.

Paper 1 Reading and Use of English   **PART 6**

You are going to read a magazine article about the causes and implications of an ageing population, using Australia as an example. Six sentences have been removed from the article. Choose from the sentences A-G the one which fits each gap 37-42. There is one extra sentence which you do not need to use.

Ageing Populations

In the past Australia was a relatively youthful country. In 1970, 31 percent of the population was aged 15 years or younger, while by 2002 this proportion had dropped to 22 percent. Likewise, the proportion of Australia's population aged over 65 years grew from 8 percent in 1970 to 14 percent in 2012. It is expected that by 2040, the proportion of the population over 65 years will have almost doubled by around 25 percent. At the same time, growth in the population percentage falling within the traditional workforce age parameters of 18 to 65 years is expected to slow to almost zero. The population is ageing rapidly.

This is not an incidental pattern unique to a particular time and place. **37** **C** Barring an unprecedented change in fertility rates, the age structure of the population is likely to stabilise with a far higher proportion of older Australians. This phenomenon is not unique to Australia either. In fact, birth rates have been falling in a similar manner in all the advanced industrialised countries.

Ageing populations are caused by two factors. Firstly, families are having fewer children. **38** **B** Low birth rates largely reflect the increased choices available to women, including access to birth control, access to education and employment and higher living standards. For the last 20 years or so the birth rate has fallen below the replacement rate in Australia — meaning that without migration, the population would eventually begin to fall. The second factor contributing to ageing populations is that people are living longer. For example, in 1960 life expectancy at birth for Australian males was around 68 years. **39** **A** Similar increases have occurred for females. With fewer babies being born, and more people living longer, it is inevitable that the population will get progressively older.

These changes are definitely a cause for concern. The decisions that are made today will affect future generations. Societies will, unavoidably, look quite different to how they do today. To stay with the Australian example, the number of people aged 65 and over, which was around 3.2 million in 2012, is projected to increase to 6.2 million by 2042; that is, from around 14 percent of the population to around 28 per cent. At the same time, growth in the number of people of workforce age is expected to fall from the 1.2 percent per year that has occurred over the last decade to almost zero in the same amount of time. In 2012 there were more than five Australians of working age to support every person aged over 65. **40** **F** Who will pay the increasing cost of the ageing population's healthcare, among other things?

Governments have several options about what to do about this problem. They could elect to do nothing now, and raise taxes in the future to cover budget deficits as they occur. Some argue in favour of this position, noting that in 40 years average incomes will be substantially higher than they are today due to continuing economic growth. However, we are not talking about a minor tax increase. For this method to work, an increase in personal income tax collections of over 40 percent would be required. **41** **G** But again, the dimensions of such spending cuts are enormous. For example, the sorts of expenditure cuts required in Australia could include the entire amount now allocated to health, or over half the social security and welfare budget. Clearly neither of these options could ever seriously be contemplated. **42** **E** But this is not a sustainable or responsible solution, as it merely passes the problem on to our children's children. Interest payments on debt would grow at an ever-increasing rate, reducing the money available to pay for pensions and health care. It is not a solution that any responsible person would be prepared to contemplate.

A. Today it is 79 years, and in 2042 it is projected to be around 83 years.

B. Birth rates started declining in the late 1960s, and have been falling ever since.

C. It is undoubtedly a permanent change.

D. Yet, it is not the role of governments to tell citizens how many children they should have.

E. Instead of cutting spending, governments could run deficits and hence increase debt.

F. By 2042, there will only be 2.5.

G. An alternative approach would be to cut future government expenditure.

37. The correct answer is **C**. The topic sentence of this paragraph states that the pattern is not only present in this time and place. Later in the paragraph, place is discussed, so this gap must concern time. Something that is permanent does not change with time, making C an appropriate choice.

38. The correct answer is **B**. The gap is surrounded by the topic of *fewer children and lower birth rates*, so it follows that the correct choice would share this topic. Choice D might also be considered, but while it sort of fits, the topic of the paragraph is that lower birth rates are one factor that causes an ageing population, so the goal is to point out that lower birth rates do indeed exist. There is no mention anywhere in the paragraph of the government's level of influence on birth rate, so D does not support the paragraph's aims.

39. The correct answer is **A**. The second gap in this paragraph deals with the second factor - people living longer. Life expectancy at a past time is mentioned before the gap, and after the gap "similar increases" in life expectancy are mentioned, so we would expect the gap to provide us with proof of an increase in life expectancy. Choice A does just this, with "it" refering to life expectancy today and in the future. It makes sense for "it" to refer to life expectancy, because "it" is measured in years.

40. The correct answer is **F**. The topic of the paragraph is *changes causing concern*. Before the gap we are given a statistic in the past, in the form of a ratio. We would expect the gap to provide us with a worrying example of how this ratio is changing - from 5 to 1, decreasing to 2.5 to 1 - as choice F does. Other choices that show changes do not express them in a way that fits this ratio.

41. The correct answer is **G**. The paragraph where the next two gaps are located discusses what might be done about the problem, and a number of options are given. The first gap is sandwiched between a sentence about huge tax increases, and enormous spending cuts, so we would expect the correct choice to transition between the two ideas, which choice G does using "An alternative approach...". Choice E has a similar role, but instead prantices between spending cuts and a deficit, which is required for gap 42.

42. The correct answer is **E** which uses "instead" to provide a transition between impossible budget cuts, before the gap, and irresponsible dept, after.

Paper 1 Reading and Use of English   PART 7

You are going to read part of a blog on the internet, where four people have sent in accounts of their earliest childhood memories. For questions 43–52, choose from the people A–D. The people may be chosen more than once.

Which person:

has a memory that involved not having something in their room?	43	B
had their age at the time of the memory verified by someone?	44	A
has an upsetting early memory?	45	D
had the earliest first memory?	46	C
surprised a relative with their memory?	47	A
remembers a parent working?	48	B
does not have clear and detailed early memories?	49	D
recognised something years later?	50	C
remembers a positive feeling?	51	B
remembers one season more than others?	52	D

Practice Test 9

Memories of our childhood

Michael Richardson A

My earliest memory is of being held on some-one's lap on a porch swing in front of my great grandmother's farm house. I was describing the memory once to my mother and I gave her a walkthrough of the house, the layout of the rooms and the memory of two bench swings facing each other on each side of the front door on the porch. My mum got kind of quiet **47** and then called my grandmother to verify a **44** date and told me that I was describing a house that was sold when I was 18 months old. I still have never seen a picture of the front of the house to verify for myself but I'll take my grandmother's word for it.

Mary O'Malley B

The first thing I recall must have happened right after my family moved to our second flat. I was somewhere between 18 months and 2 years old and had just gotten my first "grown-up bed" which I kept falling out of. Since we didn't have one of those side-rails **43** so prevalent today, mom got creative and put the vinyl high back chairs around my bed like a fort. I woke up one morning to find myself slowly falling from the bed - the chairs push-ing out away from me in slow-motion. I thought this was great fun to fall out of bed **51** so slowly! I remember crawling (because I was sleepy and being silly not because I couldn't walk) to find mom in her bright sunny room, working at her desk on some **48** bills.

Martin Green C

The earliest thing I can remember is sitting in **46** my crib, in a house we moved out of when I was about nine months old, and leaning to try to see my mother in the kitchen, right across from my door. That is the only clear memory I have from that house, but I have many from the one we lived in for the following year. Once when I was in my twenties I walked into a pub-lic place with my mother and stopped and said, **50** "We used to have this tile in our kitchen." She looked at it for a minute, then looked at me as if she was expecting it and said, "We moved out of that house before you were two." I guess you get to know the floor pretty well when you're only two feet tall!

Ann Clark D

I know a lot of people have clear memories of their early childhood. I don't. Instead they **49** are flashes of events over a period of time. Some of the events were major and some were minor. Despite my dislike for the sun **52** they are all sun-drenched - I don't have many memories of winter in my early years, and I'm not sure why that is. The first big memo-ry I have does have a date attached: Christmas Day when I was six. We weren't able to make our annual trip to the coast that year because of financial restraints, so we were watching the news on the TV. What I **45** saw was horrible. A child standing by a destroyed house, clutching a doll, with tan-gled tinsel all around her. The night before Cyclone Tracy had destroyed 70 percent of a nearby town. I also remember the red cross vans going up our street getting donations, and the town hall where the donations were being collected. It seemed like the goods were piled to the roof.

Writing

Paper 2 WRITING　PART 1

*You **must** answer this question. Write your answer in **140-190** words in an appropriate style.*

1. In your social studies course, you have watched a documentary on the potential effects of too much pollution on the air quality of city centres. Your professor has assigned you an essay to write.

   Write an **essay** using **all** the notes and give reasons for your point of view.

> Keeping the air quality in city centres at healthy levels for their residents is a concern for many places. How can we solve the problem of pollution in city centres?
>
> **Notes**
>
> Write about:
> 1. automobiles
> 2. factories
> 3. .... (your own idea)

Paper 2 WRITING　PART 2

*Write an answer to **one** of the questions **2-4** in this part. Write your answer in **140-190** words in an appropriate style.*

2. Your favourite fashion magazine has advertised a contest for readers to write an **article** about someone who they admire.

   > ### Modern-day Fashion Icons
   >
   > Whose style do you most admire?
   > What is unique about them?
   > How do you think they have changed fashion?
   >
   > Write an article answering the following questions, and you might win a £2,000 shopping spree!

Write your **article**.

3. You are a member of a music club. Each month, the club publishes a newsletter with reviews of new albums that have been released. Write a **review** of an album you have listened to recently, commenting on the style of music, its good and bad points and whether or not you would recommend it to others.

Write your **review**.

4. You have just come back from seeing a wonderful play on Broadway in New York City with a classmate, and want to tell your sibling about it so that they go see the work before it leaves to tour around the world. Tell your parents in a **letter** about the play including the characters, story, direction, stage props and audience reaction, among other facets. Mention anything you would have changed or done differently, if applicable.

Write your **letter**.

Practice Test 9

Listening

Paper 3 LISTENING   PART 1

*You will hear people talking in eight different situations. For questions **1-8**, choose the best answer, **A, B** or **C**.*

1. You are at a public celebration when you hear this announcement.
   Why does the speaker want the car moved?
   A. it is parked inconveniently
   B. it is parked illegally
   C. somebody has complained

2. You have taken your camera to a shop where the assistant explains why it is not working.
   What does he tell you?
   A. the battery was too old
   B. the battery was incorrectly fitted
   C. the film was incorrectly fitted

3. You switch on the radio to find a phone-in programme in progress.
   What is the caller asking the expert about?
   A. gardening
   B. cheese making
   C. travel

4. You are in the lounge of an expensive hotel when you hear this exchange.
   What does the woman want the man to do?
   A. not take a photograph
   B. stop smoking
   C. not bring his dog in the building

5. You are in the office of a major trading company when you hear this woman talking on the phone.
   What time does she arrange to meet Peter?
   A. 3:45
   B. 4:15
   C. 4:45

6. Listen to this woman speaking on a TV travel programme.
   The company
   A. had too many clients.
   B. was the sole cause of a problem.
   C. was forced to pay out money.

7. You overhear this man talking in a fast food restaurant.
   What is he talking about?
   A. his pet cat
   B. his daughter
   C. his pet parrot

8. You telephone a number in order to hear a freephone message about a new product.
   The Brain-Booster is claimed to
   A. make the user's brain bigger.
   B. make the user cleverer.
   C. help people with poor memories.

PART 1 - JUSTIFICATION OF THE ANSWERS
1. The correct answer is **A**. "...but if your car remains there, the floats won't be able to get past..." Choice B is incorrect because "Sorry, we appreciate this is your legal parking space..." Choice C is incorrect because if the car remains where it is "...then everybody will be complaining." They have not begun complaining yet.
2. The correct answer is **B**. "Now, if you look here into the battery compartment, this should be put in this way round..." Choice A is not correct because when the same battery is used or inserted correctly they "have power". Choice C is incorrect because the speaker says "Oh, don't worry about the film, I wound it back into its container."
3. The correct answer is **A**. Cecilia is concerned about her "Swiss Cheese plant". The programme is neither about cheese or Switzerland but a living thing which grows in the garden.
4. The correct answer is **A**. "...the flash disturbs other visitors and damages the colouring in our priceless antique paintings." A flash is used to take a photograph inside. Choice B is incorrect because no mention is made of smoking and choice C is incorrect because we

are told there is no problem with the man who has brought his dog because "...he is not using a flash".
5. The correct answer is **A**. "...we can meet at quarter to four..." Choice B is incorrect because it is "the departmental heads meeting at 4:15" and choice C is incorrect because no mention is made of 4:45.
6. The correct answer is **C**. "... Horden's Limited should provide compensation of..."; compensation is money paid out because of a mistake or bad service. Choice A is incorrect because no mention is made of there being too many clients and choice B is incorrect because the company was "not directly responsible".
7. The correct answer is **A**. "...her fur did come out such a beautiful, snowy white colour..."; cats have fur, while children and parrots do not.
8. The correct answer is **B**. "...the Brain-Booster is capable of raising your intelligence level by as much as 40 I.Q. points..." Choice C is not correct because it works "...without affecting other brain functions such as memory".

Paper 3 LISTENING **PART 2**

You will hear a woman called Yvonne on a TV programme giving her opinion about children being punished at school. For questions 9-18, complete the sentences with a word or short phrase.

The strap was a long piece of leather made especially for **9** **hitting** children's palms.

Today, children who misbehave at school seldom even get a **10** **telling off** .

In the fifties, Yvonne was strapped for coming to school in **11** **the wrong shoes** .

Yvonne thought the way she was disciplined at schools was **12** **(very) cruel** and unfair.

The members of the organisation P.O.P.P.I. all had **13** **young children** .

In 1979, because of P.O.P.P.I., **14** **the government** made the strap illegal.

Yvonne describes her children as **15** **lazy** and irresponsible.

Yvonne does not think her children understand **16** **how lucky** they are.

She is now sorry that the government **17** **changed the law** .

She believes that there would be less **18** **(teenage) crime** if the strap was still used.

PART 2 JUSTIFICATION OF THE ANSWERS

9. "The strap, as they call it, was a thick piece of leather... especially designed for **hitting** small children with, on the palms of their hands."
10. "Nowadays, if you do something wrong at school, you're unlucky if you even get a **telling off**."
11. "I'll never forget the first time it happened to me...I came to school in **the wrong shoes**..."
12. "I saw this and many other examples of our school's discipline system as **very cruel** and unfair."
13. "All the other members were like me. They had **young children**..."
14. "...in 1979, **the government** put an end to the strap..."
15. "My own son and daughter have turned into **lazy**, irresponsible young adults ..."
16. "...who really have no idea **how lucky** they are."
17. "... I've begun to think - to wish - that they'd never **changed the law**."
18. "... we wouldn't have all the **teenage crime** if those teenagers concerned had ... been given the strap."

Paper 3 LISTENING **PART 3**

You will hear five different people describing different unusual musical instruments from around the world. For questions 19-23, choose from the list A-H which speaker's instrument best fits the description given. Use the letters only once. There are three extra letters which you do not need to use.

A It is entirely made of wood.
B It is similar to a guitar.
C It is played by blowing through it.
D It is difficult to transport.
E It can no longer be made.
F It serves another purpose.
G It can only be found in Japan.
H It is entirely made of rosewood.

Speaker 1 **D** 19
Speaker 2 **E** 20
Speaker 3 **F** 21
Speaker 4 **B** 22
Speaker 5 **A** 23

PART 3 JUSTIFICATION OF THE ANSWERS

19. The correct answer is **D**. "... some of these bells weigh as much as 40 kilograms."

20. The correct answer is **E**. "... since international trade in ivory has been made illegal, few of these instruments have been made."

21. The correct answer is **F**. "... the drum can be displayed outside a building of importance to drive away the evil spirits..."

22. The correct answer is **B**. "... not only its appearance but the tuning as well are similar to that of a classical guitar..."

23. The correct answer is **A**. "The curved base and supporting structure of this instrument are made of matured rose-wood while the nails ... are traditionally made of ebony ... Four different trees are used to make the blocks themselves...hammers are fashioned by hand from willow"

Paper 3 LISTENING | PART 4

As you are leaving an aeroplane at the end of a flight, you overhear this conversation between a passenger and a flight attendant. For questions 24-30, choose the best answer A, B or C.

24. What is the passenger doing in Athens?
  A. spending a holiday there
  B. trying to get a job
  C. buying a house

25. How many more hours will the flight attendant be working today?
  A. five
  B. at least five and a half
  C. twelve

26. What is true about the trips from Athens to London and from London to Athens?
  A. same distance, different journey time
  B. different distance, same journey time
  C. same distance and same journey time

27. How does the flight attendant feel about longer flights?
  A. She finds them difficult.
  B. She doesn't give an opinion.
  C. She prefers them.

28. How often does the flight attendant get to stay somewhere for two nights?
  A. almost every week
  B. once a month
  C. very rarely

29. What is the flight attendant's attitude towards going to Moscow?
  A. She finds the living conditions difficult.
  B. She is curious to find out what it is like.
  C. She is looking forward to going.

30. What is the weather like in Moscow these days?
  A. warm
  B. cold
  C. summery

PART 4 - JUSTIFICATION OF THE ANSWERS

24. The correct answer is **B**. The passenger says "I'm visiting a friend who says he can get me a job." Choice A is incorrect because "Well, actually I'm not exactly on holiday."

25. The correct answer is **B**. The flight attendant says "More like five and a half hours and that's if there are no delays..."

26. The correct answer is **A**. "... it's the same distance but from London to Athens we have a tail wind which makes it quicker ... but on the way back that becomes a head wind which slows us down."

27. The correct answer is **C**. She says of the longer flights "Well, actually they're better..." and "And sometimes, if you're lucky, you even get a two-night stop-over."

28. The correct answer is **A**. She tells the man that she stays over for two nights "About once a week usually."

29. The correct answer is **C**. "I'm doing Moscow tomorrow, that's one...and it's a nice place..." She's going and says it's nice so she is looking forward to it. She knows it is nice so she must have been before, therefore, choice B is not correct. Choice A is incorrect because she complains about the weather, not the living conditions.

30. The correct answer is **B**. "...but it's a bit chilly around this time of year." 'Chilly' means 'rather cold'.

Test 10

Paper 1 Reading and Use of English PART 1

For questions 1-8, read the text below and decide which word A, B, C or D best fits each space. There is an example at the beginning (0).

Example:

0.   A. acts   B. plays   C. creates   D. makes | 0 | A | **B** | C | D |

Transport in The City

Transport (0).......... an important role in our daily lives and in the (1).......... of life in our city. Moreover, the individual decisions we make when we choose how to reach our destination can have a(n) (2).......... on other people - longer traffic queues, (3).......... air quality, greater numbers of accidents and health problems. Providing more transport options/choices will create a transport system that is safe, efficient, clean and fair.

Increasing (4).......... of the car has led to greater (5).......... of the impact it has and the (6).......... costs to us - for our health, for the economy and for the environment.

We want our city to become a successful, cosmopolitan city by the sea, where people can enjoy a high quality of life in a pleasant environment. To achieve this we need to make sure everyone has (7).......... to the services and facilities they need, through a choice of as many different means of transport as possible. We therefore welcome the Government's White Paper on Integrated Transport published earlier this year and (8).......... their vision of *"A New Deal for Transport: Better for Everyone"*.

1.	A. quantity	B. equality	**C. quality**	D. equation
2.	A. force	B. crash	C. problem	**D. impact**
3.	A. better	B. open	C. difficult	**D. worsening**
4.	A. motion	**B. use**	C. sale	D. method
5.	**A. awareness**	B. interest	C. campaign	D. transfer
6.	A. frank	B. successful	C. greedy	**D. real**
7.	A. opening	B. contact	**C. access**	D. touch
8.	A. dream	B. spoil	**C. share**	D. ask

Paper 1 Reading and Use of English PART 2

*For questions 9-16, read the text below and think of the word which best fits each space. Use only **one** word in each space. There is an example at the beginning (0).*

Example: | 0 | office |

Life in Hertford

I picked up my bag of letters and left the post (0) ....**office**............... . The bag was heavy and I (9) ....**had**.......... a lot of letters to deliver. But I was feeling very cheerful. It was 7 o'clock on a fine summer morning. The sun was shining. It was (10) ......**going**........ to be a warm day.

I started on my long walk through the streets of Hertford with a light heart. It wasn't only the bright morning that (11) ....**made**............ me happy. We, my wife and I, had been, until very recently, living in London. I had (12) ....**been**............... a postman there for a long time. Then I had the chance to get a postman's job in Hertford and I decided to take (13) ....**it**...... . Several times I wondered (14) ....**whether/if**.......... I had done the right thing. It is not always wise to (15) ...**leave**... the place that you are used to.

But now, six weeks after the move, I know that it was the right thing to do. We'd found a comfortable little house with a good garden. We liked the atmosphere of the quiet, sleepy town and we'd (16) ....**already**........... made some friends. Life in Hertford pleased us both. I knew that we were going to enjoy living there.

Paper 1 Reading and Use of English   PART 3

For questions **17-24**, read the text below. Use the word given in capitals at the end of some lines to form a word that fits in the space in the same line. There is an example at the beginning *(0)*.

Example: | **0** | o u t r a g e o u s l y |

It's difficult when you want to buy an (0)......*outrageously*...... expensive but	**OUTRAGE**
(17)............*stylish*............ new outfit. Shop (18)............*assistants*............ can be	**STYLE / ASSIST**
very helpful, of course, but they can also be very persuasive. They want to make a	
sale and will say anything (19)............*imaginable*............ to make you part with your	**IMAGINE**
money. Sometimes they may suggest you pay in (20)............*instalments*............ or	**INSTAL**
they may use other innovative methods. However, if you have a (21)............*fondness*......	**FOND**
for good quality clothes and are looking for something (22)............*tasteful*............	**TASTE**
then you should find your (23)............*inspiration*............ in small boutiques that sell	**INSPIRE**
clothes of (24)............*excellent*............ quality – for a price!	**EXCEL**

Paper 1 Reading and Use of English   PART 4

For questions **25-30**, complete the second sentence so that it has a similar meaning to the first sentence, using the word given. **Do not change the word given.** You must use between **two** and **five** words, including the word given. There is an example at the beginning *(0)*.

Example:

0 They think the owner of the house is in France.   **thought**

   The owner of the house .... in France.

The gap can be filled by the words **"is thought to be"** *so you write:* | **0** | i s t h o u g h t t o b e |

25. If we walk faster, we will get home sooner.   **the**

   The ....*faster we walk the sooner*............ we will get home.

26. Tony began to learn the violin three years ago.   **learning**

   Tony ....*has been learning*............ the violin for three years.

27. He intends to visit his relatives next summer.   **intention**

   It ....*is his intention to visit*............ his relatives next summer.

28. I expect he was very happy to hear the news.   **been**

   He ....*must have been*............ very happy to hear the news.

29. He failed the test because he hadn't studied.   **have**

   He ....*would have passed the test*............ if he had studied.

30. Someone stole Jane's purse while she was out.   **had**

   Jane ....*had her purse stolen*............ while she was out.

You are going to read an excerpt from the novel Howards End, by E. M. Forster which takes place during a concert. For questions 31-36, choose the answer A, B, C or D which you think fits best according to the text.

"Who is Margaret talking to?" said Mrs. Munt, at the conclusion of the first movement. She was again in London on a visit to Wickham Place. Helen looked down the long line of their party, and said that she did not know.

"Would it be some young man or other whom she takes an interest in?"

5   "I expect so," Helen replied. Music enwrapped her, and she could not enter into the distinction that divides young men whom one takes an interest in from young men whom one knows.

7   "You girls are so wonderful in always having – Oh dear! one mustn't talk."

For the Andante had begun – very beautiful, but bearing a family likeness to all the other beautiful Andantes that Beethoven had written, and, to Helen's mind, rather disconnecting the heroes and ship-wrecks of the first movement from the heroes and goblins of the third. She heard the tune through once, and then her attention wandered, and she gazed at the audience, or the organ, or the architecture. Here Beethoven started decorating his tune, so she heard him through once more, and then she smiled at her cousin Frieda. But Frieda, listening to Classical Music, could not respond. Herr Liesecke, too, looked as if wild horses could not make him inattentive; there were lines across his forehead, his lips were parted, his glasses at right angles to his nose, and he had laid a thick, white hand on either knee. And next to her was Aunt Juley, so British, and wanting to tap. How interesting that row of people was! What diverse influences had gone to the making! Here Beethoven, after humming and hawing with great sweetness, said "Heigho", and the Andante came to an end. Applause, and a round of "wunderschoning" and "prachtvolleying" from the German audience members. Margaret started talking to her new young man; Helen said to her aunt: "Now comes the wonderful movement: first of all the goblins, and then a trio of elephants dancing;" and Tibby implored the company generally to look out for the transitional passage on the drum.

"On the what, dear?"

"On the drum, Aunt Juley."

"No; look out for the part where you think you have done with the goblins and they come back," breathed Helen, as the music started with a goblin walking quietly over the universe, from end to end.

Others followed him. They were not aggressive creatures; it was that that made them so terrible to Helen. They merely observed in passing that there was no such thing as splendour or heroism in the world. After the interlude of elephants dancing, they returned and made the observation for the second time. Helen could not contradict them, for, once at all events, she had felt the same, and had seen the reliable walls of youth collapse. Panic and emptiness! Panic and emptiness! The goblins were right.

Her brother raised his finger: it was the transitional passage on the drum. For, as if things were going too far, Beethoven took hold of the goblins and made them do what he wanted. He appeared in person. He gave them a little push, and they began to walk in a major key instead of in a minor, and then – he blew with his mouth and they were scattered! Gusts of splendour, gods and demigods contending with vast swords, colour and fragrance broadcast on the field of battle, magnificent victory, magnificent death! Oh, it all burst before the girl, and she even stretched out her gloved hands as if it was tangible.

31. When the writer says that Helen 'could not enter' in line 5 he means that

A. her mind was elsewhere.

B. she disagreed.

C. she had no ticket.

D. she did not know the young man.

32. Why did Mrs. Munt stop speaking suddenly in line 7?

A. She changed her mind.

B. The performance had finished.

C. She saw that Helen was not interested.

D. The music had begun.

33. As Helen watched the other people listening, she felt

A. bored.

B. fascinated by them.

C. scornful of them.

D. proud of them.

34. What best describes Helen's view of the goblins?

A. horrible and violent

B. not violent, but still disturbing

C. observant and very entertaining

D. quiet but not peaceful

35. From Helen's reaction to the music, in paragraph 3, what do we learn about her personality?

A. She is young and innocent.

B. She does not think much about life.

C. She believes life is heroic.

D. She is not an idealistic youth.

36. What is the meaning of the word "tangible" in the last line of the last paragraph?

A. something that can be touched

B. something emotional

C. something imaginary

D. something frightening

31. The correct answer is **A**. "Music enwrapped her" means that it occupied her completely, and her mind was carried away somewhere by the music and not focused on reality. B is not correct because she agrees, saying "I expect so". C is not correct because she is already in the concert hall, and the concert is in progress. While D is true, it is not the reason she was not able to speak about him.

32. The correct answer is **D**. "For the Andante had begun", the "for" here has the meaning of "because" and the "Andante" is a passage in the piece of music being performed.

33. The correct answer is **B**. Although she found the music a bit boring, she was not bored by the people. She thought "How interesting that row of people was! What diverse influences had gone to the making!"

34. The correct answer is **B**. The goblins "were not aggressive creatures; it was that, that made them so terrible to Helen".

35. The correct answer is **D**. The goblins observed that "there was no such thing as splendour or heroism in the world" and "Helen could not contradict them, for, once at all events, she had felt the same, and had seen the reliable walls of youth collapse." If you say the walls of something collapse, it means you can no longer believe in that something.

36. The correct answer is **A**. "tangible" = something clear enough to be seen, felt or noticed; something concrete and physical. She reaches out as if there was a physical thing that she could touch.

You are going to read an article about what music is, and why it exists. Six sentences have been removed from the article. Choose from the sentences A-G the one which fits each gap 37-42. There is one extra sentence which you do not need to use.

Where Did Music Come From?

What is music? Musical expression can be divided into two groups: vocal music or "song" which consists of complex, learned vocalisations and instrumental music which consists of structured, communicative sound using parts of the body other than the voice and sometimes additional objects.

Although the production of music is considered uniquely human, musical utterances of various degrees of complexity and perfection can be observed in several species in the animal kingdom. **37 E** Most research has been done on songbirds so far, but also parrots, hummingbirds, whales, seals and possibly other species show vocalisations that can be called musical according to the above definition.

Birdsong is commonly regarded as the most complex vocal utterance in the animal kingdom. **38 B** Traits of the latter such as an extensive repertoire of melodies, a sense of diatonic intervals, very precise pitch recognition and intonation, ability of transposition, melodic and dynamic variation, imitation, improvisation and composition have been observed in songbirds in various degrees of perfection.

Instrumental sound generation is very rare among animals. **39 G** Our closest cousins, the African great apes (chimpanzees, bonobos and gorillas), make drumming sounds with their hands, sometimes with both arms, on their own chest, the ground, on objects like tree roots and even on other individuals. Chimpanzees have been found readily adapting other surfaces to drumming including hollow walls. Drumming sequences typically last only a short time, between one and twelve seconds. It is currently unknown whether apes can learn rhythms. It is also unknown whether they can create more complex rhythmic patterns than the simple, steady beat typically observed. **40 C** However, using both hands to drum seems to be unique to the great apes and humans.

But why did music develop? This natural question may be asked in another way: what, if any, adaptive functions does music serve? In other words, what advantage did species with musical skills have that allowed them to have more offspring than those that did not? This is a question that interested Darwin. In fact, he was probably the first to ask it, when he said "As neither the enjoyment nor the capacity for producing musical notes are faculties of the least use to man in reference to his daily habits of life, they must be ranked amongst the most mysterious with which he is endowed".

41 F Many researchers have many different ideas. The following hypotheses about the function of music are among the most common that have been suggested so far. As a null hypothesis, it has been proposed that music has no adaptive function at all. Perhaps it is a mere by-product of some other ability that we need, such as language. Another often talked about purpose for music, prominent both in the scientific literature and in the popular press, is in mate choice. Data on birdsong and whale song support this hypothesis. Other ideas include that music might have begun with the use of song by mothers to soothe infants, or as a learning tool in the play of young animals. **42 A**

A. However, the precise reasons for the existence of music are still a mystery today.

B. Some species, such as blackbirds, nightingales and white-rumped shamas, deliver vocal performances of outstanding musical quality that come close to human music in many aspects.

C. There are a few other drumming species, including palm cockatoos, woodpeckers and kangaroo rats.

D. Simple sounds that are instinctive and serve functions like signalling danger are usually not regarded as music.

E. Vocalisations of amazingly high complexity and musicality have evolved several times in birds and mammals.

F. Few stones have been left unturned as to potential functions of music since Darwin posed the question.

G. It seems to be limited to purely rhythmical elements, to drumming, thus lacking any melody or harmony.

---

37. The correct answer is **E**. The topic of this paragraph is "musical utterances" in the "animal kingdom". E is a better choice than B, because it mentions birds and animals, covering more of the animal kingdom than B, which only concerns birds. Although choice C also mentions members of the animal kingdom, it may be eliminated because it is speaking about drumming, which is not an utterance, or a sound produced with the voice.

38. The correct answer is **B**. This paragraph talks specifically about birdsong, which makes choice B, which lists species of birds, most appropriate. Also, the sentence following the gap, speaks about "the latter" (which means the second of two) topics and "human music" which is the second of two topics in choice B, fits nicely with the meaning of the next sentence.

39. The correct answer is **G**. The topic of the paragraph is instrumental sound which eliminates all but C and G. Choice C may be eliminated because it contains the word "other" which requires a specific animal to have been mentioned previously. Also, in choice G, the words "limited to" agree with the word "rare" in the sentence before the gap.

40. It follows that **C** is the correct answer in the second gap in this paragraph about instrumental sound. The "other" species mentioned before are the great apes. Also, the list of drumming species fits with the modification in the following sentence using 'however', followed by statement of the fact that only a couple of species drum with both hands.

41. The correct answer is **F**. This gap is in the position where we would expect a topic sentence. The following sentences would lead us to expect the meaning to concern ideas about the function of music. F has this meaning, and also ties in with the previous paragraph by mentioning "since Darwin posed the question". Choice A also shares the subject, but because of the "However", it cannot take the position at the beginning of the paragraph.

42. The correct answer is **A**. The initial "However" makes it appropriate for a sentence at the end of a paragraph, emphasizing that although the paragraph mentions several ideas, we still don't know the answer. The subject matter both sums up the paragraph, and the whole composition.

Paper 1 Reading and Use of English **PART 7**

You are going to read a magazine article that contains the opinions of three people about the roles music can play in society. For questions 43–52, choose from the people A–C. The people may be chosen more than once.

Which person:

suggests that all music may be in some way political?	**43**	B
believes music can provide social unity?	**44**	B
believes music has a particularly important role in growing up?	**45**	C
personally witnessed the role of music in social reform?	**46**	B
says music can empower children facing difficulties?	**47**	A
mentions a charitable organisation?	**48**	A
does not mention his or her own occupation?	**49**	A
gives the opinion of an expert?	**50**	A
suggests how an interested person could learn more?	**51**	B
singles out the advantages of a particular style of music?	**52**	C

The role of music in our society

ANN JOHNSTON   A   49 no mention is made of Ann's occupation

For me, the power of music is just about summed up by the work of a charity called the National System of Youth and Children's Orchestras of Venezuela, popularly known as "The System". It provides poor children with their own instruments, teaches them to play and groups them into a network of orchestras and choirs. These skills are necessary to perform music: synchronisation, dependability, punctuality and collaboration. The children that secure a place in one of the orchestras are paid a monthly stipend so their parents understand that music-making has a real financial value, and don't make them stop in order to work. **48**

It was founded in 1975 by a professional economist and musician, Jose Antonio Abreu, who believed that young, deprived boys and girls could receive strong skills to overcome poverty with the collective learning experience of music. Abreu successfully identified the feelings of alienation and low self-esteem in the Venezuelan poor as some of the handicaps that forced them to remain deprived. Let me give you a quote in which he highlighted how these feelings affected the poor, much more severely than the lack of income: **47** **50**

"The most miserable and tragic thing about poverty is not the lack of bread or roof, but the feeling of being no-one, the lack of identification, the lack of public esteem. That's why the children's development in the orchestra and the choir provides them with a noble identity and makes them a role model for their family and community."

JOSEPHINE SAKS   C

Music has an undeniable effect on our emotions. Any parent knows that a quiet, gentle lullaby can soothe a fussy baby. And a majestic chorus can fill us with excitement. But more and more research is now showing that music also can affect the way we think.

Both as a parent of young children, and as a primary school teacher, this is of particular interest to me. After all, it's my job to help others get the best possible start in life. It seems music has a role to play. You see, babies are born with billions of brain cells. During the first years of life, those brain cells form connections with other brain cells. Over time, the connections we use regularly become stronger. Children who grow up listening to music develop strong music-related connections. And these music-related connections actually affect the way we think. **45**

Listening to classical music can improve our spatial reasoning, at least for a short time. Learning to play an instrument can have longer lasting effects. This seems to be true for classical music, but not other styles of music because of classical music's complicated structure. What is really amazing is that research shows that babies as young as 3 months can pick out that structure and even recognise classical music selections they have heard before. **52**

THOMAS JONES   B

Apartheid, in South Africa, when the white minority held power over the entire population, was met with strong internal and external resistance, prompting global boycotts of trade with South Africa. The most powerful form of resistance, however, was the refusal of South African blacks to remain prisoners in their own land.

In the 46 years that the system of Apartheid was in place, the resistance movements evolved from loosely organised unions of non-violent protestors to powerful armed coalitions. Throughout every stage of the struggle, the "liberation music" both fuelled and united the movement. Exiled South African singers also had a role to play, bringing the struggle into the global spotlight. Song was a communal act of expression that shed light on the injustices of Apartheid, playing a major role in the eventual reform of the South African government. **44**

I had a glimpse of this first-hand growing up in South Africa before my family immigrated to the UK in my early teens; perhaps that's what inspired me to study Human Rights Law. If you want to know more, let me recommend *Amandla! A Revolution in Four-Part Harmony*, a powerful film that focuses specifically on the 'liberation music' of the struggle against white domination in South Africa. But can music ever be separated from its political context? This is investigated with striking clarity in Daniel Fischlin's and Ajay Heble's book *Rebel Musics*. The book outlines the diverse ways in which music and song have impacted human rights and social justice issues, and explores the concept of music as a dissident practice, as power, and as the contradiction of "being silenced". **46** **51** **43**

Writing

Paper 2 WRITING PART 1

*You **must** answer this question. Write your answer in 140-190 words in an appropriate style.*

1. You have watched a documentary about young children in poor areas who leave school to work. Your English teacher has asked you to write an essay.

   Write an **essay** using **all** the notes and give reasons for your point of view.

> Teenagers are dropping out of school to find a job.
> How can we help them to continue their education?
>
> **Notes**
>
> Write about:
> 1. family problems
> 2. financial difficulties
> 3. .... (your own idea)

Paper 2 WRITING PART 2

*Write an answer to **one** of the questions 2-4 in this part. Write your answer in 140-190 words in an appropriate style.*

2. A classmate overhears you critiquing and discussing a musical theatre performance with great insight and asks you to submit reviews of other shows. He tells you to explore the characters, plot, music, larger themes, setting and production style in developing your criticism.

Write your **review**.

3. You recently saw this notice in an international magazine called *Travelling the World*.

> ### We Need Articles!
>
> We are seeking readers' articles about a memorable holiday they have taken. We want to know where you went and what it was like, what you did there and what made it memorable.
>
> We will publish the most interesting articles!

Write your **article**.

4. For a political science class you are taking, the professor asks you to conduct a small survey of students to learn more about their voting habits in elections of local officials. The professor asks that you create a **report** organising the data you collect on if and why people vote, do they vote based on single issues, party affiliation, and what do they read or consult to inform themselves about the issues and political leaders and candidates of the day. Include other factors or ideas in your report as you see fit.

Write your **report**.

Listening

Paper 3 LISTENING PART 1

You will hear people talking in eight different situations. For questions 1-8, choose the best answer, A, B or C.

1. You are in the service department of an electrical store when you overhear this technician speaking on the telephone.
   What does he want the caller to do?
   A. wait for a trained technician
   B. try adjusting the TV himself
   C. bring the TV to the shop.

2. You are in a railway waiting room when you overhear this man speaking.
   What is he describing?
   A. the weather
   B. his working conditions
   C. a recent illness

3. You are standing at the bar of an English pub when you overhear this exchange.
   What does the man want the woman to do?
   A. let him have the menu
   B. get him some food
   C. bring the food to his table

4. You are visiting the offices of a construction company when you overhear a woman answering the telephone.
   What is the caller complaining about?
   A. noise late at night
   B. damage done to his property
   C. noise early in the morning

5. You overhear this exchange in an office.
   What does the woman want the man to do?
   A. type the letter
   B. check the letter for spelling
   C. give his opinion of the letter

6. You are listening to the results of football matches on a Saturday sports programme.
   The West Bromwich-Albion game is different because
   A. it was delayed by water on the pitch.
   B. it was delayed by rain.
   C. there was no score.

7. You are at a rock concert where the lead singer makes this announcement.
   The next song has been specially written for
   A. disabled people.
   B. people with a certain disease.
   C. children in hospital.

8. You are a passenger travelling in a car when you are stopped by a policeman.
   The reason you have been stopped is because
   A. there is a fault with the car.
   B. there has been an accident.
   C. your car crossed a red traffic light.

PART 1 - JUSTIFICATION OF THE ANSWERS

1. The correct answer is **B**. "...if you can just try changing the contrast and brightness controls, they're on the back of that model, and try repositioning the aerial..."

2. The correct answer is **C**. "I had a shocking temperature...and a couple of days I felt so dizzy I couldn't even stand up"; it sounds like he had the flu or a similar illness. Choice A may be eliminated because "...feeling hot and cold all the time and shivering..." refers to how he felt when he had a temperature, not the weather.

3. The correct answer is **A**. "Can I take this over there to show my friends?" The answer comes from the context; since they are discussing price and choice of meals, it makes sense that "this" would be a menu.

4. The correct answer is **C**. "...no work begins before 7am but we can check with the foreman to see if this rule has in fact been broken..." Choice A is not correct because the topic of discussion is noise in the morning;. Choice B is not correct because when the speaker says "I think you'll find that if there's been no damage..." the "if" implies that damage is not the problem.

5. The correct answer is **B**. "I just wondered if you could read through it and see if I've made any spelling mistakes." Choice A is incorrect because Amanda says "I've just finished typing this letter". Choice C is incorrect because when the man asks if she wants his opinion she responds "Well, not really. I do know how to write a letter."

6. The correct answer is **A**. "...the West Bromwich Albion - Wolverhampton game which has been delayed by flooding of the pitch..." Choice B is incorrect because "The Fulham Brighton and Hove Albion match was postponed due to rain..." and choice C is incorrect because both of the above games are scoreless, so this is not different.

7. The correct answer is **B**. "This song is for Simon and anyone else with cerebro-spinal arthritis."

8. The correct answer is **A**. "...your tail-lights are not functioning." Choice B may be eliminated because the policeman says "Otherwise, there'll be an accident."; there hasn't been one yet.

Paper 3 LISTENING | PART 2

You are going to hear somebody giving an introductory talk about a course of lessons at a summer school.
For questions 9-18, complete the sentences with a word or short phrase.

Name of the college	**Trinity**	9
Students at the talk are studying	**History**	10
Time of seminars	**9 - 12.30**	11
Rooms for seminars	95 and 201	12
Length of course	**8 weeks**	13
Saturday 5th July, visit to	**The British Museum**	14
Students should see the Parthenon Marbles and	**Egyptian Mummies**	15
Canteen opening times [Mon-Thurs]	12 to ..2.30 and ...5.. to 8	16
Sports facilities free except for	**Aerobic classes/Aerobics**	17
Accommodation office is room 16 in	**Western House**	18

PART 2 - JUSTIFICATION OF THE ANSWERS

9. "Good morning, I'd like to welcome you to **Trinity** college."
10. "For you, the **history** students, most of your seminars will be held..."
11. "...your seminars will be held from **9-12.30**..."
12. "... in rooms **201** and **95**."
13. "...who will just be here for the **eight week** course that you are following."
14. "The highlight of this is always the trip to **the British Museum** on Saturday 5th July."

15. "This museum is particularly famous for the Parthenon Marbles and the **Egyptian Mummies**..."
16. "The canteen is open daily from 12-**2.30 p.m.** and again from **5**-8 **p.m.** although on Fridays..."
17. "These are available every day and all are free with the exception of the **aerobic classes**."
18. "...you can find the accommodation officer in Room 16 in **Western House**."

Paper 3 LISTENING | PART 3

You will hear five different people talking about incidents at work involving children. For questions 19-23, choose from the list A-H which occupation each speaker has. Use the letters only once. There are three extra letters which you do not need to use.

A	shop assistant	Speaker 1	A 19
B	doctor	Speaker 2	D 20
C	executive	Speaker 3	E 21
D	nursery teacher	Speaker 4	C 22
E	bus driver	Speaker 5	F 23
F	lawyer		
G	video games expert		
H	debt collector		

PART 3 JUSTIFICATION OF THE ANSWERS

19. The correct answer is **A**. "... just after the New Year sales..." and "he picked up a crystal decanter, looked at it and then put it back on the shelf" indicate she is in a shop.

20. The correct answer is **D**. "...after quickly phoning his mum, I asked Sam to take care of my group"; she is looking after children.

21. The correct answer is **E**. "...in the back" and "I pulled over" indicate a large vehicle such as a bus.

22. The correct answer is **C**. "... like other products when it comes to market research...". Executives conduct market research.

23. The correct answer is **F**. "In legal terms..." and "... custody of the child. And according to her rights, she should have...".These are all concerns of a lawyer.

Paper 3 LISTENING PART 4

You will hear three people, Norman and Linda Hunter, and Linda's friend Patty, talking in a shopping centre about their children. For questions 24-30, choose the best answer A, B or C.

24. How do Patty and Norman know each other?

    A. They worked together.

    B. They are old friends.

    C. They met at a party.

25. What does Norman mean when he calls Patty's child a "rocket scientist"?

    A. He is very smart.

    B. He designs rockets.

    C. He has a good job.

26. How does Norman feel about young children being encouraged to learn languages?

    A. He thinks it is easier for younger children.

    B. He thinks it is essential today.

    C. He thinks it is unnecessary.

27. When Linda says her son taught her computer chess, Patty

    A. is quite impressed.

    B. does not approve.

    C. decides to go to night school.

28. What can we guess about Linda's working schedule?

    A. She only works occasionally.

    B. She works a lot of hours.

    C. She has no time off.

29. Patty can probably afford to work less because

    A. she has financial help.

    B. her son will have a free education.

    C. she is a teacher.

30. What does Norman think is important for children?

    A. to have a lot of lessons

    B. to have the latest toys

    C. to have time to play

PART 4 - JUSTIFICATION OF THE ANSWERS

24. The correct answer is **C**. Patty says "...We met at the Thomas' Christmas party last year..."

25. The correct answer is **A**. To call someone a rocket scientist is an idiomatic way of saying they are very smart. Also, the children are very young, so B and C are not possible.

26. The correct answer is **C**. Norman says "...just what every seven-year-old needs." which is sarcastic - it means the opposite - and follows this with "It never caused me any trouble not knowing three languages." Choices A and B are incorrect because it is Patty who says "And you know, the younger you start..." and "...languages are so important these days."

27. The correct answer is **B**. Patty says "Oh Linda, you ought to find out about these things. He expects to learn from you, not be your teacher." Choice C is not correct because Patty went to night school in order to help her son and brings this up as an example.

28. The correct answer is **B**. Linda says "I could never manage that - what with the hours I work." which means she doesn't have time because she works so many hours. Also, Patty says "So you're still doing six nights a week?" and Linda replies "I'm afraid so." Choice C is not correct because Linda says "Still, tomorrow night's my night off."

29. The correct answer is **A**. Norman says "Is your husband still sending you the maintenance cheques every month then?" and Patty replies "...he's my ex-husband now, but he does still send the cheques..." Choice B is incorrect because Patty mentions "Stewart's school fees" and choice C is incorrect because no mention is made of Patty working as a teacher.

30. The correct answer is **C**. Norman says "Does Stewart ever have time to play?" Choice B is incorrect because he says "No, I mean play with other kids, kick a ball around, get in fights..." and choice A is incorrect because he says "...all he seems to do is one lesson after another. What a way to spend a childhood".